THE LONG WINTER ENDS

The Long Winter Ends

Newton G. Thomas

with an Introduction by William H. Mulligan, Jr.

Wayne State University Press   Detroit

Originally published by Macmillan, 1941.

01 00 99 98   5 4 3 2

Library of Congress Cataloging-in-Publication Data

Thomas, Newton G. (Newton George), b. 1878.
    The long winter ends / Newton G. Thomas ; with an introduction by
William H. Mulligan, Jr.
      p. cm. — (Great Lakes books)
    ISBN 0-8143-2762-1 (pbk. : alk. paper)
    1. British Americans—Michigan—Upper Peninsula—History—Fiction.
2. Cornwall (England)—Emigration and immigration—Fiction.
3. Cornish—Michigan—Upper Peninsula—History—Fiction. I. Title.
II. Series.
PS3539.H593L6   1998
813'.52—dc21   98-37105
                                              CIP

To

MY WIFE

AND DAUGHTER

GREAT LAKES BOOKS

*A complete listing of the books in this series
can be found at the back of this volume.*

PHILIP P. MASON, EDITOR
Department of History, Wayne State University

DR. CHARLES K. HYDE, ASSOCIATE EDITOR
Department of History, Wayne State University

Introduction

NEWTON G. THOMAS'S NOVEL *The Long Winter Ends* offers a rich and unusually nuanced window into the experience of an often neglected immigrant group, the Cornish, who played an important role in the development of the Great Lakes and American mining industries. The novel moves from Cornwall, at the extreme southwestern end of Great Britain, to Michigan's Copper Country, a region in the western Upper Peninsula, and follows the life of Jim Holman, a young miner looking for work and a future for himself and his family.

The Cornish are an extreme case of the phenomenon identified by Charlotte Erickson in her *Invisible Immigrants: The Adaptation of English and Scottish Immigrants in 19th Century America* (1972). As English–speaking Protestants with economically valuable skills as underground miners, the Cornish were able to enter into American society with few difficulties. This was due in part to their similarities to mainstream Americans and the rapid decline in anti–English sentiments among native–born Americans after the War of 1812.

The Cornish, who are not ethnically English or Anglo–Saxon but Celtic, had already seen their distinctive language all but disappear before they began large–scale migration to America in the 1840s. It had given way to a dialect of English that retained a large number of Cornish words, especially those involved with underground mining. Further, the Cornish had also almost universally adopted an enthusiastic, evangelical form of Methodism. Both of these characteristics made them less visible in America than the more numerous German and Irish immigrants, whose large–scale arrival coincided with that of the Cornish. Further, Cornish attachment to their traditional work in underground mining also took them to the geographic fringes of America, beginning with the Lake Superior mining districts in the 1840s. Thus, they largely avoided the conflicts that German allegiance to their language and Irish devotion to their religion engendered in more heavily populated ares of the East Coast and Midwest. American immigration officials almost invariably listed the Cornish as being from England, as did the federal census. Cornwall had been almost completely absorbed into England, both politically and linguistically, and American officials simply codified this situation. All this made the Cornish even less visible in their new home. The distinctive customs of Cornish men and women never really reached public awareness in nineteenth–century America, and only in recent years has the Cornish language reappeared and Cornish ethnic consciousness reemerged.

These distinctive customs were closely linked to Cornwall's long underground mining tradition. Before the Romans reached Britain, Cornwall's tin and copper mines were part of the world–trade system. For centuries, small villages clustered around the mines, and for unnumbered generations Cornish men went underground, deeper and deeper, to earn their livelihood. As the mines went deeper, the Cornish became leaders in developing innovative ways to get men down into the depths; ore, as well as men, up and out; and water pumped out. For generations, the rhythm of life in Cornwall revolved around the mines, as men went down each day into the bal and returned to grass at the end of their shift to their families. Despite the ingenuity, tradition, and strong work ethic of the Cornish people, the depth of Cornwall's mines made them less and less competitive in the world market. As mining in Cornwall reached an economic crisis after years of decline, the

rich mineral reserves of the Lake Superior region were being discovered. The new mines were the death blow for the ancient
mines of Cornwall, but the beacon of hope for its people; they
were drawn to the new mines in America, where their skills were
badly needed.

The new mines needed men who knew how to work the rock
and bring its wealth to the surface. The new land was like
Cornwall only in the most superficial ways, as the emigrants
quickly learned. It, too, was a remote and isolated peninsula, but
its climate was hard and extreme with long, seemingly endless
winters that brought cold and snow beyond anything imaginable
in Cornwall. In this hard land, however, the Cornish were able to
maintain their tradition and pursue the craft that gave their lives
purpose and direction.

On the Michigan mining frontier, the Cornish were not invisible immigrants and played a major role in the development of the
mining industry and its early communities. As is Cornwall, the
early settlements huddled around the mines and moved to the
rhythms of the changing shifts and the descent and return that
marked each day. The close connection between Cornish immigrants and underground mining began in the small communities
of the Keweenaw copper district and the Marquette iron range in
Upper Michigan in the mid–1840s. Because of their expertise, the
Cornish defined the language of American mining and established its earliest industrial organization. Their distinctive tribute
system is one example. In the tiny early mining communities of
the Keweenaw and Marquette range, they clung to their traditions
in the mines and in the Methodist chapels they established. They
were no longer in Cornwall, however, and everything in their new
environment conspired to challenge their old ways. Ultimately,
they faced the challenge of becoming Americans.

The Long Winter Ends brings the reader into this world, with
its hopes and fears, challenges and triumphs, in a very compelling
and human way. We follow a decisive year in the life of Jim
Holman, a young miner who has recently married, and several of

his friends from Stoke Parish in Cornwall. The Holmbush Mine in Stoke is closing as the novel opens, and a group of men from the village, including Jim, head for the Keweenaw, where they have heard from earlier emigrants that there is work in the copper mines. Jim leaves his wife Pol behind as he goes in search of their future in America.

The novel traces the emigrants' long and arduous journey from Cornwall to the Keweenaw, providing a good picture of the means and difficulty of travel to the remote Lake Superior region. Their hopes and dreams are explored through their conversations along the way. Jim and one of his companions find work in the community of Allouez when their stage coach stops there. The rest of the party continues to their original destination, Central Mine, further up the Keweenaw Peninsula. They all but disappear from the novel, which follows Jim Holman's life.

For a year, we share Jim's experiences as he adjusts to his new world, a world somewhat familiar as he lives with other Cornishmen in a boarding house run by a fellow countryman and his wife. He also works with his countrymen underground in the mine and attends Methodist chapel meetings. Slowly, however, some of the immigrants begin to question the old ways. Jim learns to read and write from one of them so he can communicate directly with Pol, despite the ridicule of some of his boarding housemates. He meets Americans and tries to speak without his Cornish accent so as to better blend with them.

He gradually, and then explicitly, abandons his hope of returning to Cornwall and realizes his future is in America. At the novel's conclusion, he is establishing a home for Pol and their first child, who was born in Cornwall after he left. Over this year in Jim's life, the reader is brought into the heart of the Cornish immigrant experience. First there is the failure of the mines in Cornwall, then hope for the preservation of Cornish traditions in America, and finally acceptance that their future is in America.

Some of the great strengths of the novel are the author's ear for the inflections and patterns of Cornish speech and his knowledge of the work routines and vocabulary of underground mining. Clearly, Thomas is drawing on his own experiences as a young Cornish immigrant in the mining communities of the Upper Peninsula. The result is a powerful novel capturing the tensions experienced by immigrants adjusting to America while trying to hold onto traditions that define their identify. While Jim Holman adjusts well to America, many of his companions struggle and cling to their traditions, refusing to acknowledge the new world in which they find themselves.

Newton George Thomas was born in Stoke, the community in Cornwall where *The Long Winter Ends* begins, in November 1878. With his parents, he emigrated to the Upper Peninsula as a child. This is a generation later than the initial Cornish migration, but is roughly the period in which the novel appears to be set; one of the weaknesses of the novel is its ambiguity about when it takes place. Thomas attended high school in Norway, Michigan, on the Menominee iron range from 1892 to 1895 and graduated from Central Academy in Pella, Iowa, in 1901. After attending Central College in Pella for three years, he received his A.B. in 1909 and his master's degree from Central in 1915. This information, and the fact that he taught school during the intervals in his education, suggests that he initially received a life certificate and completed his bachelor's degree while teaching. He may have briefly worked in the iron mines of Norway after leaving high school, but there is no evidence of this. From 1911 to 1914, he attended Northwestern University's Dental School, receiving his D.D.S. in 1914, and then taught for one year on the faculty of the University of Illinois's College of Dentistry in Chicago. He returned to Northwestern as a member of its dental faculty from 1915 to 1919 before returning to the University of Illinois, where he taught histology and served as secretary of the College of Dentistry in Chicago until 1926 when he resigned. Reviews of *The Long Winter Ends* refer to him as a schoolteacher and a professor.

His personal life, based on the little that can be learned about it, was unremarkable and is difficult to document. He married Lena M. Awtry in Pella in 1904, and they had one daughter, L. Frances, born in 1905. Thomas published a number of articles in his area of specialization, and in 1941 he published *The Long Winter Ends* with Macmillan, apparently his only work of fiction. Perhaps it is fitting that little information is available on Thomas, the man and his life, since his novel is a powerful picture of the lives of the ordinary men and women whose largely anonymous lives shaped our history.

WILLIAM H. MULLIGAN, JR.
Murray State University

Chapter One

R<small>UMOR HAD BEEN TRAVERSING</small> the lanes and turnpikes and stiled bypaths of the parish for weeks—the distressing, sickening threat that the Holmbush was to shut down. At first it was only a whisper that was passed between intimates. The whisperer touched off his announcement with an anonymous, "They say," or, "I 'eard." He advised his hearer to keep it to himself, saying finally, "Dawn't tell I told e," with no thought of the implied distrust. He was guilelessly conceding a liberty he knew would be taken just as he had taken it, but the source of the information must be withheld. Reprisals might be forthcoming from the authorities if time should prove the story untrue. So, nobody knew how it started. Many tried to suppress it: "It's just talk," they said; "the less said, the better." But the fateful words were soon on everybody's lips. The whisper became outspoken gossip. The subject was discussed at the family mealtime; it held first place at Fools' Corner; it invaded trysting places and Lovers' Lane; it was finally mentioned in the village chapels. As men might pray for the prevention of war, the ministers prayed that the shutdown might not happen. They implored the people to have faith to believe that such a catastrophe could not befall them. Thoughtful men argued that it was unreasonable: the mine was as productive as it had ever been; the market always had its ups and downs; things were a bit slack, but they had been that way before. Why should the mine close? Rumors came and went. This one would pass too. Thus they tried to bolster their own hope and the courage of the parish. As soldiers know the meaning of the order to fire, these men knew the import of a closed mine to the community it sustained.

The afternoon shift, fivescore men or more, stood around the Higher Mine shaft waiting for the captain and the whistle. They talked little in the last minutes before going down. The sun was midway down its afternoon slope, and clouds came like aimless wayfarers over the crest of Kit Hill from the English Channel. From where they stood the men could look down on the mine offices and the shears of the Lower Mine. Beyond, but still on the valley floor, was a cluster of houses that looked like discarded shards thrown there in utter disregard. They seemed suitable enough to surround the slaughterhouse that supplied the parish with meat. From the far side of the village began the ascent of Kit Hill, its lower half marked off by hedges for the laying out of which no surveyor ever had stretched a line. The enclosed fields had shapes of all kinds, approaching but never attaining the geometrical. Beyond the fields the heather-brown rise, burdened with gray, moss-covered moorstones, continued to the crest where stood an old enginehouse that from the Higher Mine looked like a monstrous tombstone. A hundred feet below the Higher Mine floors, water gushed from the adit and sped to the valley. It flashed in the sun and mimicked other streams in its chatter. Fragments of rainbows crested its spray when it threw itself against moorstones in its path, but it was murky, poisonous, sterile. Nor would it be otherwise until it had joined the Tamar and was diluted by the Channel tide.

Finally the whistle blew, and the captain in his white duck coat came from the dry. He skirted the crowd without a nod, found a wheelbarrow near the shaft, and stepped upon it, standing carefully in the middle of it to keep his balance.

His face was as white as his coat when he began to speak.

"I 'ave bad news," he said. "This be the last shift. The mine close down t'night." He stopped as though the words clogged his throat. He coughed to clear the way for what more he had to say—the men, the while, looking up at him in silence. "W'en you are through, bring your tools to the shaft. The first lift will pick them up." He stepped out of the barrow and nodded toward the waiting cage.

Before a move was made toward the shaft, a voice broke the stillness:

" 'Ow 'bout the pay, Cap'n? Be there any use goin' down? Will us get our pay?"

Again Captain Bennett stepped into the wheelbarrow to be better seen and heard. "You'll get your pay, I'm shore," he said. He paused again, his difficulty recurring. "Hi be hawful sorry, but—" Once more he stepped to the ground.

Still the men stood like graven images, faces white and muscles tense as though hypnotized by the news they had expected so long. The captain's "I'm shore" was a familiar idiom to them, expressing faith established in hope but not in knowledge. They were not assured. Bennett had to speak again to break the spell he had put on them.

"The cage be waitin', men," he said.

The men understood. Captain Harry Bennett was a product of the parish, and the older men had known him from birth as he in turn had known the younger men who worked for him. His sympathy with them and their faith in him were never debated. They spoke of him always as "Cap'n 'Arry."

With the filling of the first cage the stricken men found their tongues. It was evident that extending a drift or deepening a winze was a waste of time. Tomorrow—if they were in the bottom of the mine—both would be full of water. As a result, the men who worked in such places volunteered to help their neighbors who had "loose dirt" to get out. The captain would expect nothing else. Others who had to drill a cut and blast before they could have dirt to send up for themselves, offered to shovel or tram—anything to help another man to get out the last pound of broken ore.

But they did not all talk of the work. A man well past middle life turned to his neighbor and said: "Goin' down, be e? 'Tis the last shift, you knaw. I've a mind t' bide on top an' go 'ome."

A doubtful look came over the face of the man addressed. " 'Tedn' so much that I be afeard as 'tis that the missus do need the threp'ny bit I make. If I knawed us wouldn' get un, I'd bide on top an' go 'ome with e."

Other reluctant ones stood apart from the shaft, debating the wisdom of daring the curse of the last shift. "A bal * will always take 'e's tribbit. 'E's fool'ardy t' go down." Not a man lowered his voice as he spoke of it. Superstition had only a weakly disputed place in Cornish belief from the Tamar to Land's End.

In a quarter of an hour the last cage had made its journey to the bottom, leaving its load to candlelight and the winding underways of the pit.

There was not much work done that night, in most instances. There were more hands than were needed for the work to be done. As the captain made his rounds—more to extend a little cheer and show his interest in the men than to see what they were doing—he found timbermen and trammers and miners sitting in groups, talking and smoking, the tools they were responsible for conveniently at hand to be taken to the shaft. He stopped with each group long enough to "titch pipe" with them and to answer any question that any one might ask.

Tonight, the question was the same everywhere although worded differently: "Izza the last shift for good, Cap'n?" or, "Will they let 'er fill up?"

---

* Mine.

"The horders be t' stop the pump," he answered. And then, forcing a smile, he said: "That 'ave 'appened before. W'en steam be up an' turned on, the bob will do the rest. There's no better pump in the worl' than a Cornish pump. If 'e dawn't stay closed too long, the water won't matter." No one knew better than he that this was just talk to give them a moment's ease with a passing appeal to their pride.

Equally certain to come, was, "W'at about the pay, Cap'n? Shall us get 'e?"

He answered all with utmost patience, albeit with a lump in his throat. He knew what the few shillings they had earned meant to them, and he also knew that under previous management, when a shutdown had come, the pay had sometimes failed to follow. The question was not an idle one; it might happen again. As best he could, he tried to encourage them without deceiving them.

He found men shoveling greedily under open backs that had not been trimmed or ceiled against "drops" of rock. In spite of his sympathy he spoke sharply in such instances. He ordered them out of the danger, saying, "You knaw better than that."

Ashamed but resentful, the men obeyed, stepping under cover.

"You put up a pentis t' protect your 'eads, or stop workin'."

"That will take a hour's time, an' us'll leave dirt be'ind."

"Better that than leave a life be'ind! Doin's like yours be w'at give the last shift 'is chance."

To such he sent help from the groups who were idling the shift away.

Shift's end came at last. For the sake of those who had dirt to send up, the skip would run to the usual time; but the company-count men gathered at the shaft early with the miners who had little to do. Perhaps the captain had dropped a word with one group that he had left unsaid to another. Crumbs of information were precious. So, at the different levels they gathered in the half-light of the plat lanterns to wait for the hoisting to begin and to glean what stray bits would add to their store. Their candles were out from habit, an economy learned from the bitterness of hard living. They would have more to take home for use in bedroom, parlor, and kitchen.

Conversation, however, was at a low ebb. The captain had not said much.

"W'en all be said an' done, Cap'n 'Arry dedn' tell much," one said.

"An' us dedn' ask much—the same question awver an' awver, more'n likely," answered another.

No other subject could break through the blackness of the catastrophe that overshadowed them. What did it matter whether the lode looked good or a contract was liberal! Both were ended now. No work! No work! The family! No work! No work! The family! Few sentences dealt by law or Fate could rend a man worse. The future was empty, dark, its content, if it had any, invisible. No work! The family! Silence.

The drip, drip of the water that oozed from the back and fell on them or splashed into the little pools at their feet became monotonous. Every man who felt or noticed the falling water knew that each drop foretold the fate of the pit. In a few weeks the space in which they stood would be full of water. It would rise until it reached the adit, and then form a leat that would race down the hillside.

The hoisting began from the bottom first. The first cage stopped at each level to collect the tools. The captain and one workman came on it. Bennett stepped into each plat and asked, "Hev'rybody out?" The tools loaded and the captain assured of the safety of all, the cage was rung on its way.

It did not take long for the cage to make the journey; soon the rumble of its return brought the men to attention and they gathered closer to the shaft gates. Those on the upper levels listened for the first creak of the bell line and watched for the tightening of the capstan as it took the weight of the cage. On each level some one was sure to announce, "He've started!"

Usually the lift-loads sped their way to the surface with talk, jokes, laughter; some one aboard the lift would call a taunt to each waiting group as it passed a level. But tonight the loads were silent.

On the eighteenth was a group that customarily sang as the lift tore its way through the shaft. Fellow workers gave way to them so that they might ride together and those who waited might hear their song. But the waiters did not expect singing tonight. The anxious cargoes already on surface had gone up in silence. These would too. A man on the twelfth spoke about it.

"Do e think they'll sing t'night?"

"Men dawn't sing a welcome t' mis'ry," came the reply.

Three loads had already left the bottom, and the rope was twisting to the weight of the fourth. It was the last from the eighteenth. Easily enough the singers might have gone to grass unrecognized in the silent bundles packed into the cage.

Suddenly, breaking the silence of the waiting plats came the familiar sound from below, not one but many bound into a harmonious whole. It smote the silence with magic and filled the place it had occupied—a pianissimo as faint as an echo on a distant hill. Slowly it grew into a moderato, increasing in power until in a bursting crescendo made perfect by the approaching cage, it matured to its fullest strength as the singers dashed by each listening, waiting drift. As perfectly it graded away—from crescendo to moderato, to pianissimo, until, as echoes die, it died—died as it was born.

"Diadem," said a listener when silence had returned. "A brave tune."

"Did e ever 'ear a baas like Craze?"

"Small as 'e be, too, you wonder w'ere a voice like that come from."

"An' Holman's air be as true an' certain as Pompey Passon's floot."

"They Collinses would make their mark too, if they awnly knawed 'ow."

"E seem out of place, singin' a night like this."

"If 'e did any harm. But I dawn't see 'ow cryin' will do any good."

"Little they care 'bout th' ol' bal if w'at I 'eard be true. All of min, 'cept Craze, be goin' abroad."

"W'ere to?"

"Hameriky."

The last cage reached the surface, only the lower half of it occupied. A half-dozen men stepped out. Five men were waiting for them. They lingered, curious to see what would happen. Captain Harry was one of the waiting group.

"Ring 'er hup a bit, men," he ordered.

A man stepped to the shaft side and pulled the bell. Slowly the cage rose out of the shaft mouth, rose until its bottom was the height of a man from the collar of the pit.

"Stop!" ordered Bennett.

Again the man pulled—a single stroke—and the cage hung motionless.

"Hall right, men," said the captain, and the four slid large, squared timbers over the shaft mouth until it was entirely covered.

"Ring streak," he said.

Again the bell was rung, and the cage dropped slowly to rest on the timber.

Bennett reached for the bell rope and gave a signal to the engineman. The engineman knew that was the end.

The miners stood by in silence like watchers at a bedside. For a moment the captain with the rest was motionless. They stood with eyes fixed on the "bob" sliding up and down and listened to its heavy moan as it took the weight of the water. Once more Bennett moved to the shaft. He raised his hand to another lever and pulled once. The bob was on the up-stroke. It began its descent, shuddered, and came to rest. The heart of the mine had stopped.

Some of the men in the dry changed their clothes hurriedly as though glad to get away, while others lingered for desultory, hopeless talk or, perhaps, because they dreaded the increase of their pain when they reached home.

A score of lanes and open roads or narrow footpaths, like slivers ripped from the pike, wriggled their way across open, rock-strewn wastes, through plantations between fields and orchards, to end in village and hamlet or at the door of a cottage tucked into a hollow or grove. Along all of them men, in pairs when possible and alone if need be, fretted and puzzled their way on worry-burdened feet. While it was to them the captain had spoken, and their hands had performed the last rites of the mine, they knew that two other shifts shared the calamity. Two hundred men had been made jobless, helpless, hopeless. A single man without work found courage for his quest in the fact that other men were at work; but when men were forced into idleness en masse hope found neither root nor light nor air.

The situation was new to all of them. The mine had stopped before for reasons unknown to them but had started again before the worst could happen. They had not hungered. "Give us this day our daily bread," was an easily said petition while the mine worked. With steam up and sheave wheels turning they could do much toward answering the prayer themselves; but when the mine closed, the words were a full-grown supplication with a burden to bear, a burden of women and children. Again and again they sifted the captain's words for any grain of hope, but the effort was in vain.

Until now they had discussed a rumor. "W'at shall us do

if 'e close?" The *if* eased the jab of the question. Now the rumor was routed by the hard, actual fact. The formless shadow had become an oppressive substance—something they felt, something as real as a load on their backs. No *if* dulled the points of the issues they had discussed. No work meant no food, no rent, diminishing clothes—sickness of spirit. They felt themselves affected by a wasting disease that lowered their self-respect, lessened their importance, debased their worth in the world. "Us be like they leaves blowin' from they trees —drawve by the wind," said one. "Aas," said another, "and like they leaves, stamped under foot." Only Providence stood between them and the woes they had forecast, and few of them could trust Providence with the mine idle. So thoroughly had the results of the rumored shutdown been discussed, the report to the families waiting at home would be simple and brief: " 'E 'ave 'appened! The bal 'ave knocked." Husband and wife and children would stare at one another in full understanding and in wordless despair.

One miner said bitterly, "T'morra I'll be a stonecutter an' strike the quarry for employ."

"An' Hi'll set hup for a mason an' look for work in town," said another, catching thought of the first.

"No, my sons," said a third, "it's the mine for you. But where?"

All the other mines in the parish had closed. The Holmbush was the last to go. From the West End word had come from time to time of the same portent. Well known lodes were being abandoned, and hundreds of men were already adrift. Each man touched walls with his fingers, was imprisoned, condemned without a cause.

America, Australia, Africa were the possible havens for the miners of Cornwall, but the way to get there had to be found. Few or none could have saved enough for the journey had they known a year in advance that the emergency would happen. Some might count on the confidence of the shopkeeper, the doctor, the landlord or a well-to-do farmer friend. Some knew their credit would not suffice. A friendship with a fellow miner now in a foreign field came to mind. "I'll write to 'e an' ask un if 'e can take me out." That meant weeks of waiting because of the distance, and always a sickening uncertainty accompanied the attempt. " 'E 'ave been abroad a twelvemonth, an' 'e never wraute. P'r'aps 'e wouldn' care." Such a despair was not to be wondered at. "Write to me," was not a common phrase when friends parted. So few could write. Even the families of such—expatriated either by conditions at home or by a passion for adventure—did not hear from the absent ones for months if ever. Long partings and long silences were accepted as inevitable. Only deep affections could bridge the gap. "W'at sh'll us do?" was the unanswerable question.

Among the last to leave the dry were the men who had sung their way so often from the black depths to the top and sang it tonight for the last time. As they left, Captain Bennett joined them to walk with them until their ways parted for their respective homes.

In single file they went down the side of the burrow, following the path that had been etched there and kept firm by generations of feet. They made the descent to the turnpike in silence, rigid and inclining backward like men descending a stair. Every man glanced at the silent adit and the bed of the stream, now only a wriggle of bronze mud in the starlight, spotted here and there with tiny pools that would vanish with the next sun.

Leaving the turnpike, they continued their way between moorstones and patches of furze, the captain leading until, in front of the offices and shops, they reached a single-track road. Path and road lay on the open, hedgeless, treeless hillside, past the Lower Mine, across the narrow valley almost to the village of Windsor. There the small road divided, and its branches became compressed between hedges and overhung with shrubs and trees that made them tunnels of darkness. Now that walking was easier, the captain spoke.

"I want t' thank e for the hymn," he said. " 'E broke the strain I've been hunder since I got word t' close. Some of the men took un purty 'ard, an' a few talked like I was responsible. Poor fellows! I dawn't blame mun. The closin' mean a lot t' they. Many of mun 'ave no idea w'at they will do. W'at be your plans?"

"Goin' to Ameriky," said Holman. "We 'ave our bookin's made. To Michigan. Us leave nex' week."

"I'm glad you'm goin' there," said Bennett. "Ev'rything will be new to e. The work bayn't no 'arder there than 'ere. You'll like it w'en you get used to it. We sh'll miss e 'ere—all of us. Hi shan't forget the hymn."

"Some of the men climbed up, Cap'n," said Bill.

"Aas. 'E was the last shift, you knaw. They wouldn' trust the lift. I be glad nothin' 'appened t' nobody, though."

" 'Ow do such fancies live?" asked Tom. "A score of last shifts with nothin' 'appenin', an' they chaps would still think the same."

"You'd knaw if you'd seed w'at I seed," said Bennett. But he did not explain.

"Do e think the bal will ever open again?"

They had reached the end of the road, where the captain would leave them. They stopped to wait for his answer.

"No, Jim, I dawn't b'lieve 'e will. W'en you get t' Michigan you will see copper mined like you've never seed un afore. Masses of pure metal. I've been there an' knaw." He hesitated a moment, then said: "That's w'ere the blame be—if blame's the word—for 'appenin's like this. Mines like 'Olmbush can't compete." Bennett faced away from his companions as if to hide his grief. "Good night, men," he said. "I'll see e afore you go." A half-dozen steps, and he was out of sight.

The brothers and Holman strode on in silence, their hob-nailed boots striking fire on the hard road. They passed through Windsor, a half-dozen cottages on the left, slaughter-house, barns and pens on the right.

"Hi be glad cattle an' sheep dawn't leave ghosts be'ind," Joe Collins said.

A murmur of amusement came from the others.

"Hi'd hate t' breathe thicky stink day and night," said Bill.

"If you did, you wouldn' knaw there was a stink, 'tis said," added Jake.

"B'lieve trade like that do e?" asked Joe. "I dawn't. I'd still 'ave my nawse, wouldn' I?"

"B'lieve! B'lieve!" said Jake. "Did I say the word?"

All hands laughed at Joe.

At times they could see the stars, but for longer periods the lane was as black as a drift in the mine. They knew the way well enough to keep within the hedges but not so well that they did not stumble at times. Jake twisted his foot on a loose stone and grasped his brother in the darkness.

"Better strike a light, comrade," said Bill.

But no light was made. Jake hobbled for a step or two but was soon comfortable. A short distance, and they were on the turnpike. Following the strip of unobscured sky, they kept in the middle of the road.

"Masses of pure metal," said Tom, the youngest of the brothers. "I should like t' see they."

"You will soon anough, my son," said Joe, "an' get tired lookin' at mun."

"I wish us dedn' 'ave t' go away from 'ome t' see mun," the boy continued.

"Showin' the w'ite feather, be e, boay?" asked Bill.

"No, I bayn't," Tom answered emphatically. "I was thinkin' of Father an' Mother. Us empty the 'ouse w'en us go."

Jake, the eldest, saw the trend. "I'm proud of e, boay, t' 'ear e say that. A lot of boays go an' forget they 'ad parents.

Fitty an' proper anough for birds an' baysts, but cruel for a human cheel, seem t' me like. But dawn't worry. They still 'ave Sister, an' we c'n keep mun in comfort. As for we, us will try t' bide t'gether."

"You spayk as if you was shore of work w'en you get there," said Bill. "I wish I felt as shore."

"Us be spendin' a lot of money t' be unb'lievin'," said Jake. "I'd ruther stay 'ere than do that."

"In that case, one could go as a forerunner an' write back w'at 'e find."

"If 'Olmbush dawn't work no more, I hate t' think w'at will 'appen in the parish," said Jim.

"Then dawn't, my son," said Jake. "You can't see further 'n t'morra night, an' that not very plain. So w'y worry? 'E'll be 'ard shore 'nough, but folks 'ave a way of keepin' on. You an' the Collins boays will do w'at us can. Let un drop at that."

They were passing through the village of Holmbush, a mile from the mine, when Jim spoke. The houses nearest the road were visible, but those farther back were mounds of blackness. Not a light shone anywhere. The little village nestled tenderly in Jim's heart. It was here he had courted Pol, his young wife, who was waiting for him at this moment. Perhaps that explained his repetition, for he said again, "I 'ate t' think of un."

"That's awnly Cap'n 'Arry's opinion," said Joe. "Cap'n 'Arry edn' no prophet."

"If they Yankee mines shut un down they'll keep un shut so long as they'm good," said Jake. "All us c'n do be wait an' see."

Chapter Two

The Collins brothers and Jim lived under one roof in a double house. Their two-mile walk made lingering at the gate unnecessary. There at last, they merely said good night and parted.

With the click of the latch, the short path was suddenly lighted and Jim's wife stood in the open door. For a moment he held her in his arms; then he kissed her and said, "Hi'll stream my 'ands, maid," and went into the kitchen. He noticed how the large blue stones of the dining-room floor shone in the light of two candles and the small blaze of the fireplace. The red coals, the small yellow and blue flames, the bellows on a stool near by told Jim what had been Mary Ann's last touch to add coziness to his welcome. She went to the fireplace for the teapot and filled his cup while he washed. When he came back, they both sat down, Mary Ann on a small bench at the end of the table and Jim on a longer one at its side. Jim offered thanks. The amen said, she reached for the bread, spread the end of the loaf with butter, and cut a slice as thin as cardboard and handed it to him on the knife. Jim's plate, she had already served with salmon, decorated with sprigs of water cress she had taken from the spring at the foot of the garden.

"American fish," she said, a smile twitching her lips.

" 'E make a nice endin' for afternoon shift," Jim replied, "a miner's dogwatch."

Mary Ann's face sobered. "You'm a bit late, Jim. I'd commenced t' fret about e. Jan Cloke told hev'rybody the bal 'ad closed. Jan was afraid. 'E said it was the last shift an' nobody would catch 'e goin' down. Though I knawed you bayn't moved by such fiddlesticks, I was frettin' afore I knawed it. I'm glad you've come."

"Aas, maid," he said, "the bal 'ave shut down."

"Will a hever open again, do 'e think?"

"No, chul, I dawn't think e will. Cap'n 'Arry said 'tis too aysy t' get copper in Michigan."

Mary Ann raised her cup, and for a minute her blue eyes looked into its amber depths. Jim noticed that her face was white, but knew it was not the pallor of fear. Brave maid, he thought.

"I 'ope us won't be parted long," he said.

Mary Ann smiled although her heart ached. She would go to the ends of the earth with Jim, but she loved Downgate, the fields and moors around it, the buttercups, primroses, and honeysuckle. Jim sensed the effort back of her parted lips and asked, "Will a be 'ard for e t' leave 'ome if 'e come t' that?"

"You'm askin' awnly 'alf a question, Jim—all for me an' none for you. W'at about you?"

"Hi was thinkin' about Mother," he said.

"Hi bayn't thinkin' about leavin' Mother now. I bayn't leavin'. It's you that's leavin'." Mary Ann hesitated for a moment to steady herself. "If 'e come t' that, Mother have Lizzie Jane t' see after 'er." Then the smile that was always peering from her eyes took possession. "It's you an' me for it now, comrade, w'atever come."

Jim finished his meal with less food than usual, leaving a half of what his wife had put before him. He got up, stepped around the table and sat down beside her. He put his arm around her and drew her close to him. For a moment he held her so, her smoothly combed head nestling on his shoulder. "I want t' keep e this way for hever, maid," he said.

Mary Ann raised her face to his and smiled.

"Hi never seed a smile like yours on any face," he said, and he kissed her before she could answer. "Hi was thinkin', comin' through Holmbush, 'e's a cruel thing that 'ave 'appened. 'Ow many famblies will it shake apart like we? No tellin' w'en they'll come t'gether again."

"Us will, Jim," she said. "Us will. Somethin' inside say so."

"Aas," he said, answering her faith rather than expressing his own. "An' I was thinkin' too w'at travelers we two be. You 'ave never been out of the parish, an' I 'ave been awnly t' Calstock an' Plymouth. You nineteen an' me twenty. Now I 'ave bookin' for Michigan."

Again Mary Ann smiled. She knew what it did for Jim. "Aas, an' you'll go—an' come back if that's t' be. If 'e edn', then I go t' Michigan too. The Cap'n 'ave set you an' me a contrac', comrade. Us'll work un till 'e's finished." Seeing what she had unintentionally done for him, she stroked his young beard, wound it around her fingers, and teased him for mimicking Jake who wore his beard full and long.

Jim caught her spirit and said, "I wonder if men let mun grow in America!"

When Mary Ann spoke again her voice was no more than a whisper although the walls around her were stone and the hour was midnight. As a little girl would say it, she said, "Jim, I 'ave a secret."

"W'at izza, maid? You look like somebody left e a fortune."

"Somebody did," she said. "I thought I wouldn't tell e afore you left—afore you got yer bookin', that is. I was afeard you wouldn' go. Not that I dawn't want e 'ere. I want e t' go more. Thee'd go maze if thee'd stay 'ere. 'Ere 'tis: Us be goin' t' 'ave a cheel!"

For a moment his mind was in a tumult of happiness. He grasped his wife, a hand on each shoulder, and held her at arm's length so that he faced her.

"Pol!" he exclaimed. "Be e shore?"

She nodded, her face glowing in response to the joy she saw in his. "Aas, I be."

Jim drew her to him again, his thoughts leaping from peak to peak of a father's experience, with a child to nurture and guide. But the brightness of his vision faded. What a time for a child to come! His voice took on a new pitch when he spoke again.

"But, Pol, maid, I should be with e! I want t' be with e!"

"Aas, Jim, I knaw. But Lizzie Jane will be close t' hand, an' Dr. Davey will take care of me. 'E 'ave knawed us both from chuldern an' will do 'e's best." Pol's lips trembled for a moment, but she went on. "I want e t' go! Dawn't e see? 'E'll be better for 'e or she too. There be no place 'ere for one or tother. For a maid, service; for a boay, mines—if they open again—or a farmer's hind! You must go for the baby's sake, Jim."

The clock struck twelve. They both got up, and Jim, carrying the candle, led his wife up the narrow stairs. Ready for bed, Jim pinched the flickering wick, and Sunday began in darkness.

"Jim."

"Aas, chul."

"I forgot t' tell e, S. P. R., was 'ere a bit after you left for work t' tell e be at the Prayer Meetin' Wednesday night. The Class want t' 'ave a bit of a good time for e."

"Thank e, maid."

Jim put his arm around her and drew her close.

"Seem like I can't give e hup," he whispered. "If us awnly knawed 'ow long 'e'd be!"

"'E won't be long, Jim. 'E won't be long. You'll find a way."

Jim wondered how he would do it, but he said: "I'll shorely try. You'm worth all I can do."

As she lay in his arms, her breath in waves passing over his cheek, the smell of her hair stirring him like the fragrance of spring, the thought that had tortured him most, as he knew it did her too, came to his mind. It had come first the day he got his passage in Plymouth, come like the thrust of a knife. At the pain of it, words burst aloud from his lips as he walked. "I can't write t' 'er n'r read w'at 'er write t' me!" Pol felt his body tense and asked, "W'at izza, boay?"

When he did not answer, she said: "I fancy I knaw, dear. You'm thinkin' of letters, bayn't e? Did e 'ear me say, 'You'll find a way?' You will, Jim. An' I'll read in ev'ry word, no matter 'oo write un, ten more I knaw you'd say if you done un with your awn hand."

Pol kissed him and said, " 'E's a short night. Best go t' slayp. There's a good boay. Good night."

"Good night, maid."

Jim still kept his arms around her but let her relax for the sleep she needed. Immediately his most worrisome problem returned. He remembered the morning his father took his hand and led him to the mine. He bestrode his father's back for the descent. He fetched a drill or a tin of water for his father's use. At the shift's end his father carried him to the top and most of the way home. Father and mother needed the extra pennies he helped his father earn more than he needed school. They never thought of a time like this. Finally he fell asleep.

When morning came, both had resolved to begin the day as though it were no different from the Sabbaths that had preceded it. Jim lent a hand where he could in getting breakfast, but he watched Pol more than he helped. She chattered about the things her hands were doing in a brave attempt to keep her resolution. At the table, the barrier she had tried to build gave way. The pressure of her heartache was too great for her will. Her voice was strained when she spoke. "W'at izza, Jim, that do things like this? Us 'ave been 'appy not knawin'; now us be un'appy not knawin'."

"So 'tis, maid. Jake called un a careless Providence that feeded us sometimes an' let us go 'ongry others."

"That sound like 'e's father—a sharp-tongued ol' man—but 'e dawn't hexplain."

"Jake be like 'is father in a lot of ways. The ol' man said, 'The mine comp'nies be Providence for we—they an' the markets.' The markets be for we, like the weather for a farmer —ayther fayst or famine."

"I dawn't understand," said Pol.

"N'r me," said Jim. "The ol' man like t' spayk in riddles."

Mary Ann shook her head, her face showing the perplexity of her thought.

"I've 'eard he crake about the consols, markets, Parliament an' gover'ment, but they'm awnly shaddas t' me. Goblins. Us dawn't knaw 'oo they be or w'ere they be, but us eat or starve at their fancy. Us be nothin' t' they."

Jim felt her bitterness and a wave of hatred for the fantastic causes of it. "Aas, maid," he said. "P'r'aps 'tis a good Providence that take me to Michigan."

Jim and Pol got ready for chapel, a custom they never thought of breaking. But there was one they would break today: They would sit together in a pew instead of in the choir. This was the last time they would worship together for . . . That, only God knew. Yes, they would sit together. The Collinses sang as usual, two at each end of the choir. They would understand, and so would the others who saw Jim and his wife in the audience.

Jim paid small attention to sermon, reading, or prayer. He was attracted by the faces around him. He had never seen them as they appeared today. They were kind faces and friendly. He read neighborliness in them and saw graces he had never thought of before. He listened to the singing and heard in it a new quality, a new richness. He picked out voices without turning his head. They were really musical, he thought, although he knew they had never been regarded as singers. The little mannerisms that had brought a jesting comment on previous days, he did not hear. Every sound was full of praise.

To him, the chapel was a huge cube of sound. Everybody sang, sang without fear or shame. How good it was! Singing was the biggest interest of the community, the peak of its social life. To have a voice and an ear were the best of gifts. The choir gave the whole a solid core; two rows of singers across the width of the house, divided in the middle by the harmonium, a toy of a thing, important only as a guide in practice and a stay to pitch. It filled the bare spots when the choir rested, or changed the key. The singers stood with their backs to the audience and faced the pulpit, a tribute to the high spot in the Wesleyan service. Jim's place was between Bill Collins and the harmonium. He thought of the space left when he and the boys had gone, and wondered who would fill it. He waited for the anthem. They would sing "Vital Spark of Heavenly Flame"—"Vital Spark" only, when the singers referred to it. It began as a minor—weird, gloomy, tricky—but graded later into a triumphant major. The choir sang it with ease and certainty, and the last measures left the listeners tingling with victory. As he listened, Jim wondered why the theory of worship set the pulpit high on the wall.

From his pew, Jim could command a half of the chapel walls. He sought every detail with a heart hunger that was almost a greed. Two black slabs high on the walls, inscribed with letters of gold, commemorated the consecration of two ancestral worthies. Jim knew the epitaphs by heart. His eyes lingered on the swallow's-nest pulpit. He had stood there once, "on trial" to go on the circuit. The remembrance of that agony flushed his face. Under the pulpit were the wooden plates upon which the small gifts of generations had been placed for the maintenance of the house of God. All these things he sought with the eye of affection, that their forms might linger in his memory. " 'Tis all because I shan't see mun again," he said.

Jim turned to Pol. "Be e list'nin', maid?"

"Not close, Jim," she whispered.

Occasionally the words of the preacher reached Jim's ears. "Born in sin and shapened in iniquity." "Born to trouble as the sparks to fly upward." "I strive to keep my body under, lest I become a castaway." Jim knew the man, remembered when he was converted and went on the plan. " 'E knaw the Scripters," Jim thought, "the 'ard ones."

Jim's eyes dropped from the preacher on the wall to his four friends in the choir. They had often talked about the hard demands of the chapel on their way to and from work.

"I tell e w'at, comrade," Joe said one day. "I can't live up to min. Afore I knaw w'ere I be I've sinned—slipped from grace."

Jim lingered over the memory. He was as fond of Joe as a brother and had not known what to say. Joe broke in on Jim's helplessness, apparently understanding why Jim was silent. "If God was more like Father or Jake even, 'oo dawn't profess, 'e'd be aysy."

For minutes Jim's eyes rested on Joe and Jake: Jake tall, spare, square-bearded; and Joe short, round, heavily mustached. His hair bristled like a doormat. Both were dark. Then he glanced at Bill and Tom, smaller patterns of the other two—Tom the round one, and Bill thin but not as tall as Jake. Both were lightly mustached and fair. Tom promised to be as stout as Joe.

The preacher got Jim's attention again, announcing the Prayer Meeting and mentioning the five young men about to leave. He repeated the saying that "a man can't take his religion across the sea," and hoped that these would prove the saying false. A hymn and a prayer ended the service.

When dinner was over and the table was cleared, Jim left his wife while he made the call on his father and mother which he had made weekly since his marriage. They lived in a thatched cottage at the foot of the hill, close to the leat. With the click of the gate his father came to the door to watch Jim's approach and to welcome him. "It's the boay," Jim heard him report to his mother. Inside the gate Jim stopped and looked around as if he had never seen the place before. The sunken path to the door was girded with low walls. Flowers bloomed in unarranged profusion along the top; others grew out of the chinks between the stones from the sides. "A king never walked a purtier path," Jim murmured. His father had put the plants on the rim of the wall but gave them little culture. There was no plan to their setting, no sequence to their blooming. Those in the cracks and crevices were the overflow of plenty from those above.

Beyond the wall to the left, stretching to the brook was his father's garden, harvested now, but clean, the black soil stoneless and weedless—well kept. Back of the house two oaks rose to thrice its height. Under them and in them Jim had played in his short childhood. On the right was orchard—a half-dozen cherry trees, as many pear trees, and double their number of apple trees. Just to think of them brought the taste of their fruit to his tongue. Around it all were hedges to the height of a man, and on these swaying shrubs which shut out the village and the world and doubled the Sabbath quiet of the place.

"Be e comin', boay?" his father asked.

Jim moved slowly down the path. He looked at his father as he had looked about the chapel and the garden. Every feature of the man before him was important—something to prize: the shining, bald head streaked over with a few carefully swept strands of hair; the whiskers, beginning as a narrow strip at the ears and becoming a roll under his chin. Father be still strong for 'is age, he thought. Jim noticed the

Sunday clothes, knowing that they and his retreat from his garden were the old man's nod of regard for the day. It was difficult for him to stay inside, and he observed the rule only because Mother had made it. Jim knew that a dozen times during the day he would walk to the gate and back—" 'e's Sabbath day's journey," Jim called it—stopping here and there to stay a bloom with his fingers while he touched his nose to the petals. "Nothin' but looks," he muttered when disappointed. Jim had seen him and heard him often. If a flower was fragrant, he inhaled the fragrance with slow delight. An unpromising bloom sometimes surprised him, and again he found what to his sight and smell was neither beautiful nor odorous. "Flowers be like folks," he said.

Jim reached the door, and his father put a welcoming hand on his shoulder, saying, "Come in, boay, come in."

Inside the dimly lit room, Jim said, "Hello, Mother."

She was sitting in a short settle at the end of the table where the light from the only window fell on the pages of a pictured "Pilgrim's Progress." She raised her eyes from the book and with no change of expression said, "I thought you was never comin'."

"Service was a little longer t'day than usual," Jim said.

"Poor hexcoose be better'n none, I fancy," she said tartly. "Moonin' awver leavin' Pol, more'n likely. Leavin' Mother dawn't matter."

"Mother! Mother!" said the old man reproachfully.

"You spayk w'en you'm spawk to," she retorted.

"You spayk t' me though you dawn't mean to, w'en you spayk t' 'e that way." He turned to Jim. " 'Er be grudgin' hev'ry minute 'er lose with e, boay." He leaned toward the hearth and raked a small ember to its edge with a calloused finger and toppled it into his pipe. The tobacco afire after a few puffs, he dropped the ember upon the hearth again. The bit of coal bounded from the brick to the floor. Quickly he picked it up and flipped it into the fire.

"You'll burn the 'ouse down some day," she said harshly.

The old man looked around at walls and beams and ceiling, his eyes full of merriment. "I was borned in this 'ouse, Mother, an' my father afore me. I learned t' smawk from 'e."

Jim mentioned the service again, and some of his reflections while it was in progress.

"You dedn' listen much, seem t' me like," his mother broke in.

"No, Mother, I can't say I did. It bein' the last time an' all, my mind kep' wanderin' hoff."

"Tomfoolery! You'm soft, Jim, like yer father."

" 'Oo'll take the Collinses' place in the choir, do e s'pose?"

"An' yer awn an' Pol's?" added his mother. "Dawn't think they'll be 'ard t' fill, do e?"

"Pol will go on," Jim said.

"Not for long, if my heyes bayn't seein' double."

Jim flushed and wondered how his mother knew. There were ways she might have heard—Lizzie Jane and Pol's mother—but she wanted credit for having seen some early sign. He was about to speak of his plans for leaving when the gate clicked, footsteps and the sound of a man's cough came to their ears. Jim's father went to the door.

"Hi wonder if Mrs. Holman would sell me a 'apporth of peppermint sweets." He coughed again. "I 'ave a ticklin' in my thrawt; 'e won't stop."

On the two-foot-thick window ledge were three glass jars containing the sweets Mrs. Holman made to attract stray coins that could find no other haven on the Sabbath. She looked at the jars with an air of reluctance.

"I knaw 'e's Sunday," the man said apologetically, and coughed again.

Slowly the old woman rose and reached for a jar.

"Thank e, missus," the man said, putting a halfpenny on the table, and coughed his way to the gate.

"You'm the awnly shopkayper open on the Sabbath, Mother," the old man said playfully.

"If a hox fall in a pit on the Sabbath, the Scripters say," the old woman began, when her husband interrupted.

"Thicky ox will be out of 'e's pit w'en the gate shut be'ind un is my belief."

The old lady looked at him belligerently. "Jedge not lest ye be jedged," she retorted.

"Mother dawn't jedge w'en there's a 'appenny t' get," he answered, his eyes sparkling with playful intent.

She turned her eyes toward him for a moment in silence. "I'll spayk t' you w'en 'e's gone," she said, nodding toward Jim.

The old man's smile faded away.

"I'm sorry thicky chap 'ad a cough," Jim said, and rose to go. He looked at his mother, stepped to her side and glanced out the window. He saw long shadows across the garden; the quiet of the Day was on the place outside. He smiled before he spoke. "You like the Scripter, Mother; the sun will be settin' soon. I'll say another for e: 'Let not the sun go down on your wrath.' Us was awnly 'avin' a bit a fun."

"Go 'ome with e," she said as Jim patted her shoulder. "The Sabbath bayn't a day for fun."

"Good evenin'," he said. "I'll come in t' see e t' say good-bye."

On his way home, Jim wondered if his father would ever give up trying to change Mother's humor. He wished Mother's hair was gray or white instead of staying black out of season. And her glasses with their shiny rims made her face look hard—" 'ard as a moorstone." He questioned how she would say good-bye. "Come t' think of it, I've never seed 'er kiss nobody."

Wednesday night came, and Jim went to the Prayer Meeting. Simon Rattenham—"S. P. R." to the whole parish—was the self-appointed leader of this usually rudderless service.

When the first hymn was called, Jim looked around to note the size of the audience and gleaned many smiles from faces that were stolid when his glance found them. Some, he knew, were ill at ease in the pious surroundings. They had come as friends, not as worshipers.

The devotional service done, the men present filed into an adjoining room. Jim and the Collinses stayed together until their places at the table were shown to them. Steaming cups of tea were already set upon the table, and along its center were plates of buttered rolls as well as of saffron stained cakes from the Rattenham bakehouse. Jim and his friends were assigned to places on S. P. R.'s right, Tom sitting next to their host. The chair opposite Tom was tilted against the table, the cup before it was empty. Jim wondered if it was Cap'n Bennett's place. He hoped his surmise was right: this was the only chance that remained to see him. They were to leave for Southampton in the morning.

Joe nudged Jim. "Look around, boay, an' see w'at's 'ere," he said.

Jim looked and realized that these men were the strength of the chapel. But he was sure that was not what Joe meant. He looked again. They came from all walks of the parish life. Rattenham's miller and wagoner sat side by side. A mason chatted with a quarryman from Kit Hill. Bill Downs, whiskered and bald and stooped, the best hedger in the community, talked with Rattenham's hind between sups of tea. A half-dozen miners wearing a look of dejection that all present understood, sat together in silence. The teacher of the parish school was at the end of the table opposite S. P. R. Jim noticed how pale he looked and how frail beside the laborers next to him. He preached occasionally in the chapel, sermons that were oddities for the village pulpit. One morning he left his home at the parish seat two miles away, with no thought of what he might say. Along the road he picked a leaf from a plantation tree that had begun to color, and a sermon grew to full proportion as he walked the rest of the way.

"W'en 'e beginned t' praych about a oak leaf," said Bill Downs, "I thought 'e was maze. W'en 'e was finished I thought I'd never trim a hedge with a free hand again."

Jim looked from the teacher to the hedger and back again. He felt himself drawn by something that he fancied united the teacher and the hedger; but he could not make it clear, give it shape, call it by name. The only thing he was sure of was that that something was real. The sound of a trap stopping at the chapel door caught Jim's attention, and in a moment Captain Bennett came in and took the empty chair. He spoke cordially to all the men, calling them by their first names and shaking hands with those nearest his chair. He refused to eat or drink and asked that the meeting be not delayed because of him.

Rattenham called for the attention of all without rising and told why he had asked them there. He urged them to feel at home and free to speak as they felt. A few responded, but more kept their thoughts and feelings to themselves or for an easier expression to their departing friends when the meeting was over. Finally, one said, "Simon, us would like t' 'ear from the boays 'oo be goin' away. Can't us 'ear from they?"

Simon turned to the lad sitting nearest to him and said, "Tom, my son," and smiled the rest of the invitation.

Tom stood up. "Us can't say much, Mr. Rattenham. Would e mind if us would sing instead of spayk?"

Immediately the brothers were on their feet. They sang as readily as they laughed or bantered one another in conversation. For a moment the four waited in silence; then Joe put his hand on Jim's shoulder. "Come, Jim, boay. Pitch the tune for us. Us can't do nothin' without thee."

Jim stood, pitched the tune, and with the first note their voices fell into place and filled the room with music.

With the last note a sigh that was half groan came from the

listeners. "God bless mun, hev'ry one," said the hedger aloud.

The teacher arose and asked to say farewell. "I have far to go," he said, "and it's a lone road." Rattenham nodded permission, and the teacher said, "I want to speak of America." He did, with the fluency of one who had been there and more. Of its size, its wealth, its resources, its new hard ways and of its future, he talked with the certainty of prophecy. "I envy you," he said. "In a few years, America will lead the world. America will never be cursed with a history such as England has had. She began with the mistakes of Europe to warn her. Her founders were men of scholarship, wisdom, ideals. No child born there need be bereft of the opportunity given by education. For the man who is not afraid of work, the man who invests himself, the intelligent man, it is a Land of Promise." He walked around the table, shook hands with Jim and the Collinses, and left the room.

Captain Bennett stood up. "I know w'ere you are goin'," he said. "I 'ave been there. The country is different, mining is different, the way the people live is different; but the facts of life—the foundation facts—are the same." He stopped, gave to each of the brothers and to Jim a package, and continued: "It is a book. Dawn't make the mistake made by many. The secret of life be in that book w'ether that life be lived 'ere or in America. Hi couldn' think of nothin' better. My best wishes go with e."

The chairman stood but said nothing. To each of the five young men he passed an envelope. This done, he continued to look around the table helplessly. At last he said, "With my best wishes and faith in each one of you." Again Simon lost control. Captain Harry saw his plight, pushed back his chair, and the meeting ended.

At the door an old woman was waiting. She touched Jim on the arm and said: "Jim, my son, my boay Jan be awver there, somew'ere. If you see un, tell un Mother would like to 'ear from un."

"Aas, Mrs. 'Enwood. I'll tell un if I see un," said Jim. " 'Ow long is a since 'e wraute?"

"Lawzee, chul, Jan can't write," replied the old woman. " 'E 'ave t' ask somebody t' write for un. The last word I got was a year ago w'en Dick Griffin comed 'ome from there."

"Aas, Granny, I'll tell un," Jim said, and she went up the road wiping her tears with her kersey shawl. Jim recalled that Griffin had been in Colorado—how far from Michigan, he did not know.

Jim left the chapel and took a back lane for home alone. He would be hidden in the darkness. He wanted to see nobody, to talk to nobody. He kept asking: " 'Ow will 'er stand it? . . . 'Er will say little—but the strain! I almos' hate t' think of the mornin'." Her words of Saturday night came back: "Not that I dawn't want e 'ere. I want e t' go more!" " 'Er be some brave," he said, and emerged from the lane which opened opposite his house.

Pol spoke first in the morning.

"Jim."

"Aas, Pol."

"After breakfas', afore the trap come, let's go down by the spring an' bide a bit like us did w'en us was married. Our last chat will be like the fust ones."

"Aas, chul."

And this they did. The dew glittered on the grass and sparkled on the leaves of fruit bushes and trees. They stood by the bench on the edge of the pool into which the water curved from a small wooden chute like a thread of living silver. Apple trees near at hand and hedge growths farther back and all around their little plot made both sacred and secure for them all of the world they asked.

Finally, Pol said: "W'en warm weather come, I sh'll come 'ere t' write to e, Jim. You'll be able t' read w'at I write then, boay."

Jim held her hand in silence.

"One thing more, Jim. I won't go to the trap. . . . There 'e be now, Jim."

Back in their house again, they saw through the window that the Collins boys had loaded their carpetbags and had said their good-byes. Jim took his wife in his arms and held her without a word. Their lips met. Pol slowly pushed him from her and slipped to a form beside the table. "Go, Jim," she said. And Jim turned away, picked up his bag, and joined the others at the trap. He shook hands with the elder Collins pair and started up the road.

The boys had determined to walk to Callington and chose the upper pike. It ran along the line between fields and moors. From its height they could see the hedges that marked off the squares and rectangles of the fields of the parish, fields they had seen red or yellow with trifolium, green after the spring rains, or swaying with loaded ears of waiting grain. From its height they looked upon the thatched roofs of three villages. They could name every dweller in each of them. Across the valley, crowning its own elevation they saw the Holmbush again, looked at it for the last time. The last to disappear was the tower of the parish church. Its bells had pealed for the marriages of generations and tolled for the spirits of the dead journeying their soundless ways. Roads and lanes, as familiar as the paths of the family gardens, they followed with their eyes until they were lost in the far country of a neighboring parish. Again and again they stopped and looked in silent longing. This was all they wished to see. The rest they would look upon would be England; that did not matter. Again a look—the last. This was home.

Chapter Three

FOUR WEEKS LATER the five travelers stood together on the wooden platform of the little station at L'Anse on Keweenaw Bay. The name of the town painted on the station end meant nothing to them. Tom tried to pronounce it but was baffled by the isolated letter and the capitalized second part. What concerned them most was that it was the end of the line. They knew they had some time to wait so they watched the unloading of luggage, their own bags within hands' reach at their feet.

With them on the platform stood several men whose mission there was only to see the train arrive and the little activity stirred by its coming. They were dressed oddly. Their caps covered ears and necks. Their coats were checked with red and black and green squares. The collars of their coats were turned up and reached the top of their heads. Their trousers of blue denim were cut off just below the knee and hung loosely around the top of their boots, which in all cases were laced their entire length. They spoke to one another in a foreign tongue. Their replies to the greetings from the station and train men were in English with a peculiar inflection. The travelers caught only an occasional word, and that uncertainly. Suddenly, as though they had formed where they stood, a half-dozen others appeared. "Look see," Tom whispered. "W'at be they?" Except for their footwear the new onlookers were dressed quite like the rest, but their clothes were ill-fitting. Their faces were uniformly dark, their eyes black, with a fixed look that approached a stare. They said nothing, and nobody spoke to them. They seemed to regard all they saw as puttering futility. Tom stepped up to a trainman. " 'Oo be they?" he asked. "Indians—red men," the trainman said. Joe looked again. "If they'm red, I dawn't knaw my colors," he said. The engine was disengaged from the cars and rattled away, its service done until later in the day.

The boys were tired. They were disheveled; they felt disrespectable without shame. For four days they had ridden the cane-seated coaches from New York; and they had not washed since the train left Chicago the preceding morning. The washrooms of the day coaches had discouraged them. They had slept each night, bent and knotted in the discomfort of the car seats, without undressing. They were hungry. The small stock of food they had bought in New York had given out the previous morning. In Chicago there had not been time to make other purchases. They had been afraid to trust the "Fifteen minutes for lunch" stops lest the train go on without them. Once Joe and Tom dared it. The "All aboard" of the conductor came before their meal was half eaten. Tom left the counter, his money and what remained of his food. Joe left his money but took his plate and, before the objection of the restaurant keeper could become effective, boarded the train. He seated himself at a window and watched the little flurry of excitement his escapade had caused. The restaurant man stood in the door helpless and angry. Fingers were pointed, and laughter went round as explanations were made. Joe held up his plate tauntingly, enjoying his joke. When the little station was out of sight, he turned his mischievous attention to his companions. With his spoon he pushed a piece of potato to one side and said, "Jim, my son, that be for you." He separated a small puddle of gravy. "William 'Enry, that be for you." He herded a half-dozen peas and said, "Jacob, they'm your allowance. Now hopen your mouths an' shut your heyes." The boys laughed at Joe's generosity but kept their eyes open. "You baynt 'ongry, I see," he said, and cleaned the plate. Then he opened the window and threw the plate and spoon away. "Not 'nough silver in thicky spoon t' keep," he said.

When the engine left the scene, the spectators filed away. Jim and the Collinses picked up their bags and followed. As soon as they stepped off the platform out of the shelter of the station, they shivered in the wind that came over the water.

"The water look cold an' the sky look cold, spite of the bit of sunshine," said Jake.

"An' I knaw I be cold," said Bill.

"That wind 'ave a clean sweep for a long way, seem like," said Joe.

From the track they could see the wharf through the leafless trees. A footpath led to it—a shorter route than that of the road. The idlers from the depot headed for the dock with the earnestness of men paid for serious employment.

Despite the sharp wind, Jim and his friends put down their bags to view their surroundings more easily. The wharf was a wooden structure supported by wooden posts sunk into the bottom of the lake. Everything about them was wooden—the walks, stores, station, dwellings. This was the climax of the day-long impression that their ride had given them. The occasional villages of wooden houses nestled in spaces hewn out of the endless forests. Those villages sat in a welter of logs, of sawdust, of bark and chips. Beside the tracks vast piles of logs were reared higher than the coaches they rode in. They had passed trains loaded with logs which indicated endlessness of supply. They had seen a mine or two as they came along, and each was set in timber piled as high as the houses and covering what looked like acres. They scanned L'Anse with its feet in the cold water of the lake, its back against the forest. Across the bay, three miles away, forest ranged north and south and west as far as the eye could see, its farthest edge meeting the sky. At two points a few houses cringed on the shore as though courting the open space in fear of the black distance behind them, in half-confidence of escape should need arise—escape to the open sea.

The waves, rising and falling before the wind, seemed to hurry for the shore. Their white crests flashed and disappeared in endless procession. They rolled under the pier with savage purpose but broke on the rocks or flattened on the sand, their strength gone.

"They look brave anough comin' in, but they'm limp goin' back," Jake said.

"Us 'ave seed bigger ones, comrade," answered Bill. "I 'ope the boat can ride mun."

"There her is now," said Tom, pointing up the bay.

All turned to look. For minutes they watched her approach, then they turned away to find a place to eat. A sign saying "Meals 25 Cents" caught Tom's attention, and toward it they went without question.

When they came back to the wharf they went immediately into the little cabin to be out of the wind. A half-dozen others, all men, constituted the list of passengers. Refreshed by food and a wash, they felt more like themselves again. Joe and Bill and Tom sat on a bench fixed to the side of the boat. Joe was observing the strangers seated around the wall. Tom took his concertina from his bag and held it in silence on his knees, the look on his face showing that his mind was not made up about playing. Bill was watching him caress the instrument, and smoked while he waited for results. Jake and Jim stood together looking through the window toward the open door of the bay. In the farthest distance a pennant of smoke lay across the sky.

"Do they call this a lake, Jim? 'E's big anough t' be called a sea."

"I was wonderin' if 'e froze in winter," Jim replied.

"Seem like they'm all strangers t' one 'nother," Joe whispered when he had satisfied his curiosity.

"That, or they'm tired of one t'other an' talked out," replied Bill.

"They could talk 'bout we," Joe said. "Us look comical anough to mun, no doubt—us with our tubbers, bobtailed coats, an' 'lastic side shoes in this climate. An' they awver-sized frails!" He kicked Bill's carpetbag in emphasis.

"They'll 'ave their fun w'en they get 'ome, likely."

"Likely."

Encouraged by Joe's talk, Tom's fingers found the keys of his instrument, and faint sounds trickled through the barriers made by the stroke of the engine, the whir of the propeller shaft under their feet, and the *slap, slap* of waves against the boat. When no one objected, Tom's courage increased. Scraps of tunes that had blown from the easier life of Plymouth to his moorland village came from the responsive keys. Bill and Joe added a hum or a word in scarcely audible voices. Jim and Jake still found interest in the lake and the receding shore line. Then more sober strains from their chapel life came in odd antithesis. Joe's mellow bass grew more audible in response to Tom's whispered melodies. Jake and Jim turned from their sea and landscapes and stepped across the cabin and made easy union with the wistful, half-expression of the little instrument. Pipes and song were their stepping-stones to ease. A haze came over the waters that cast a silver grayness of late afternoon. Tom's fingers moved in unconscious response to the muse that rode the mist. A few lines only, and the little group forgot their strangeness, forgot their remoteness from the scenes of their heartache, took charge of the place, and sang as of old. The other passengers looked and listened. New faces came to the door, smudged with grease and streaked soot. Between songs, Tom's fingers chased fugitive cadences here and there until another song took hold. Finally the muse suited itself to both scene and circumstance. Tom played a line, nodded, and they sang verse and chorus:

"One day nearer, sings the sailor
As the eve is drawing on;
Slowly drops the gentle twilight,
For another day is gone—
Gone for aye and its race is over,
Soon the darker shades will come—
But 'tis sweet to know at even,
We are one day nearer home."

Tom folded his concertina and put it away. "That's anough," he said when Joe laughed.

"W'at's the matter? Maze, be e?" asked Tom.

"If I be, I be glad," he answered. "Your faces was as long as the tossels on a 'earse. An' did e knaw w'at you was singin'?"

Joe's eyes still sparkled while the others look bewildered.

"Did e forget 'ow far you be from 'ome, my sons? You've crossed a 'alf of England, the 'Lantic Ocean an' rode four days an' nights on the train! 'Ow can e be nearder 'ome?"

Bill and Tom laughed with him as he explained. Jake's eyes only showed agreement with Joe's humor.

"Be e shore you'm goin' back, Joe?" Jake asked. "If you bayn't, 'ere's w'ere yer 'ome will be. W'at do e say, Jim?"

Ordinarily Jim stood aside when the brothers stirred up an argument. Called on to referee, he said, "It be a fambly affair," and enjoyed himself on the sidelines. This, however, was his affair too. He had helped with the song, but he had sung it with an entirely different meaning and was a trifle shocked as the rest were at Joe's funmaking. Only Joe could be expected to give the song a meaning like that. Joe would see fun in a funeral sermon.

"Maybe you'm right, Jake. 'E's likely all of us won't go back."

Some of the listeners asked for another song, but Joe still saw mirth in the last one.

"Best not t' sing no more if us want t' get *'ome*. Us 'ave t' 'ave somebody run the boat."

Joe's emphasis on home made some of the audience smile. One man said, "Thanks for the singing, boys, and good luck." He left the cabin, and the others settled themselves for the remainder of the ride.

It was dark when the *Mary Sutton* scraped and creaked to rest at the Hancock dock. Two runners reached for Joe's bag at the same time, urging their hotels.

" 'Old on a minute, boays," said Joe, resisting the pull on his belongings. " 'Old on a minute. Us five be t'gether an' must stay t'gether. Us will go with the purtiest of e. Let us 'ave a look!" He scanned the two with a serious eye and said, "Us will take thee," pointing to the one all the others said was the uglier. With a sheepish smile the rejected runner went away.

Assigned to their rooms, they reassembled in the one Jake and Tom were to use.

"The beds do look brave anough," said Bill. "Hi'll sleep without rockin', I knaw."

"Thicky pitcher an' bowl look encin' t' me," said Jake. "A foo drops of water do 'elp a man's morals no tellin', if they be used right. You all get out w'ile I wash."

They obeyed Jake's orders and left him alone. In a short time he called to them, "All's clear." Tom came back and found Jake in bed, his face to the wall. Then Tom took his turn to help his morals. A half-hour, and the two rooms were quiet.

To Jim sleep came slowly and with mincing steps. His mind was too full of the varied scenes of the day, his heart with the ache that the scenes could not dispel. The girl he had left clung to him with an all but tangible grasp. "Go,

Jim," she said as clearly as if she had been beside him. The unanswerable query of their last hour together seemed to sneer at his weakness. Joe's jest about the song and Jake's answer tormented him. Where would home be for him and her? He stared through the darkness past the days and months to the time of her pain and hated himself for leaving her. At times when he verged upon sleep her voice, audible, half frightened, called him back:

"Jim!"

"Aas, Pol."

His own voice brought him to full wakefulness.

Again he was on the struggling train, looking from its windows. He saw the futile villages held in the palm of the black forest. He compared them with the little hamlets of Cornwall so snugly safe in the protection of their fields and hedges, so peaceful under their bonnets of thatch, so quiet that he wondered how ills or misfortune could find them. And how close together they stood! A strong halloo would carry from one to a half-dozen of its neighbors. But, today, the train ran, it seemed for hours from one little nursery of human life to another. Each town must provide for its own emergencies, must, single-handed, grapple with its foes. The schoolmaster's words came back to him as he measured the vastness of the new world and the fortitude required for its conquest. At last he fell asleep.

Breakfast over, the boys, with bags in hand, started for the depot, the hotel man leading the way. A snow had fallen during the night, and the wind was searching and cold. With the first step from the hotel porch their congress shoes filled, and the day began in discomfort. The depth of the snow and the intensity of the cold told them that a Michigan winter was a full-grown, an oversized thing in comparison with the light snows of southern England. In single file they followed in the path the hotel man broke. During the few minutes they waited for the train they stood around the depot stove.

"That's the coldest I've hever been," said Bill. "Dedn' knaw weather got so cold."

"Might's well 'a' 'ad no clo'es on for the good mine done," said Joe.

The conductor's "All aboard" called them to the train. It was a toylike thing that clicked and careened over infant rails set close together. The snow made the train slow and, the boys thought, dangerous. But it was warm as long as it lasted, and that was something.

At Calumet a coach stood waiting for the train and whatever passengers it might bring. Runners had taken the place of wheels overnight. It was closed in all around except at the back. The floor was covered with straw, a consideration shown to newcomers who were almost a daily occurrence. A long bare bench on each side was the principal accommodation. The bags of the passengers were placed on the top; the driver sat out in the weather. He seemed a mountain of clothes. The face his scarf did not cover, whiskers and cap did. Only his eyes braved the cold.

There were four other passengers, a woman with two children and a man. The man was comfortably dressed, but the woman and children shivered visibly, as did the five men opposite them. Cold wisps of the bitter air bit their ankles while their toes and fingers tingled. Joe and Bill tried to beguile themselves with their pipes and occasional comment.

" 'Ow did e sleep last night?" asked Joe.

"After I started, well anough. But I couldn' start for thinkin' of they towns—'ow far apart they was, an' 'ow aysy t' burn down. All made of wood—ev'ry one of mun."

"I s'pose Central be the same," said Joe, "an' from the looks of things dawn't 'ave a railroad."

"W'at would us do if us couldn' find work there?" asked Tom.

"One worry be anough, my son—one at a time," Joe answered. "Atween work an' catchin' my death of cold, gettin' work be a small matter. I'm goin' t' try walkin'."

Joe stepped out, and Bill followed him, each taking a runner rut for the experiment. They flailed their arms, rubbed their hands and ears, and occasionally ran a few steps to overtake the coach. The other three sat in silence, finding it difficult to keep their eyes from the woman and children, knowing that they suffered.

The little girl whimpered and began to cry. "I'm cold, Ma," she said.

"Yes, yes, we'm all cold," the mother said, drawing the child closer to her. "We shall be there soon. Just think, us shall 'ave supper with Da! Won't you be glad t' see Da?"

The woman spoke without a glance at the men opposite.

"Cornish too," Jake whispered. "Comin' to 'er man."

The comfortably dressed man called to the driver to stop. He got off the coach, went around to the side and took a bundle from the top. He loosened the straps around it, removed an oilcloth covering, and took out a blanket. He secured and replaced the bundle and stepped into the coach. "Take this, madam," he said. "Wrap the children in it. I am going to the end of the run. Use it till you get home."

The woman said, "Thank you, sir," and tucked the blanket snugly around the little boy and girl.

Joe and Bill watched the man open his pack. Immediately Joe reached for his bag and took it inside.

"Take off they boots an' stockin's, my son," he ordered Bill. "Your feet be as cold an' wet as mine," and he began to take off his own. He opened his bag, took out two pairs of socks and a soiled shirt. "Dry yer feet with this, boay, and put they socks on." Both rubbed their feet vigorously, Joe talking as he rubbed. "Feet bayn't very hornamental, but I'm glad I washed mine last night." He shoved the open bag toward Bill. "Now stick yer 'oofs in the bag t' keep mun warm." Both sank their feet into the bag among Joe's other belongings.

" 'Lastic sides was never made for weather like this," said Bill.

Joe's little show stirred the group to sociability. The woman asked the man who had lent her his blanket how long the snow would last.

"This is an early fall and a heavy one. It looks like a long winter ahead. Snow will probably cover the ground till March."

"An' it be awnly October now!" said Tom, shocked into speech.

The man turned to Tom and asked, "Did you just come over?"

"Yes, sir, we just landed. We'm goin' t' Central Mine t' look for work."

"I hope you find it," the stranger went on. "Winter is usually a bad time to find work in the mines. I hear Central is slowing a little too. You will pass several mines on the way. Why don't you inquire as you go? The stage will stop at Allouez long enough for you to go to the mine office."

That sounded reasonable to the boys, and they all thanked him for his advice.

"What will you do if you can't find work underground?" he asked.

Tom's question again. Fate seemed to have the habit of repeating the disagreeable; perhaps because Fate is so mockingly reasonable. What would they do? They had dismissed the question when Tom asked it to keep their own courage up, but the stranger must be answered.

"Us dawn't knaw, sir. Us be miners, you see."

"I understand. It might happen that you can't find what you are looking for. If it does, I am looking for men for my camp at Baraga. Lumber camp. My name is Roach. Look me up."

Again the five thanked him.

The lumberman's words and their approach to the first

mining town after Calumet compelled them to face the possibility. They couldn't evade it. "If you can't find it." The first try was just around the next bend in the road. Then what? The answer was always the same to them. Another mine. That was a part of their history; it was written in their marrow. Another mine and another until in some dark gut of the earth they found a place for their skill. Every Cornish miner answered the question, met the emergency so. It mattered not to him what the ore might be that he mined. Mining was his trade. For generations his ancestors had picked and pried, mauled and shoveled, blasted their way by candlelight in the Cornish pits. They knew ground, how to break it, to timber it, to channel its water and dispose of it. They knew the whimsy of veins and followed them as if by scent. In the narrow ways they cut to obtain the precious dirt, they acquired a skill with their simple tools that has been equaled by no others. Given a hammer and a few drills, these men would make passage through anything that steel would dent and powder break. On the other hand, they could push their way through dirt that crumbled at the touch or ran like quicksand. Their pride in their tools and their own skill never abated. When the small bits of their drills were insufficient and their shoulder muscles inadequate for the tonnages demanded from the thick veins of the Peninsula and together gave way to air-driven machines, they still persisted that a man was no miner if he had no skill with a hammer and drill. Wherever they went, they found that their methods had preceded them; wherever they went, the copy of their work made them feel at home. In mines everywhere their terms were established. What would these men do? They would go to another mine and would mine.

For a time the plan to seek employment in Central was unsettled. Thought of another place had not come to them. They felt familiar with the place because of Captain Bennett's description and recommendation of it. The mines of

Hancock and Calumet were behind them, passed without a thought. The practical suggestion of the lumberman must be discussed.

Tom was impatient to be sure of a job. He was uneasy, worried. The prospect of a return ride in the coach sapped his courage. He was impetuous in his insistence: "Us bayn't shore of anything up there, an' us might get somethin' 'ere."

Here meant Allouez. They were within a half-hour of the place.

Tom turned to Jake and Jim for support. "W'at do you two say?"

"Speak up, Jim," said Jake.

"Us dawn't knaw anybody there, an' us dawn't knaw nobody 'ere," said Jim slowly. "The chances be the same— even."

Jake agreed, and it was settled to try Allouez.

At Allouez they could not overlook the mine. Its structures towered over everything else in the place. Shaft houses, trestles, rock burrows, enginehouses and stamp mills. A small building painted white stood apart, indicating its importance —the Office. Jake and Jim led the way to it.

It was not quite noon, and the captain had just come in from his round in the pit. He was a tall man, full-whiskered, stout. He had an air of authority tempered with affability. One might have expected firmness from him or kindness as the need arose. He looked at the men and frowned. He understood before they spoke why they had come, and wished he might escape the refusal he felt bound to make. He surmised that not much stood between them and hunger. A look told how little stood between them and cold. Each face was pitifully anxious. He was sorry, but—

"Could e give us a job, Cap'n?"

In spite of the urgency of the question the captain did not answer it. Instead, he asked one:

"W'ere did e come from, my sons?"

There was always a chance that the dimming lanes and fading hedges, the dying sound of parish bells might be revived by a new arrival.

"W'ere did e come from?"

"Stoke Parish," Jake answered.

"Did e work in the Holmbush or Redmoor? I 'eard both 'ad closed down. I come from that parish twenty year or more ago. W'at be your names?"

The bus was waiting. Their bags were still in it. Work seemed within reach. The air quivered with anxiety. The captain's face darkened.

"Things is kinda slow," he said, "but I'll see w'at I can do."

Captain Chenoweth went into an adjoining room, leaving the men in a confusion of hope and fear. A few minutes, however, and he was back.

"We 'adn't expected t' take on no more for the winter. I can't take e all on, but I'll make room for three of e. You can split up as you like. I'll leave e alone t' talk it over."

In a few minutes full of protest and argument the matter was settled. Jim because he had a family, Tom because his savings were small, and Jake, the oldest, as a companion and adviser for Tom were to stay. "Father would like to 'ave un that way," said Bill.

The captain waited for their decision, called a clerk to take down their names and went to the door with them. He pointed to a house and said: "That is a boardin' 'ouse an' a very good one, I'm told. English—Cornish, that is. Come t' work t'morra night."

The five said, "Thankee, Cap'n," in unison.

At the coach, good-byes were said again.

" 'E's 'ard anough," said Jake to the two that were going on, "but not so 'ard as the last."

Joe took Jim's hand. No mischief shone from his eyes when he spoke.

"Maybe thicky song was right after all, boay. Maybe you be nearer 'ome. 'E look like it."

Jim, Jake, and Tom watched the stage until the forest hid it from sight, picked up their carpetbags and went to the house the captain had pointed out to them.

Chapter Four

JAKE KNOCKED ON THE ONLY DOOR to which a path had been made through the snow. It was the back door. They knew that because stovewood was piled within two feet of the stoop. A narrow cleft in the snow no more than shovel wide ran from the stoop between the house and wood rick to the back of the lot. A worn broom stood beside the door, the especial use of which the newcomers did not know. They kicked the snow from their boots as they mounted the steps. The door opened, and a middle-aged woman, stout, bare-armed, hair closely smoothed back to a knob, blue-eyed and dispirited, stood before them.

"We'm lookin' for board, missus," said Jake. "The cap'n sent us 'ere."

"Come in aout of the cold. I've room for e," she answered, and stepped aside to let them in. "Put your bags in there"—pointing through an open door—"an' find seats. There be men still abed, so I can't take e hupstairs."

Without question or comment she resumed her work at the kitchen table.

Four night-shift men who for some reason had risen early were sitting on a form set against the wall, smoking. Not a word passed between them until the strangers had found

places to sit. Jake and Jim sat on the form with the others;
Tom took the corner of the woodbox.

There were no introductions. All seemed absorbed in the
"boardin' missus' doin's." She was loading the pails for the
men who went to work that night. She scanned each one for
initials or other mark scratched on the tin to indicate its
owner. She put slices of cold beef between cuts of bread
spread with butter softened on the stove, and adjusted them
in the upper half of the pail. Then she tucked a bit of
"tetty cake" in one, a "seedy nubby" in another or a saffron
bun. A store cooky topped the meal for all. When she put the
lid in place, Mrs. Uren said, " 'E's a pity they can't all eat
the same, 'twould save a lot of work." Nobody answered.
She've prob'ly said the same times on end, Jim thought.
Into the large compartment of the pail she poured a bounti-
ful supply of cold black tea, added sugar to one, milk to
another, both to the next.

That job done, Mrs. Uren took a shawl from the wall,
threw it over her head and shoulders, fastened it under her
chin, and went out to the hydrant for water. When she came
back her bare arms were red as was her face, her eyes watered,
and she was breathless. She put the bucket in place and
fetched two armfuls of wood for the stove. Then she removed
the shawl and wiped her cheeks and nose with the underside
of her apron. Nobody volunteered to help her. Every man
there regarded that as her job. The "boardin' boss" was responsible for the pile outdoors; she was responsible for the
woodbox behind the stove. The men paid their board and
were expected to do no more. None of them wished to be
tagged a "fancy boarder."

Jim tried to sum the things the woman had to do. She
cooked—for how many, he did not know—and cleaned and
scrubbed, made beds, fetched wood and water and what more
he couldn't imagine—unless she had a servant who at the
moment might be out on an errand. Jake nudged Jim and

nodded toward her warming her hands at the stove, and said, "Comp'ny count an' long hours." Jim made no reply. "An' t' make un more discouragin', low pay." Still Jim did not answer. Then one of the men spoke.

"Do e 'ave a bit of bacca, Northy?"

"Iss, you, Griffin. 'Ave some." And Northy handed Griffin his pouch.

"W'at are e doin' t'night, Allen?"

"I bayn't shore—timbrin' maybe."

The fourth man was ignored and therefore nameless for the time being.

"W'at kind of a crossin' did e 'ave?" asked Northy, addressing Tom who sat opposite him.

"You choosed a bad time of the year t' cross," said Griffin.

"Us dedn' 'ave no choice," answered Tom.

"You'll fin' the weather 'ere some diff'runt from 'ome," continued Griffin. "Look see, they boots be sawkin'-wet naow!"

"This bloody country bayn't no place for a w'ite man," said the man whose name had not been mentioned. As he spoke he turned toward Jim and Jake for appreciation of his remark.

"Dawn't e 'ave money for a passage 'ome, Sims? They trains an' boats dawn't stop for a bit of snow."

" 'Oo's spaykin' t' you, Hallen?" retorted Sims. "You spayk w'en you'm spawk to."

"I've 'eard e say that afore, Sims," continued Allen. "I been thinkin' of a collection t' send e back, my son. Ev'ry man in the 'aouse would give somethin' gladly, I knaw."

Jake's eyes brightened at the sharpness of Allen's retort. He gave Sims a second look to see the effect of it. A face like a thundercloud, he thought. Hair standin' straight, like a 'edge'og. Eyes dawn't look for no good an' mouth 'ave forgot 'ow t' spayk un. 'E'd make a good 'angman.

Allen got up from the form and came to the strangers.

"As you 'eard, I be Allen, Bob Allen. W'at be your names?"

"I be Jake Collins. This be Jim Holman, an' the cheel on the box be my brother, Tom Collins."

Allen smiled and shook hands with Tom.

Allen was as tall as Jake, the tallest of the brothers, and spare like him too. He had no beard, however, and was of light complexion. He was perhaps in his middle thirties.

"If you'm like I was w'en I come 'ere, you dawn't 'ave the coats an' footgear for this climate; but you'll 'ave t' 'ave they." He pulled a large silver watch from his pocket. "Us can still do un afore cribtime. Come with me, my sons, an' I'll shaw 'e w'ere t' go." He put on his coat and hat and led the way to the road. Two blocks, and they were on Main Street. Another block, and Allen led them into a dry-goods store. A clerk came to serve them.

"I want t' see the boss," said Allen.

A few minutes, and the boss emerged from his official coop on the balcony and came down the stairs. He was short, and overweight, wore a black skullcap and a full silky beard. On his feet were carpet slippers. His brown eyes shone with welcome as he addressed Allen.

"What can I do for you, Bob?"

"Mr. Marx, these 'ere boays be jus' come awver an' need some clo'es. Fix mun hup, 'ead an' feet—diggin' clo'es an' all." He turned to the surprised trio. "I 'ave t' be goin'. Marx is all right; 'e won't sell e w'at you dawn't need." And then in a lower voice he added: "If you run a bit short afore payday, let me knaw. Never mind sayin' nothin'. W'en I come awver, ol' Joe Dingle steered me. 'E ain't 'ere no more. I be jus' squarin' accounts. So long."

When they got back to the house they put their bundles with their bags, and Mrs. Uren told them to sit down to tea.

By three o'clock the men were all down, and Mrs. Uren took her new lodgers upstairs. As they crossed the living room with their bundles, not a man spoke. Greenhorns were too common to merit attention. In the bedroom the boys put their packages on the beds and waited for orders.

"You can sleep 'ere, one in each bed," she said. "You get 'ome at six in the mornin', an' the men 'oo sleep in they go t' work at seven. If you weren't all the same shift two of e might sleep in the same bed. Hang your clo'es on the wall. Look see." And she pointed to a row of nails just below the ceiling.

The woman did not stay to talk after the instructions were given. She had no time to waste. At the door she turned and said, "Naow my beds be all full again," and went down the stairs.

The boys looked the room over. They could stand straight only in the middle of it. There were four beds, the head of each touching the ceiling which sloped still lower, leaving a space usable only for stowage between bed and side wall. In this space were five carpetbags. Along the other wall was a long bench for convenience in dressing, and over it the row of nails Mrs. Uren had pointed out. Only a few of the nails were in use. Coats hung from the corner posts of the beds, and trousers were draped over head and foot boards. Small piles of underthings lay on the bench, and there was an array of shoes beneath it. The beds were as the night men had left them. Under each a "cloam pot" was visible. On the back of the door was a small mirror and a tin combcase. The room had a peculiar odor which the boys noticed but did not mention.

After the look around, Jim said, " 'E'll look better w'en the beds be made." To which Jake added, "A little."

There was one window in the gable end of the room. The lower half of it was boarded up, and the intervening space filled with sawdust. The upper half was sealed between sash and frame with rags.

"Us might as well get comfortable," said Jake, whereupon they changed stockings, underwear, and shirts.

Dressed again, Jake said, "I want to look at the place that 'ave 'dopted us," and went to the window. Jim and Tom followed him, and together they looked on a block of back doors, back yards, woodpiles, and two parallel rows of "little houses" separated by the alley. The snow was still clean and scarcely broken. Gusts of wind continued the storm of the preceding night by swirling the snow from the housetops. Beyond the square of dwellings the white spread rose steeply to be lost in the darkening forest.

Suddenly all heads turned to see a neighbor come from a near-by porch and go to the little house at the end of the lot. They watched in silence till the privy door sealed its flimsy seclusion.

" 'E mus' be hawful t' sit 'alf bared in a place like thicky," said Jim.

"Aas, an' winter edn' really come yet, I fancy," added Tom.

"Seem like our winda face the wrong way," said Jake. "Let's go down an' see w'at the comp'ny's like."

On the landing they saw two doors, one open and one shut. They looked into the open room in amazement.

"That's a new one!" Jake exclaimed.

The room was higher than their own, and along the side walls were bunks—six to a side in tiers of three. A form was set down the middle. The bunks were homemade of two-by-fours and planks.

"Look like steerage on the boat," said Jim.

"Us be favored, seem like," said Tom, nodding toward their beds.

"I s'pose the bunks give way t' beds as the missus c'n afford mun," said Jake. "Make me think of bolts of drap'ry on S. P. R.'s shelves."

"Us be learnin'," said Jim.

"Fast," answered Jake, "an' awnly arrived. Stoves in the middle of the room, sawdus' in windows, an' beds in ricks. Necessity do spawn a lot of things."

When they went downstairs five men were sitting around the room, three astride their chairs with arms resting on the chair backs and two tilted against the wall. No one spoke. "They'm too fresh from bed," thought Jake, "t' be talkative. The door op'nin' an' closin', lettin' in fresh hair, will wake mun." A long table occupied the center of the room. It was covered with a hugely figured cloth, mostly red. On it, in the center was a revolving caster.

The new arrivals accepted in silence all they found. Jake and Tom lighted pipes and added to the thickness of the air already carrying a full load of reek from the others and the kitchen stove. So they sat, some watching as the smoke they blew expanded and lost itself in the haze. Others stared at spots on the opposite wall or through the window across the street. They appeared to be buried in deep speculation. Jim speculated, too. He thought a man lucky who smoked because he made a smell of his own, could make his own atmosphere. He pondered on the tempers of the strangers, whether he would like them, what was their history. The quiet was embarrassing, but the greenhorns would not tempt an hour as tricky as this when men were freshly from bed but unrefreshed by their sleep.

"Is a goin' t' snow some more?"

The question was to anybody, a sign of recovery.

"The sky do look low anough."

" 'E wouldn' s'prise me if us 'ad t' shovel a tunnel from the door in the mornin'."

" 'E's a caution the way 'e can snow in this country w'en 'e's a mind to. Las' winter 'e was two feet awver the door."

Jim, Jake, and Tom knew these remarks were for their ears. They were toned with the pride of experience.

"Hi remember—let me see, was a five or six year ago?— w'en the stage dedn' go through for two weeks! 'E's a purty country."

"W'en did e land, my son?"

This was to Jake. With wakefulness came curiosity and friendliness.

"Four days back."

"Do e 'ave work?"

"Aas. Start t'morra night."

"I heard they wadn't takin' on no more."

"They did this mornin'. Took on three."

With that, questions stopped. All that was left to know, these men knew except names. Names were not important at the moment. They would leak out in time. The strangers were not from the parishes of the questioners; their brogue showed that. But they were from Cornwall, and there was nothing worth telling about the Duchy that all did not know. Work was slack there or entirely gone, and any change could only be for the worse.

"Hi need stretchin' a bit," said one, yawning and raising his hands toward the ceiling. "W'at do e say t' a turn with the ax? The air will do us good."

"Hi'm with e."

"Hi too."

Accordingly, three of them got mittens and caps and went out to the woodpile. That was within the code. Helping the "boardin' boss" did not make a fancy boarder of a man.

The younger of the two men left said: "Hi be Jack Spargo; 'e be 'Arry Jenkins. W'at be you called?"

Jake answered.

Spargo was, in the Cornish term, "a bit sandy." He looked older than Jim but not as old as Jake—probably close to thirty. He was of medium height, walked with a forward tilt of his body as miners habitually do, and wore no whiskers. Harry Jenkins was tall, mustached, and gave an impression of serious-mindedness.

"I 'ope you like it 'ere, my sons," said Spargo. "Us do 'ave plenty of snow, an' the winters be long, 'tis true; but us do make a livin', an' that is the big thing. W'at's more, the bal edn' goin' t' strike t'morra or next week. This country be a safe place t' live for years t' come."

Jim listened, bewildered. There was something hard and cold in Spargo's words. "A safe place to live for years to come!" While he spoke, Jim's mind raced a half-dozen times over the four thousand miles of distance he had come in the last weeks. Didn't home mean anything to this man? He spoke of the years to come as though England, the old associations, meant nothing to him. At the same time Jim was aware of a strong appeal to something inside himself in Spargo's words. Also he thought Spargo spoke as though he had been waiting for the chance to say these things.

"You be lucky t' get work," Jack continued, "an' this be a fair place t' live. You can make aout t' be 'appy if you want to."

Jenkins had said nothing. He only nodded when the new-comers had given their names. At this point, however, he took his pipe from his mouth as though loath to part from its savor and said, "I be 'avin' my maid aout come spring, if all be well."

Jenkins spoke like a man under a powerful compulsion. Jack had tossed England aside as a miner discarded the remnant of a used candle. Jim's eyes returned again to Spargo; his heart went out to Jenkins.

The children came in, bringing snow and fresh air with them, a boy of ten and a girl slightly younger. They threw their books on a chair in the room where the men were sitting, glanced at the new boarders and went out to play. Children from five to fifteen went by the window, laughing and screaming with the delights they could extract from the snow. Jim arose and went to the window to watch them.

"The parents of most of they come from the ol' country— that is from one ol' country or another," said Spargo.

"Iss, you, an' a lot of they chuldern come across too," said

Jenkins. "They'm 'appy anough, seems like. That comfort me. I 'ave two."

"Happy" was the word in Jim's mind as he watched them. He tried to think if he had ever been as happy as they were. They lay in the snow to make figures of themselves; they threw snow at one another in handfuls; they tripped one another and laughed at the one sprawled at their feet. There was no restraint. Care for their clothes seemed not to enter their minds. Jim made comparisons. When he was nine—he picked a child he thought was nine to illustrate his thought to himself—when he was like that, he went underground to work with his father. A child miner! And he had worked ever since! He had had no childhood. He wondered what a childhood of labor had done for him. "S'pose I 'ad played like that an' gone t' school till I was growed?" he asked. But he couldn't answer. The problem was too much for him. A heavy footstep on the porch recalled him to his surroundings. He turned and took his chair again.

The footstep Jim heard was of the first day-shift man coming home. One after another, they came in quick succession. Boots thumped on the porch or were kicked against the step; the door opened, and they passed through the kitchen to the "dry" or "change room" at the other end. Shortly, washed and dressed in their "second best" or daily-wear clothes, they came into the room where Jim was sitting. Some sat down, but more of them stood the few minutes they must wait for the supper call.

Little conversation accompanied the meal, and again no one paid any attention to the strangers except to ask that something be passed. They were hungry and "mealtime be no time t' talk in a boardin' 'aouse." As each man finished he arose, stepped over the bench, and left the room. Jim and Jake and Tom stayed until all three were done. Jim counted them—twenty men.

Jim listened in vain for a Devonshire accent as he heard

the men talk, both at the table and as they lighted their pipes in the middle room. "They'm all from the west," he said. "They spayk softer an' sing their sayin's. Yet they say some words the same." He heard Jake and Tom speak as the others spoke and remembered that the Collins family had come from St. Austell. But when he was in the talk, the two brothers stood by and spoke the Devonshire brogue with him. One boarder, Jim noticed, was markedly different. When he asked for food he said, "Please," and "Thanks." He was young, smooth of cheeks, and his eyes had a light in them when he looked around.

Ten minutes after the meal most of the men had disappeared. A half of them went into the washroom to change and be ready when the whistle blew at a quarter to seven. Others went to town. Two men of the day shift stayed at home. Those who went to town went as they were at the table save for a cap and coat. The boy Jim had marked put on a tie and wore gloves instead of mittens.

" 'E's aour Yankee boarder, a bit of a dude," volunteered Penglaze.

Penglaze was forty past, short and square. He had a large face, made larger by muttonchop whiskers. He had an air of self-satisfaction. He spoke always as if making a correction. He was a religious man and took the role of setting an example. Jake said, " 'E's good but 'is goodness 'ave gone sour."

The other man was Johnson, tall, blue-eyed and redheaded. He came from Carn Brea, he said. At the table one of the men had called him Fire-and-Flame Johnson. He pulled his chair near to Jim, sat astride it, and essayed to be friendly. While he loaded his pipe he talked of the early snow and the unusual cold for the time of the year. " 'E's a good thing the mines 'ere be all close t' taown," he said. "Hi'd hate t' 'ave t' walk six miles across the moor in weather like this like I did back 'ome."

Johnson struck a match, and while it burned and before he put it to his pipe he said, "Be you married?"

"Aas," Jim replied.

" 'Ave a fambly?"

"No, sir."

"Let me advise e a bit. Get your maid aout as early as can be, my son. 'E'll be aysier for you and she. Cornwall won't never turn a w'eel again, I dawn't b'lieve. These little taowns be growin' fast, the mines be rich in min'ral. Hamerica is a comin' country."

And then, like an afterthought, but in reality, Jim thought, the reason for his speech, he said, "My missus be comin' in the spring."

"W'en she come, you will be 'ere t' stay."

"Iss, you, that will settle it."

"This look like a 'ard place for a woman," said Jim. He was thinking of the snow that might cover the door in the morning and of Mrs. Uren at the hydrant in the icy wind.

As if reading his mind Johnson said, "My woman won't keep boarders. And his face hardened at the thought as though the suggestion of his own making insulted her. "My woman will make a 'ome for me, 'erself, an' 'er chuldern. 'Er won't slave for strangers."

"W'at would us do if all feel like you do?" asked Jim.

"Iss, you," added Penglaze. "W'at would you done we'n you come? You'm selfish, Johnson."

Johnson's blue eyes changed to steel as he spoke. "Selfish, iss, in a fitty way, but not greedy. That answer one part of your speech, Penglaze. I dawn't care w'at you'd do, any of e," added Johnson bluntly. "I'd ruther build a shanty with my own 'ands an' batch than see any woman slave like this one."

" 'Ear, 'ear!" said Jake.

Jake's approval softened Johnson noticeably. "The mines must 'ave men; the men must live some place. The comp'nies could make shift for the men like the lumber camps do.

Men cooks, men dishwashers, men bedmakers, an' men wash-women for that matter."

"Did e ever eat men's cookin'?" asked Jake, his eyes sparkling with enjoyment.

"Not that I knaw by," answered Johnson, "but I hear say no woman in taown can cook like they lumber-camp cooks. Be that as 'e may, my wife cook fur me an' nobody helse."

"Spaykin' of 'ome an' chuldern," began Jim, "I've been told—" When he realized that he did not know this man and that, what he was about to say might be unwelcome or worse.

"Iss, iss, boay, I knaw," said Johnson, stopping him. "A lot of nonsense 'ave been told." A smile spread over his face, and Jim felt easier. "Us do 'ave churches an' schools an' wages. W'at more do e want? That's more than you'd 'ave back 'ome naow. If all the married men in the bal 'ad their fambles 'ere, they would be better men; an' us would 'ave a better taown. I've been 'ere five year. I made a mistake. A place that give a man a livin' deserve all 'e can give back. Hafter all, we an' aour fambles do make a taown."

The men who had gone to town began to return. As Jim and Jake and Tom were starting up the stairs for bed, one man said, "Nothin' us took hoff will dry t'night."

"I'm takin' my hunderwear t' bed with me," said another.

"Better not let the missus see e," said a third.

"That's a idee! Two of mun in fact," said Jake, but neither of the others answered.

Jim felt a deepening sense of loneliness in spite of those about him and the talk he had heard. It was the loneliness of a stranger in a crowd. The day had seemed endless to him in spite of all its newness. He felt neither weariness nor desire to sleep. In their room, Jim said, "Seem like a lot be thinkin' the same thing."

"Aas, comrade," said Jake. "Two! 'Ow many do e add yerself up to?" He laughed and winked with assumed slyness, knowing that Jim saw him. "Joe would say they do want their women; but 'tis deeper than that. 'Ome mean more'n that. Necessity be spaykin'. Necessity do work wonders. 'E will change Englishmen into Hamericans."

Each took the bed Mrs. Uren had assigned to him. Neither knew who had slept in the bed before him, and neither would know until Saturday night brought two to each bed.

As Jim lay waiting tensely for sleep to come, he tried to adapt himself to the group that filled the house. It was his first experience in such close contact with so many men. He assorted them as they had impressed him. Spargo and Jenkins seemed likable. Penglaze— He wasn't sure; he might like Penglaze better if he knew him better. Johnson was a solid sort, dependable, of a sensible turn. Allen came to mind. Allen paid no attention to him or the Collinses at the table. Allen made a different impression from the rest. Jim's mind leaped the vast distance he had traveled. Simon Rattenham had loaned him money, but Simon had known him from infancy. This man had never seen him before or Jake or Tom! Allen's retort to Sims came back. His words had cut like a knife. Allen was different, sure enough.

But more than of all these he thought of Mary Ann. He wanted to tell her everything that he had seen, heard, experienced. The journey, the captain, the job, the men, Allen. He opened and clenched his fingers as he wondered if he could teach them to write. He fancied letters full of the stories he would tell of the new land. The new land! He recalled lakes he had passed—more than he could count— streams he had crossed, forests of different woods his train had cleft. He fancied himself looking down on it all like a deity, before the whites came to mar it. What a sight! What beauty! He gave way to the Deity he trusted. "An' he kept un for 'Is awn enjoyment, 'ow long, nobody knaw. Now 'E give it t' we." "Hev'ry day I could plod with 'er," he muttered. His voice broke the silence.

"Dreamin' already, my son?" asked Jake.

"Dreamin' shore 'nough," said Jim.

Again his mind filled with candlelight. "Hi want e t' go, Jim. It will be better for 'e or 'er." Again he put out his hand and pinched the wick and together went to sleep.

In the morning Jim found Tom in the middle room writing.

"Be e writin' 'ome, Tom?"

"Aas, Jim."

"Tell thy sister to tell Pol somethin' for me. Dawn't forgit t' say I told e to say it."

A half-hour later Tom read to Jim and Jake what he had written. It was a simple message—the day of their landing and the choice of Allouez, that they had work and a place to live, that Joe and Bill had gone on—little more.

"Tell 'er our haddress, Tom."

"I've done un, Jim."

"That's brave, my son."

Jim went to the window and stared across the white distance. Such was all he would send her for months while his heart and mind burst with more. He raised his hands to the sash and said, "You sh'll write 'er some day—more than that."

Chapter Five

THE FORECAST HAD FAILED. Snow did not cover the door in the morning. More snow had fallen, and Mrs. Uren had swept the small stoop while the kettle was "coming to a boil." The sky had cleared, and stars were shining. In the next hour the beds would be emptied, breakfast would be eaten, and the beds filled again. It would be a busy, noisy hour, after which voices and activities would be hushed until the men began to come downstairs in midafternoon. The newcomers had risen early to "stream hands and faces," and be out of the way before the rush.

After the last man had gone upstairs, Jim and Jake and Tom went into the middle room and sat down. At this hour in the light still uncertain and wavering between dawn and day, the silence required by the men in bed best suited their mood. They waited for their minds to clear as they waited for the day, waited for the shapeless ghosts that filled their heads to take form as the houses and trestles and burrows would emerge from the gloom and become recognizable in clear daylight. They were in no hurry for either speech or action. The day was ahead of them, and the night—twenty-four hours of wakefulness. Nor did they think they were wasting time; time was not a responsibility at the moment.

Jim was puzzling over his sense of oddity, of newness, of isolation. If he had been dropped upon another planet he could not have felt more apart from all about him than he did here. Not that others remarked it. His clothes did not distinguish him. None of his fellow lodgers followed a style. Not that his dialect marked him. The community accepted speech of all sorts without comment. Any speech that accompanied a pair of strong, willing hands was acceptable. His sense of separateness, of not belonging, of being a foreigner did not come from the outside. It arose within himself. As he pondered, his brow furrowed, and he closed his eyes to see himself better. Was it because he had left all that was dear to him—Mary Ann first of all, his parents, and so many friends—so far away? That was only a part of it. Back there he had had no such sensation of being apart, odd, foreign, strange, alone. Why? Slowly an explanation emerged from the misty chaos of his thought. That was the place of his birth. He had grown up in the lanes, among the cottages, the hedged fields, the neighbors of the place. Wherever he looked or went, he was a part of the scene. He ran together with them, fused with them. He was a part of the whole, and all that surrounded him was a part of him! He opened his eyes like a man who had made a discovery. Jake was looking at him. Tom had found a toy in the charm that hung from his watch chain.

"Well, my sons!" said Jake at last.

Tom came out of his reverie and let the charm fall from his fingers.

"The journey's awver, an' life in America begin t'day."

"Wha's tha mean?" asked Tom.

"You 'eard me, chul, an' understand Henglish."

"You speak in riddles all the same," said Jim.

"Us 'ave work, a place t' live, an' we'm a part of that." Jake's hand indicated the town and all the outdoors visible. "That be a part of America."

Nobody answered him. Jim merely emitted a small sound of surprise. Jake had been thinking his own thoughts, but had gone a step farther! Jake was ready to merge himself with his new life—or so it seemed. The ol' fox! thought Jim. P'r'aps 'e spawk awnly for Tom an' me.

Tom arose, got coat and cap, and said, "Let's go out an' see w'at 'e's like."

Side by side where they could be, and at times in single file, they walked toward the town. A few teams pulling heavy sleds passed them. Sleds and drivers took their eye, the teamsters, standing as they drove, wearing German socks and rubbers, heavy clothes and caps that covered head and ears. Their lines dangled from their hands to the sled floor. Stakes, set upright in the squared timber frames of the sled, told their purpose.

"They'm common anough t' show they belong, but they'm new to my eyes," said Jim.

"New as bunks in a bedroom," answered Jake, "and practical."

They turned a corner and were on the business street of the town.

"I s'pose this be Main Street," said Tom.

"King's Row, or Raygent's Lane," Jake replied.

Jim chuckled. "Better forgit they," he said. "You'm in America."

But Jake had dismissed that item for something else. He was looking at the high, square fronts of the frame shops. He looked as solemn as a sexton at a funeral. "False fronts!" he said. "Each tryin' t' be as brave as tother. See! The awnly hones' ones be the two bricks. They 'ave flat tops. Tothers be like little men wearin' 'igh 'ats."

"Makin' fun of yer new 'ome, be e?" reproached Tom.

"No, boay," answered Jake. "I like t' see a man or a 'ouse put on a brave front. I really fancy a bit of d'ceit in some things."

Here and there they looked at window displays, glanced into empty saloons.

"Too early for they; seein' 'e's not yet the third hour," said Jim.

Strangers greeted them reservedly but kindly.

Suddenly the school bell began to ring; children seemed to pour around every corner. Jim and Jake stepped to a store platform to watch and listen. Tom stayed on the walk. A small boy stopped in front of him, looked him up and down, and said, "Hello, Old Country." Tom flushed and grinned but could think of no reply. The boy laughed and went on. "Saucy beggar," Tom said, still red but amused.

"Better get up 'ere out of the way, boay," advised Jake. "They might take e along for a penny-peep."

They watched the children until the flurry and chatter had subsided.

"That be a sight t' do the 'eart good," Jake said, his humorous mood passed. " 'E give e faith in the footure."

The others remained silent.

"There be the comp'ny store," said Tom, pointing to a large, square-front, squat building on the next corner and across the street. "Some of the men said they was goin' there last night."

They crossed the street for a closer view. A porch stretched the full width of the building. A large window on each side of a centrally placed door displayed clothing and foods and tools.

"They bayn't put there t' attrac'," Jim said, "awnly t' be seen."

Under each window was a long bench.

"Thicky forms welcome in the summertime, likely," said Jake.

They peered through the windows and saw only two clerks cleaning and arranging the place. They turned away, apparently satisfied.

"Buildin's be just buildin's 'ere, same as back 'ome," said Jake. "They awnly say somebody live 'ere, work 'ere, buy 'ere."

"Let's see the mine," Tom suggested. "Us 'ave t' get acquainted sooner or later."

Without argument they left the street to see the mine. They stood in the doors of stamp mills and shops. They went to the shafts and sniffed the thick breath of the pit. Here and there they got a nod or a word from a workman, but no more. Everywhere was activity—steady, productive activity, without hurry.

"I like the looks of un all," Jake said. "Ev'rybody work like 'e awned a bit of the place—a good sign, t' my mind."

Together they clustered in the doorway of the enginehouse. The floor was so clean they refrained from crossing the threshold. "Thicky floor, say, 'Stay out,' plain enough fur me," said Jim. The bell rang, and the engine began to turn. Fascinated, they watched it come to speed, hold it for a brief time, and then slow to a stop.

" 'E creak and groan like's if 'e dedn' want t' stop," said Jake.

" 'E be some diff'runt from the man-engine back 'ome," said Tom.

" 'E look trus'worthy t' me," said Jim.

They turned to go but stopped again, all eyes caught by a rugged mass of metal beside the door. Snow and ice filled the crevices and hollows on its surface. It was shaped like a large, short-necked bottle. Jake put his hand on it as if to move it, but its own weight anchored it.

"A ton, aysy," he said.

"Copper!" said Tom in a low voice.

"Pure copper!" said Jim, awed.

When the whistle blew a quarter of seven the Devonshire men, as they were called, took their cribs and left for the mine.

Already it was dark and, to their unaccustomed skins, the wind was penetratingly cold. The snow crunched under their digging boots or screeched under the runners of passing sleighs. Collars were turned up to protect the ears that digging hats did not cover. With the first dozen steps from the door, toes tingled threateningly. Each intake of breath seemed to cut the inside of the nose and returned in jets of vapor.

"They all smawk t'night, comrade," said Jake, turning toward Jim. "Look see."

The miners were gathering at the shaft eager to go down. In their new clothes Jim and Jake and Tom contrasted so strongly with the others that all eyes turned toward them as they came up.

"Hi thought they wadn' takin' on no more!" one man said in surprise.

"Green'orns, too, seems like," said another, indifferent to the new and sensitive ears.

" 'Ad some pull, mor'n likely," said a third.

"Not a bad sign," said still another.

The pit was breathing a cloud of vapor into the cold night, making the shaft invisible and the swinging lantern almost useless. Here and there a man cursed himself for coming so early, and all wished the whistle would blow. They rubbed their ears and stamped their feet or kicked the rails that led to the collar of the shaft, to keep their toes warm.

The man who had seen the new employees as a good sign spoke to Jake.

"I'm glad I dawn't work on top a night like this."

Jake nodded a friendly agreement but did not speak because at that moment the whistle blew.

The captain came from the bosses' dry and joined the men at the shaft.

Those whose partners had failed to come out reported to him, and those who had a complaint or request to make.

When Tom approached, the captain called a young man back to him.

"Walters, take this boay with you t'night," he said. And to Tom: "You will stem * for a shift or two till I find a steady place for e."

Tom recognized his partner as the "Yankee dude" who had worn a tie and gloves the previous afternoon. Walters held out his hand and said, "I am glad to have you for a partner."

Walking together into the white cloud that came out of the mine, they disappeared.

Jim and Jake waited on the fringe of the group around the captain.

"You boays go daown t' the bottom an' stay there till I come."

Evidently Jake and Jim were to be partners. They had discussed the matter and hoped the dice would fall in their favor. Both were happy at the prospect. They knew what it meant to spend shift after shift in the intimacy of stope or drift with a disagreeable partner. Under the rub of such a condition dispositions wore to the quick. Mining captains could not select men or appoint them to suit the taste of the persons concerned. The men in most combinations were partners by chance. A good man—good as a miner and as a man—might have a partner who never did his share. It happened that two men who spent long shifts together underground barely nodded to each other on the street. As often two comrades in the pit were inseparable friends on the surface. Some pairs stayed together for years, stayed together until sickness or accident or age parted them. Jim and Jake felt relieved of their first anxiety.

At the bottom the strangers looked around the plat. It was larger then any they had seen in England. The timber was larger, some of the legs being three feet in diameter.

---

* Substitute. (A stem is a day's work, a shift.)

The back was twenty feet high, and there was floor space for four tracks. The back and sides converged to the drift, which was a patch of inky blackness fifty feet from the shaft. Seeing a bench nailed between two sets, they sat down to wait.

"Hi'm glad 'e dedn' part us, comrade," said Jim.

"Aas, I'd ruther work with thee than some Finn," Jake replied.

"At least thee's understan' me," said Jim laughingly.

"Sometimes I can," Jake answered, "but dawn't try me too much. 'Eadwork be 'ard work, you knaw."

'E's feelin' good too, Jim thought, but he only smiled at Jake's humor.

"Look see they buggies," said Jake, pointing to some cars on the farthest track. "They be as big as farm wagons."

"Bigger wagons, bigger 'osses, comrade."

" 'Ark to thicky bob slippin' hup an' down! An' the way the water roar in they pipes."

"Aas. 'E give me a twitch of 'omesickness w'en I seed un this mornin'," Jim answered.

For a minute neither spoke. That was a subject to be shunned. But both were what Jake called "too tayzy like," too easily agitated by their adventure to be silent long.

" 'Ow old is this mine, Jake?"

"Somebody, Jinkins, I b'lieve, said twenty-five years."

"An' 'e must be eighteen 'underd foot deep or more. Holmbush was three 'underd fathoms. Do e knaw 'ow old Holmbush is?"

"Never 'eard tell; I knaw my gran'fer worked in un."

"There's the cage!" said Jim, and they strained their eyes toward the shaft. Suddenly, like a mass of the roof broken loose, it dropped into view and splashed to rest. The captain stepped out of the darkness into the circles of light made by their candles. He took a light from them and said, "Follow me, my sons."

As Jim walked, he counted his steps. One hundred yards

from the shaft the captain stopped. Straight ahead lights were visible, and the sound of work came back to them. At their right a crosscut had been started but was only a few yards deep. Its end was within the reach of their candle rays.

"You will work 'ere," said the captain. "The direction will be straight ahead till further orders. We 'ave been runnin' one shift 'ere, but we will go a little faster naow."

The captain told them the contract their partners were working on, and turned to go. In a friendly way he held up his candle and looked into their faces.

"You both look purty young—you in partic'lar," he said to Jim; "but Cornwall do breed miners. I guess you can do un all right."

"We been underground ever since we could work, Cap'n," said Jim.

"I spect so, my son. Some chuldern was put undergraound awver there before they could work. I was one of um." He turned to Jake: "We 'ad t' let your brother stem awhile." And then to both: "I 'ope you get along," he said, and went away.

The day men had blasted at quitting time, and the crosscut was full of dirt. That meant they would shovel most of the night. They went back to the drift and found a car, ran it into their place, stuck their candlesticks into a leg, and began work.

Shoveling could be hard or easy as they made it. Their pay depended on the footage they produced. When they tired, they turned their shovels, placing the handles on a rock, and sat on them.

"Minin' 'ave some consolations, boay," said Jake. " 'E edn' zero down 'ere."

"An' 'e's safe anough too. 'Ard ground and a 'underd-foot-thick roof between we and the workin's."

"An' no boss but our pay envelope. Foo jobs better'n that," said Jake.

"An' 'e's dry. That's a comfort."

"Unless us get too far in; then I'd like un a bit moist."

"I'd rather 'ave a raise put through for a draft," said Jim, catching Jake's point. "Dust an' poor draft make a bad place."

By eleven, enough dirt was removed to allow "trimming of the back." Taking a pick, Jake stepped upon the loose pile under the naked roof and stood close to the breast. With the poll of his pick he tapped lightly here and there over the roof, and with its point removed such fragments as threatened to fall. This done, they could take out the remaining dirt with no fear of pieces dropping on them.

At midnight they put on their coats and started for the shaft to eat. They remembered the bench and thought it preferable to a shovel handle for so long a spell. When they reached the shaft, they saw the trammers sitting in a small alcove they had not noticed before. It was behind the shaft, and in it was a small engine used to lift from the cage timbers too big for men to lift by hand. The warm pipes and cylinder kept the place cozy. In a few minutes the pair from the drift head came out and joined them. There were nine men in all: the cage tender, four miners, and four trammers. The miners were Cornish; the trammers, Swedes. The Cornishmen were middle-aged; the Swedes were in their twenties.

The trammers sat apart and talked in their sibilant, musical speech, much to the interest of Jim and Jake who had never heard the language before. They all talked as long as their food lasted, and then they made themselves as comfortable as they could and slept.

At one o'clock they arose and walked back to their work in silence. The small scrap of sleep, so desirable when they lay down, had made them strangely miserable. Speech was distasteful, and silence bitter. Life was flat—stale. Everything had lost its savor. Without as much as a look at each other, Jim and Jake took off their coats, picked up their shovels,

and went to work. They filled a car, shoved it to the switch
for the trammers, and brought in an empty. They filled it
and shoved it out and returned as before. Jake turned his
shovel over and sat down.

"Is a safe t' spayk now, comrade?"

Jim grinned sheepishly.

" 'E's a good thing us dawn't 'ave no weapons after a nap
like thicky."

Jake lighted his pipe and smoked. Jim watched the operation until Jake sat back to enjoy his success.

"I feel like I b'lieve in signs t'night, you," Jim said.

"W'at now, my son?" Jake asked.

"A new job on a new level; new timber, ties, rails; even
the shovels an' picks be new. Ev'rything do drum that idee
into my 'ead. New! New! New!"

"An' you bayn't so old yerself, boay. You 'ave a new wife
and will soon a new baby. Seem sorta fitty like."

Jake smiled at the serious look on Jim's face.

"W'at be afraid of, boay?"

"I bayn't afraid, Jake, but I wonder will I crave the set
ways of the old country so 'ard I'll want t' go back."

"If you do, that bayn't no shame to e. Others 'ave done
un," said Jake soothingly. "Is yer mind made up t' stay
so soon?"

"That bayn't the question, Jake, an' thee's knaw it.
Poverty do make up a man's mind for un sometimes. You
call un necessity—a purty word. W'ere did e learn un?"

Jake was silent. He was older than Jim by ten years, a
bachelor. He had never shown a symptom of wanting to be
otherwise. He had not thought of America as a permanent
home. His trip was a bit of a lark. He could take care of
himself anywhere. He often said that. He had saved a little
money and had no immediate worry. He wanted to be with
his brothers and with Jim—to see them safely started, established. His whole appraisal of American life was biased

differently. He took his pipe from his lips, looked at it a moment as though trying to see what gave it its charm, and without taking his eyes from it began to speak.

"Look t' me like you'm fitted for this thing. New ought to fit new. You won't break your bones bendin' yerself to the shape of things 'ere. T' my mind, you'm startin' a new venture with a bit of a lark mixed in." Jake spoke slowly and with vibrant earnestness. "W'y fret, my son? You 'ave lots of time."

By four-thirty they had removed all the loose dirt and uncovered the bottom holes—six of them. Plugs of wood had been driven into their mouths to keep out dirt from previous blasts. They removed their tools to a place of safety lest they be buried or broken by the blast, and "charged up." Then they waited until the men in the main drift went back to the shaft, as it was too early to fill the place with smoke and inconvenience the others. When each fuse began to spit and its tape to blister from the trickle of fire at its core, they hurried to the drift to await the explosion. The first hole put out their lights. "Two, three, four, five, six," they said in unison. Each blast boomed dully, softly, breaking the ground easily. The smoke would be out by the time the next shift came on. A match flashed in the dark, and two lights took life from it. Their shift was over.

On their way to the shaft, Jake said, "I be anxious t' knaw 'ow the boay got along."

"I be, too," said Jim.

Tom had found Walters a pleasant partner. He was near Tom's age, active and willing, helpful with suggestions, and he assumed responsibility for the work to be done. Timber of all kinds, they loaded upon their truck and sped to the men who had ordered it. Although the miners asked for their timber before they actually needed it, to save time, the timbermen often had difficulty delivering it before the miners were ready to set it in place. Their progress depended largely upon the cooperation of the timbermen. Walters tried hard to keep the miners from waiting, and Tom soon saw that his partner was popular with them.

Doing the best they could, the timbermen sometimes got behind with their deliveries. Some of the timbers were long, heavy, and difficult to load. Because of their length the big stocks required careful steering at the curves; without it they teetered the truck, which readily left the track. Sometimes the miners were not ready to receive their order, which delayed delivery to the next group. Some places were of difficult access, and there trouble piled up, to Walters' distress. His widespread service kept him constantly deserving of praise and expectant of blame. Tom did his best to adapt himself to his partner's needs and felt a growing regard for him. Walters was easy to work with, considerate of a new man, and patient.

Just before midnight Walters said, "We are behind with one delivery. We shall get hell for being late, too."

"The chap 'oo hordered it was only a boay," said Tom wonderingly, "a foreigner!"

"Right you are," answered Walters. "A Swede. I was thinking of his partner, an unreasonable beast. Sims never does what he can make the kid do. When the Swede makes a mistake Sims cusses him. He can't understand Sims' Cornish and can't speak any better than he understands."

"Cornish bayn't the best Henglish that's spawk, I knaw," said Tom, smiling.

"I don't find fault with the Cornish, partner. It ain't the fault of the brogue in this case but of the fool who speaks it. Well, we're in for it anyhow."

At supper Walters told Tom something of himself. He came from Wisconsin, he said. He had lost both of his parents and was making every effort to carry out his father's wish that he go to school. His people were from New York for some generations back, but still farther back had come from England. He did not know what part of England. He said, "I might be Cornish, too, partner, but the brogue was washed out of us a long time ago."

" 'Ow many years do a take t' do that—wash out a brogue, I mean?"

"Some do pretty well, I've noticed," Walters said; "others are dyed fast and never wash out. Last winter, I worked in the woods, but that was too cold and too dirty. A fellow had to go too long without a bath, and he got creepy—crummy, the lumberjacks call it. The mine isn't any more dangerous, and the temperature don't change."

Tom thought of the man on the stage who had offered him and his brothers a job, and wanted to ask more about it; but that would come later. So he let Walters continue without interruption.

At one o'clock they started with Sims's timber. As their truck neared the drift end where Sims worked they heard his voice bawling at his partner.

"Call thyself a miner, dost tha? Thee couldn' 'it the end of a beer keg with a 'ammer!"

Sims turned from the Swede to Walters.

"Hi hordered that bloody stuff for 'leven, an' 'ere you be at two! I'll report e to the cap'n!"

"It is one-thirty, Sims, but you are not ready for it yet," said Walters. "You can't stand a leg in that corner."

"I knaw it," said Sims, his mind turned again to his first grief. "That corner hole was short. Us 'ave t' drill a pop in that nuck an' blaw un aout afore us can stand the leg. I was tryin' t' drill un, but that bloody Swede couldn' hit the drill!"

"I can't help you, Sims," said Walters, "even if I wanted to. It's the wrong hand for me. Help yourself to your trouble, old man, and be damned for all of me."

Sims glared but did not answer.

Tom saw the situation, he thought.

"W'y dawn't e beat the drill yerself, Sims?" he asked.

" 'E would 'ave a core in the hole in the first six inches," said Sims, nodding toward the Swede.

That was possible, Tom knew, but scarcely necessary if Sims would take the time to show the boy how to twist. The hole had to go eighteen inches to make room for the leg.

Tom turned to his partner.

"W'at more do us 'ave t' do?"

"This is all until other orders come or the boss finds a job for us."

"Git a hold of thicky drill, Sims, an' I'll beat un for e," said Tom.

Sims hunched himself into the corner again, muttering, "The bloody Swede 'ave awnly one 'and, an' 'e's no good."

"You've said anough, Sims. Let's git t' work. Both of mine be good."

Tom's hammer fell squarely on the head of the drill and the hole sank six inches before Tom stopped to rest.

Both Walters and the Swede watched the performance with admiration.

"I have heard Cornishmen say of another, 'He's a purty man with a hammer,' " said Walters, laughing. "I know now what they meant. They were talking about you."

Tom picked up the hammer for another round. Three inches more, and he stopped.

"I'll change places with e now, Sims. Let me twist a bit."

Sims arose reluctantly, took the hammer, and Tom leaned against the breast to steady himself as he twisted.

Sims's hammer fell on the drill as though it weighed seven ounces instead of seven pounds. Tom looked up and saw that Sims's back hand was ten inches up the handle. His arms moved as though every joint from his wrist to his backbone were stiff. Tom had felt a growing dislike for the man with each sight and sound of him at the house, but now he was disgusted.

"The bloody Swede 'ave awnly one 'and!" Tom sneered. "An' 'e's no good."

Sims took the taunt with a black scowl.

"Come, my son, squat in yer corner again. You've got t' 'ave thicky 'ole, an' you couldn' drive un in a month."

Sims obeyed, and Tom took the hammer again. He stayed with it until the bore was sixteen inches deep, threw the hammer into the corner, and started out of the place.

"Tim'erman," the Swede said, "Ay ban no meener. Ay tank Ay trade yobs med you."

Tom smiled. "I'm sorry, boay, but I dawn't 'ave patience t' work with that image."

Sims had recovered somewhat from his chagrin and spoke to Walters. "Iss, I'll trade partners with e."

Walters was enjoying the little drama and was glad Sims gave him a chance to speak.

"I'm not Tom's boss, Sims. If I was boss, you wouldn't be here."

The trammers bent over their truck and started for the shaft.

"All Cousin Jacks are not gold-plated miners, Tom."

"No. Some be awnly brass, look-like, an' some not that."

"Just like all folks: good ones, middling ones, and fakers."

Tom didn't know what a faker was, but he got the idea.

The rest of the shift was light. The boys found a comfortable place to sit and wait for orders. Only two came. They did not talk much. After so long a stretch of wakefulness, sleep was too insistent. They nodded instead.

When Tom finished his report, Jake stood up, stretched, and yawned. "They beds be cooled a bit by now," he said. "I'm for turnin' in."

Together they climbed the stairs. At the top Jim said, "The evenin' an' the mornin' of the fust day."

Chapter Six

"Hi wonder w'at they'll do t'day," said Tom. "If they all bide at 'ome the 'ouse will be like a ant heap."

He was speaking to Jim, but Mrs. Uren, passing through the room at the moment, answered.

"Two of um be gone already—huntin'!" she said. "They got hup afore six. More's the pity they must hunt on Sunday. Some will go to Sunday school, an' some—well, some 'ave a weakness."

"W'at time be Sunday school, missus?" asked Jim.

"Ten a clock w'en us don't 'ave praychin'; us dawn't 'ave praychin' t'day."

That was the first mention of anything religious that had been made—Mrs. Uren's regret about hunting. The thought came to Jim that religion was a close-mouthed affair except under the rules of the chapel. Few men discussed it freely even there. At chapel they were persuaded, urged, sometimes all but compelled to talk about it; but that did not lessen the difficulty of it. He had himself been persuaded to talk about it when he didn't want to. Was it too private a concern to prate about, or was it too sacred? Perhaps most people felt as he did: he didn't have his ideas well enough shaped for words. Was it true that the cause was hurt by silence? He had heard all these possibilities argued often, but he still wondered.

At ten, he and Jake and Tom went to the chapel. A little group of men sat just inside the door in an alcove—a class, obviously. The three added themselves to this group. As in England, they bowed their heads for a moment, and then sat straight and still. In a few minutes the superintendent gave a hymn number. The little organ sounded the first notes of a prelude, and Tom, to his surprise, saw that the organist was Walters. Tom had never heard the prelude of a chapel song played as Walters played this one. Nor had Jim or perhaps any other in the assemblage. Into it the timberman put volumes of sound and whispers of it. He carried the air with a positiveness that never faltered, and spun around it harmonies that thundered and showered and shone as he willed. Walters' fanciful digressions were criticized by some—" 'E should play the songs as they be," they said; but Tom exulted in it. Something new came to Tom with the music. Did the light of the morning take on a new brightness, or did something akin to a Presence fill the little cubicle of a chapel? Tom was no analyst. He let himself go, felt himself expand with a strange delight as a bud might be thought to feel in opening to the sun. Jake and Jim were bewildered—music without words was vanity to them; but music without words was more potent with Tom than music with words. He had no problem with blended sounds, only enjoyment.

Tom knew the song: the boat song of the New Testament; a song of distress, of power, of peace. The Captain of the boat lay asleep in the storm. According to the tradition he might bid the stars to come at his call or the wind to shorten his way. Tremulous waves might steady for his feet, or flowers bloom in desert places for his pleasure. The music made his majesty glow as from a throne. Walters' fancy threw lines across the storm and the Ruler of Storms together, and strained the little instrument to tell it. The cry of frailty that would disturb the Sleeper, he kept audible through the tumult, through the roar of the wind and the sea, until the Captain, awakened, commanded wind and wave and the wail of fear to be still. That was what some said he should not do. That was what he must deny himself with the means of expressing it at his fingertips! That, such listeners as Tom should do without! Walters broke over at times as he did today in an ecstasy of wilfulness.

The new voices had good company as they sang, and the singing gave them a heart's ease they had not known till now. They were at home; strangeness had gone, introduction had found its perfection in the blend of their voices. Jake and Jim were content to find the harmonies they could command, and sang for their own ears and sense of content. Tom, in the mood that Walters had created, sang without restraint. Eyes turned to see whence the new voice came; ears stayed half turned to enjoy it to the full.

As they all sat down, Jim nudged Jake and whispered, "The boay was singin' 'is 'omesickness away."

Spargo and Jenkins had come in, two of the wood choppers, and Penglaze. The boarding house was well represented. Evidently, some had "carried Christ" over the sea or found Him there. Jim watched for Allen, but he did not come.

The superintendent arose and said, "We will read the lesson responsively." He read his verse and started the school with "All together," on theirs. For most of the audience it was, evidently, the first reading. Occasionally an overattentive reader broke over into the superintendent's verse and then attempted to hide the blunder behind a cough. After the final verse the superintendent bade the classes come to order. There was a shuffling of feet and a rattling of leaves. Teachers stood up and faced their scholars.

Penglaze was the teacher of the men's class. He read the first verse again and tried laboriously to extract a moral.

"Will you read the nex' verse, Absalom, playse, an' tell us w'at 'e mean?"

Absalom read and remained silent.

"Anybody spayk t' that verse?" asked Penglaze.

Nobody responded.

Penglaze skipped the next man and called on the next. He read as requested and commented too, starting a brief discussion. "That's brave," said Penglaze. He again skipped a man and called on Jim and Jake. Both shook their heads, hoping he would understand and remember next Sunday. This method continued until the bell announced the end of the lesson period.

As soon as the benediction was said, Tom sought Walters.

"W'y dedn' you say you played?" asked Tom.

"You didn't say you sang," retorted Walters, smiling.

Together they went out of the chapel, friends.

Jim and Jake left the chapel in silence. Jim was fighting off the humiliation that had smitten him when Penglaze asked him to read. Penglaze was considerate, though; that helped. Jake was not embarrassed. He said once, "There's wuss things than not readin'." To Jim's "What?" he added, "Bein' able to an' makin' no use of un."

What Jake was thinking, however, Jim did not know. Jake was in one of his I-spayk-w'en-I'm-spawk-to moods. Jim spoke.

"W'at now, comrade?"

"Aas, w'at now?" repeated Jake. "Well you might ask. Us 'ave been to the Fountain of Life an' found un dry."

Jim was silenced. Jake had a way of snuffing out talk as he snuffed a candle—with a pinch of finger and thumb.

At last Jim said, "But there be the Words."

"Hempty cups, comrade, most of the time." Another silence. "Sunday-school classes be all infant classes, seem t' me like."

Penglaze, who was a short distance ahead of them, heard their voices and stopped to wait for them.

"I was glad t' see e this mornin'," he said, "an' t' 'ear e too. You sing better than common, I'd say. I hope you'll be faithful. Few be."

"W'y dawn't the chapel use local praychers 'ere like 'e do back 'ome?" asked Jim, thinking of the serviceless day.

Penglaze's eyes darkened as he turned on Jim. "'Ave somebody been talkin' abaout me?" he asked.

Before Jim could answer, a smile teased Jake's lips and he turned to Penglaze. "Be you onfaithful t' somethin', comrade?"

The question brought the three men to a standstill. Jake still smiled, but Jim was uneasy. Penglaze was what Jim called a hard man. Penglaze looked from one to the other before he said a word. His code called for honesty, and honest he would be at any cost. "If somebody said I was a local praycher back there, 'tis the truth 'e spawk," said Penglaze.

"Nobody told us nothin'," Jim interposed, but Penglaze ignored him.

"'Tis diff'runt 'ere," he said. "People be more edicated. Life be aysier, an' aour hard lines wouldn' suit. I bayn't gifted with spaych." He hesitated. "Bein' laughed at wouldn' keep me awake. 'Tedn' that. I bayn't fitted for un. I do w'at I can w'ere I can."

He stopped talking but made no move to continue his way home. Jake and Jim both felt an admiration for the man despite themselves.

"The class be made of Cornishmen. Hi do feel more at 'ome there." Again he sorted out what he thought needed to be said before speaking. "You seen the pious ones of the 'aouse this mornin'," he continued, dismissing his confession. "Some of min was pious till they got 'ere—some be aout an' aout worl'ly." And without hesitation he named the men in each group. Again they fell into step for the boarding house.

When the boys entered the middle room they noticed that the parlor door was open—the first time since they arrived. The curtain to the single window was raised; a fire had been started, and some boarders were sitting in the twilight. Jim and Jake went upstairs.

"Penglaze 'ave 'e's parts, comrade," Jake said. "If the truth be as hoogly as a porcapine or as cross-grained as a sack of nails, 'e'll tell un."

"An' 'e dawn't spare 'is self," added Jim.

"Sparin' bayn't in 'is book," said Jake.

Both men chuckled at that with no discredit to their subject.

"That's a word of praise, seem t' me like," said Jim.

" 'E may be, comrade, accordin' to the judgment that go with un. Tellin' the truth can be 'ard or cruel, an' sometimes silence be better. Penglaze dawn't knaw that."

"In 'e's way, 'e's brave, Hi say."

"Let un go at that. Men like Penglaze dawn't get many purty words from their boardin' mates."

Mrs. Uren's voice came up the stairs announcing dinner.

After dinner Jim walked out alone—to be alone. The cold had lost its sting, and the wind had fallen. He followed the street to where it joined the stage road to Calumet. It was the road by which he had come two days before. Paths cut by runners of cutters and bobs he found to his convenience. "A lot of things 'ave 'appened in they foo days," he muttered. The time seemed much longer. "A man dawn't live so much by days as 'e do by w'at 'appen to un," he said aloud.

A few yards beyond the last house the forest began, the naked limbs of the trees overarching the road. The road was fenceless. An occasional cutter came along, its bells ringing cheerily in the vast quiet of the cloudless sky and voiceless forest. He stepped into the snow to let the horses and cutters by, and each time got a pleasant greeting from the riders. Riding over snow and ice seemed to make people sociable.

He pondered the matter for a few minutes. More like play, maybe. The carriages slid along so easily. Going downhill the things went by themselves. The horses played, then, too. He smiled at his own fancy. The pull never seemed as heavy as it did on bare ground. Another rig approached, and he noted how lightly the horses stepped; they appeared to enjoy the music of the bells. The bells helped, then! Children climbed a hill to ride down. These older ones had the same fun without climbing. Jim estimated the distance to the brow of the hill before him and determined that its crest should be his turning point. That would make two miles, he thought.

From the top of the hill an open space stretched back from the road, an area of several acres. The trees had not invaded it; the glaciers had not left a single boulder on it. Nothing marred the snow that covered it. Jim wondered while he admired, believing that no human hand had cleared the space. While he looked, from the right forest wall came a deer, antlered, graceful, weary. It hesitated a moment as if loath to mar the ermine whiteness, the smooth spread of the snow, and then continued on its way. Jim was glad no bells had sounded to frighten it. He had never seen a deer before. In the middle of the primeval field it stopped again and raised its head to listen. " 'E's that proud," Jim whispered. " 'E knaw w'ere t' stan' t' set off 'e's good looks." It sniffed the air, scanned the looming darkness of the opposite forest wall, and went wearily toward it.

The deer had scarcely disappeared, and Jim still stood in his first amazement, when from the farthest corner of the field a man appeared. He came steadily on with a peculiar shuffling gait, his body bent forward, a gun in his hand. Across the trail of the deer he came without apparently noticing it. Jim wanted to see why he walked so strangely, so clumsily, but, rather than appear rude, turned to go when the man got close to him. As he turned, a familiar voice shouted:

"A great day, Jim. It do make the blood sing in your veins t' go far on a day like this."

It was Allen. He came to the road, removed the snowshoes from his feet, took the shell from his gun, and started toward town.

"I was lookin' at thicky field," said Jim. "I never seed anything smoother, w'iter, purtier. I was wonderin' w'y no trees growed there."

"An' then the buck scratched a path through un," said Allen. "A lot of aour purties' fancies 'ave that happen to um."

"Did you see un? W'y dedn' e aim at un?"

" 'E looked purtier there, Jim, than 'e would hangin' from a pole atween you an' me."

" 'E made a purty picter, shore 'nough."

"The field was purty afore 'e come. The buck was hextra— throwed in for good measure. Nature is purty gen'rous 'ere, Jim."

Allen looked at Jim to see the effect of his remark, but Jim's winter cap hid his face as he looked straight before him.

"An' the scene change with the wind an' cloud an' each fall of snaw. There be scenes from the 'illtop that hold e till the cold reach your marra, an' from the valley that give e thoughts like a psalmist."

Jim was listening to Allen's words with interpolations of wonder. This sort of thing must be a gift. Allen was the only man in the house—in any of the houses, perhaps—who found pleasure in this way. How far had he walked? Miles, perhaps, and yet when he removed his snowshoes he strode along as easily as Jim himself—and he had not been afoot an hour. Jim eyed the tall, slender man momentarily. " 'E mus' be made of steel."

"Was e ever alone, Jim? Hi dawn't mean lonesome, but halone, covered with distance an' buried in silence—aout of sight of anything a man ever touched, w'ere your mind could catch the ebb an' flow of things natural? You can feel as weak an' no-important as a worm, or grander than the hills you stand on. 'E's pleasant, my son, t' get away from the brawl of words an' hopinions, from baccy smawk an' the smill of the missus' kitchen t' w'ere the wind, fresh from the pole, blaw e clean." Allen laughed at his own fancy, and Jim joined him, scarcely knowing why.

" 'Aouw would e like a tramp some Sunday, Jim?"

"Hi be 'fraid I can't go with e on Sunday, Mr. Allen. Thanks, just the same. An' I never shot a gun in my life."

There was no self-praise or censure in Jim's words. He spoke simply. Allen sensed the reason back of them.

"W'y were you on the road, Jim?"

"T' stretch my legs a bit."

"Was that all?"

"Not all," said Jim honestly and hesitatingly. "You see, a lot of things, new things, 'ave come t' me the last foo days, an' I was tryin' t' sort mun out. I couldn' do so well in the 'ouse."

"That is w'y I go aout too, sometimes," said Allen.

Almost unconsciously, Jim's eyes fell on the gun, and Allen saw it.

"I dedn' kill the deer, Jim," he said.

Jim felt his face flush with embarrassment. He had not meant a discourtesy. He had not thought to censure Allen's gunning. Hunting and a Wesleyan Sabbath did not to-gether. Perhaps Allen was not pious; Jim himself professed. That was the difference.

"Hi meant no offense, Mr. Allen. I dawn't judge. I awnly try t' guard my own feet."

Allen found himself enjoying and liking this whiskered youth. He knew the lad was striving to be honest with his profession, and it pleased him that Jim did not change the subject with his apology. Allen was serious for his own sake and Jim's when he next spoke.

"W'at is there bad abaout this, Jim?" He held out the gun. "Did e ever see a man cheat with a pick an' shovel? A lead pencil is a 'andy tool for deceivers in banks an' shops, my son."

"W'y do e carry un?" asked Jim.

"Dawn't e knaw, Jim? Then, boay, thee shouldn' find fault with me."

Allen saw that the newcomer got his meaning. Finally Jim broke the silence again.

"I expec', Mr. Allen, God's 'ouse 'ave took so much of my Sundays I feel agin a thing that will take a man away from un."

"Jim!"

"Aas, Mr. Allen."

"I dawn't want t' stop e, my son. But, afore us go further, would e mind callin' me Allen or Bob? I bayn't used t' maister."

Allen smiled as he requested this familiarity to make address easier for Jim. Then he continued, lightness and reverence blended in his remarks.

"Jim, did e ever see a carpet in a church as purty as the one in thicky field till the deer come? Do e s'pose that buck would tell a lie? Do e think the trees backbite one another, a birch damn a maple, let's say? Did any harmonium or choir ever make moosic like the trees do an' the birds? An' w'at do e s'pose He made um for if 'E dedn' want we t' admire um?"

" 'Thou shalt 'ave no other gods afore me,' " quoted Jim.

"Brave, my son. Your maid will say, 'You shan't 'ave no maid afore me,' too; but w'en you praise 'er frock or 'er hair, 'er won't be vexed."

Jim smiled. He was not used to such easy parallels, but he was thrilling to Allen's clean-cut thinking, and was envying him.

"But the 'ouse of God, Allen!"

"A little handful of miners put up that box awver there,

an' a praycher prayed awver un. That made the thing a 'aouse
of God! 'Oo builded thicky hill? 'Oo spread thicky carpet?
'Oo tuned the winds? 'Oo hanged the lights in the ceilin'?
An' 'E said twas good, dedn' a, Jim?"

Jim did not answer. He went out to walk and think, and
at the end of the way this man of the woods loaded his mind
with more ideas to sort. He felt a new happiness as he realized
that he was thinking, analyzing, solving. And he was not
afraid to think! Oh, if Pol were only back there in one of
those houses, or if he could only go back to his room with
a pen and tell her all about it!

He had had enough for one day. Now he would change
the subject.

"Dawn't e ever kill nothin', Bob?"

"Sometimes, for the reason that the missus do, to 'ave a
change of meat. Never for fun, Jim. Killin' a chicken edn'
fun. 'Ere we be, boay. I'm glad you come t' meet me. Too bad
us can't keep air pure in the 'aouse as 'e is 'ere."

Allen went into the washroom, and Jim into the middle
room, where a half-dozen men sat in smoke and conversation.

"Been a-'untin', my son?" asked Jake banteringly. "W'at
would Simon Rattenham say to that?"

A few minutes, and Allen came into the room.

"W'at did e bring 'ome, Bob?" asked Spargo.

"Jim," said Allen. "Found un walkin' back t'ward Hengland."

"Did e see nothin'?" asked Jenkins.

"Iss, you, that I did. A fine buck."

"Fired an' missed," said Sims.

"No, Sims, I dedn' even haim."

"A purty tale t' tell," said Sims. "W'at kind of a man izza
'oo wouldn' shoot a deer—if 'e could, that is."

Jim sensed trouble and hastened to divert it. "I seed the
deer too, an' I seed Allen an' knaw 'e dedn' shoot."

Jenkins saw a possible opening after Jim's words and resumed the subject Jim's arrival had interrupted. "Hi 'ave been in this country long anough t' 'ave my papers an' dawn't 'ave mun," he said. "I be a bit ashamed about un."

"W'at are e ashamed of?" asked Sims. " 'Shamed of bein' a Englishman, are e?"

" 'Shamed of not bein' a 'Merican," retorted Jenkins.

"Once a Henglishman, always a Henglishman, I say," said Sims. "Hi wouldn' give up my nationality for any bloody country. 'Oo want t' be a bloody traitor like that?"

Sims knew that Allen was an American citizen, as the others did, the only one in the house. All eyes turned to him. Allen had listened in silence but in tense contempt. The time had come to speak.

"I get e, Sims," he said. "Naow, if thee will keep thy maouth shut while somebody else 'ave a say: W'y did you leave England? W'y did thy father? W'y did these boays leave England? England, like other countries in Europe, took little account of 'er workin' classes except w'en she went t' war. W'en you lost work there, 'oo cared if thee starved or no?"

Sims did not answer.

"Hi've 'eard thee cuss the mines in Hengland an' the weather 'ere. 'Oo dost thee think thee't cussin'? W'en England let e starve, America said she'd feed e; an', t' save your bacon, you come awver like all of we did. I 'ave 'eard that a jackass will sometimes bite the hand that put straw in 'is manger. I dawn't want t' be unfair even to a jackass."

"W'at's the use of you claimin' t' be American?" snarled Sims. "Your Cornish crake will always give e away."

"Iss, my son," Allen said, "my crake will give me away in some things, but 'e dawn't tell everything. They two greenhorns be Cousin Jacks the same as thee, but they talk the Devonshire lingo. And another thing. Crake dawn't tell whether a man be honest, decent, fit for good comp'ny. I've 'eard some Cousin Jacks talk of bloody Swedes an' damn

Dagoes but us all knaw the cap'n will trust some of they t' do a hones' day's work before 'e will some Englishmen 'ere-abouts. Be I plain, Sims?"

Sims did not answer, but all saw that he could not take much more.

"The Cousin Jack be the best miner in the world, but that dawn't say they can all be trusted. Try t' get a little tick from Marx on that ugly phys'og of thine, an' I'll try a 'alf-dozen Swedes I knaw. Dost tha understan' that, Sims?"

Sims did. He got to his feet and walked across the room, his short legs, his powerful arms, his bull neck tense with rage.

"Damn thy bloody soul, Allen! If thee will come aout in the snaw, I'll shaw e w'at a Henglishman can do to a cheap-Jack of a traitor like thee."

Allen stood before him, tall and spare, his slender body looking inadequate for a fight with Sims. The other men stood, too, expectant of trouble. Allen spoke again, and his voice was cold, smooth, distinct.

"Hark t' me, Sims. Afore we go any farther—w'ether you beat me or no—w'at I 'ave said will stay true, like I said it. You an' me have no right t' disgrace Uren's 'aouse, an' on Sunday too. T'morra us be day shif', more's the pity, but I'll meet e any place you say after work. You take somebody with e an' I'll take Spargo if he'll go t' see fair play. You say time an' place, an' I'll be there by the clock. In the meantime, t' keep your courage up, I'll tell thee again, thee't a damn fool."

Tom Collins and Walters entered the room, their faces fresh and ruddy from their walk. A change of atmosphere entered with them.

"Walters, my son, will e play a bit for us?"

Walters went into the parlor; some followed him, others grouped about the door. "What do you want?" asked Walters as he seated himself at the little cottage organ.

" 'E's Sunday. Let's 'ave a meter."

But feelings were too tense for sudden change. The voices were forced, the organ was disappointing, the meter failed. A man or two standing near the door slipped away. Jenkins said, "I need fresh hair," which proved to be the right excuse for all to leave—all but the brothers and Jim. Walters said, "Excuse me," and the three were alone. The place empty and quiet, Jake said: "Blessed relief! An' no disrespec'."

" 'Avin' trouble, was e, w'en us come in?" asked Tom.

"Aas," said Jim, "Sims an' Hallen. They'm poison to one t'other, seem like. Citizenship talk brought un on. Touchy subjic'. I dawn't understand."

Jake smoked as if time and eternity were one to him. Hurry was an unknown impulse in his life. When he spoke his words fitted lazily between puffs from his pipe. They seemed of equal importance in his own esteem.

"Cornishmen in Cornish boardin' 'ouses, eatin' boiled beef an' cabbage an' pasties w'ich be Cornish, talkin' Cornish an' sleepin' Cornish. They go t' chapel, an' Cornishmen praych to mun. They patternize Cornish saloons. I fancy there be the trouble."

"Would a be better if most was convinced they'd never go back?" asked Jim.

"I dawn't knaw, boay. I awnly knaw the get-up be wrong. I dawn't knaw 'ow t' make un right. I feel sorry for min." He turned to Tom. "W'at did e do t'day, my son?"

"Went t' chapel mostly. Walters 'ave a key. Went there t' practice a bit, 'e did, and me t' listen, but talked instead— that is, 'e did. Afore comin' in, us took a turn on the road."

Jake said, "Aas," and Jim, "Spayk on."

" 'E told of 'e's home, 'e's father an' mother, their 'opes for their boay an' plans t' make a moosician of un. They died —close t'gether—an' left the boay alone in the world. Last winter 'e worked in the woods t' make money t' go some place t' study. 'E dedn' like the woods."

"W'y?" came from both listeners together.

"Cold, dirty, tough, no instrument t' play."

"W'at about the work?" asked Jake. "Did a say?"

" 'E helped the cook. 'Cookee,' 'e called 'isself."

"But lumberin'?" asked Jim.

Tom told all he could remember of lumbering; cruising, cutting, scaling, swamping. He told of the lumberjack's skill on the runs and the dangers of breaking jams. "They use a hax like us do a 'ammer."

"I be glad us dedn' take the lumberman's offer," said Jim reminiscently.

"Go on, my son," urged Jake.

"Aas. W'at about 'is moosic?" asked Jim.

"Hard work be ruinin' 'is 'ands for playin'. If 'is father an' mother had lived, he wouldn' 'a' 'ad t' work. He still think 'e c'n write moosic an' teach."

" 'E won't be a miner, then?" said Jim.

Tom laughed. "Jim, you'd ought t' 'eard un say, 'No minin' for me!' Not that 'e looked down on minin' but, 'e said, 'I like sunlight too well,' an' 'there be no footure in un for a boay.' Minin' be awnly a steppin'stone for 'e."

Jake and Jim looked mystified. Jim said, "Usin' work t' get away from work, usin' one kind of work t' get to another kind, be new t' me." Jake said nothing.

" 'E said," Tom continued, " 'I wonder sometimes if Father an' Mother can see I'm tryin' t' go as far's I can.' 'E wiped 'is heyes w'en 'e said that, an' then 'e smiled. 'Tom,' 'e said, 'will you sing a song I 'ave wraute already?' He went to the horgan an' played from notes an' words in pencil. I think I can play un."

Tom went for his concertina, and after a little searching of the keys found the air and harmony. Jake and Jim listened in amazement. "There 'tis," Tom said, and repeated it.

The three were silent for minutes. Then Jake spoke.

"Thicky be some plod!" He blew a mouthful of smoke into the air and watched it as if his thought expanded with it.

"Some plod," he repeated. "Fancy Ol' Parent or Uncle Ned
—our fathers—plannin' for their boays t' go t' Parliament."
He stopped for his idea to take root. "Us was born t' labor
like a hox to the plow. 'Ere a boay say, 'I will be this or that,'
an' go after un." Jake's eyes glowed; Jim and Tom waited.
"Our fate was Cornish; thicky boay's dream be American.
Thicky tale be a capsheaf for Allen's argymint, shore nuff!"

" 'Oo was a said, 'With a great sum obtained I this citizenship'?" asked Jim.

"I dawn't knaw, my son," said Jake, "but this one can be
'ad for the askin', an' I fancy 'e's the best the world 'ave t'
offer."

Chapter Seven

JIM GREETED MONDAY MORNING with a lighter spirit than either of the night shifts had permitted.

"This is better," he said as he dressed. "Day shift."

"A man wadn' made t' work nights an' sleep days, t' my mind," Tom replied. "Day sleep dawn't rest a man like night sleep. 'E take a 'alf a week t' get t' sleepin' just so-so by day, an' then you change shifts again."

They went in to breakfast, which they found a sour affair. The food had no cheer to it—sliced, cold meat left from yesterday, and tea. There was no art in its arrangement and none in its service. The men ate moodily. They were morose, from the thick air of their bedrooms, the crowded beds, the disturbances of late arrivals. Mrs. Uren added no lilt to the occasion. She moved from stove to table and from table to stove, with plodding steps and in soggy silence. She seemed charged with a stolid resentment. She was assigned to a job that would wear her out; she expected no reprieve. No talk broke the monotony. Walters nodded to Tom when he took his place, the only evidence of cordiality that appeared. The rattle of cutlery, the thump of dishes set on the table, the blowing of tea in saucers gave the scene only a mechanical animation. This was the first stint of the day of labor, and all hands made a job of it. Heads combed and heads uncombed bent to the task, to rise only when saucer or cup was raised to be drained.

As they left the table one man said, " 'E snowed last night an' blowed through the roof onto my bed."

"Hi put my foot in a drift from the winda w'en I stepped out of bed," said another.

They were not complaining—just paying their respects to the weather. Half of the men filed into the washroom to change for work, Jim and Jake and Tom among them. The others, who had the day before them, went into the middle room to devise ways of killing time or merely to let time kill itself. A few minutes, and the day men reappeared, took their cribs, and left for the shaft. On the way out one of them playfully nudged a night man as he passed and said tauntingly, "Night shift, comrade? 'E's a purty thing, edn' a?" The night man grinned and thumbed his nose—his easiest and most effective retort.

On the way to the shaft Tom said: "Us 'ave seen all us will ever see there. Day in an' day out, 'e'll be always the same."

"Right, my son," Jake answered. "The 'ouse be too full t' change. W'at 'ave 'appened this far be a 'is'try an' prophecy all together."

" 'E's a hawful way t' live," said Jim.

" 'Oo be e talkin' about—the men or the fambly?" Jake asked.

"Both," replied Jim.

"The boardin' boss an' missus be workin' for money, my son—money. They be givin' hup comfort an' 'ome for money. They think they will 'ave both some day, but w'en thicky day come they won't knaw w'ere t' look for nayther one."

"W'at about the men?"

"They? Most of they be awnly markin' time till they go back 'ome again. The boardin' 'ouse be somethin' t' put up with in a new country. Thee's knaw they will be disappointed. Hev'ry new green'orn 'oo come say there be nothin' t' go back to—an' they keep comin'. Then the mine will get some; free livin' will get some; some will learn an' git their famblies out."

Jake stopped as though what next came to his mind needed a second look.

"Some," he said slowly, "a foo, will forgit the ol' place an' famblies too. Not many, but some." He stopped.

"Spayk on," said Jim.

Jake shook his head.

"That woman!" said Jim. "That woman! She 'ave the hardes' lot."

"I 'eard they 'ad slaves in America fifteen, twenty year ago. I'd say there be some left."

"You forgot the chuldern," said Tom aiming to taunt them a little. But they had reached the shaft, and he got no answer.

Tom was again assigned to Walters for the day. He was beginning to hope Walters' partner would not return. Jim and Jake took the first cage down.

From the bottom of the shaft they walked to their place without talk, as if loath to disturb the stillness that had settled in the pit since Saturday night. They were alone, and the spell of the place, its cathedral quiet hushed them. Their footfalls were dissonant, intrusive, sacrilegious. After the first few steps both, moved by the same impulse, put their feet down carefully to lessen the noise. The staccato drip of water seemed to protest their coming. A profound, unanalyzed respect for the spirit that pervades natural fastnesses had come upon them in this man-made depth. A half-dozen men would invade such a place with chatter and laughter, but one or two could scarcely escape the impression of a restraining presence. These two knew their place; their spirits were figuratively hat in hand as became them.

In their crosscut they found their tools as they had left

them. Drills, hammers, shovels, picks, gads, axes, all stood together against the wall—futile-looking things that in the hands of these men became effective in the process of gutting the earth.

"Nobody 'ave took mun away, comrade," said Jim, "or moved mun."

"I never 'eard of a sperrit doin' a day's work in a man's absence," answered Jake. "Sperrits be the most uselessest fancy of man's mind, 'e seem like."

The last set of timber, erected by their own hands on the preceding Saturday night, looked neat and trim. It gave the place a housed-in appearance that pleased them. They looked around with appraising eyes as if they had never seen the place. Then Jake turned a shovel and sat on the handle. Jim did the same.

" 'E's a brave job, I'd say," Jake said drolly.

" 'E should be, comrade. Us be old hands at un," Jim replied, following Jake's lead.

"Seem like a shame t' bury timber like thicky," Jake remarked.

" 'E do, but w'at else?"

Jake did not answer immediately. He seemed to be searching for words or striving to clear his thought. "I be w'imsical, I s'pose," he said slowly. "Trees be made for sunlight an' wind an' rain. Their place be under the sky, not under the ground. This be a shame to mun, some way."

"I dawn't see it," said Jim, puzzled.

"I dawn't nuther; just feel it."

Both looked around again as if to find what Jake wanted.

"I knaw, I knaw," he said as if some one had spoken to him. "W'en a drift be new and the ground not too 'ard, they sticks pertec' our skulls agin drops. One skull be wuth a lot of timber. Still I feel the same."

Jim did not answer.

"Us knaw timber do more than pertec' our polls. They

sticks show a lot of things that be important for we t' see as time go on. Shore, us must 'ave mun, but my feelin' be unchanged. Soft, I s'pose." He bent his head as if ashamed of his softness or of a fancy that he could not bring to a head. "Aw, go es 'ome with e," he said, dismissing himself.

Jim laughed. "Thee's make me think of a picter I seed once: a small boay, hat in 'and, lookin' up at a tree. I dawn't knaw w'at 'e was seein'—a bird prob'ly or a squirrel or maybe just the quiver of the leaves—but 'is face was all wonder."

"You 'ave un, comrade," said Jake, relieved. "That's me. I be the boay."

Just then footsteps became audible; a pair of lights bobbed and blinked past the mouth of their drift, and two voices shouted good morning. Jim and Jake answered, and the sound of the steps was lost.

"I be glad they be 'ere, comrade," Jake said. "I dawn't like silence you can 'ear."

"Do e 'ear un or feel un, Jake? Hi be never shore w'ich 'e be."

"I dawn't always 'ear un either—just sometimes. In the middle of the week 'e is never as plain as of a Monday mornin'."

"Aas, I 'ave thought of that. 'Ow do e hexplain un? Do e s'pose a man in the woods feel the same? Tedn' fear; us bayn't afeard. W'at izza?"

" 'Ark, comrade!" said Jim.

They listened a moment, and a measured beat came to them through the rock overhead. Somewhere a pair were drilling.

" 'E's a purty man with a 'ammer, 'ooever 'e is," said Jake. "Let's answer un back."

Jim picked up a hammer and twirled it playfully. " 'E dawn't weigh so heavy as 'e will t'night."

They stuck their candlesticks into the timber so that

a steady light would shine on the drill head. Jake selected a drill, and the day's work was on.

The first hole was pointed in the angle made by leg and cap. It pointed upward and outward, to make ample room when blasted for the leg and cap of the next set. Jake stood against the breast, his hands slightly higher than his eyes as they gripped the bitted steel. They were close to his face also, as they had to be to give him control and ease in twisting. It was not an easy hole to drill for either of them, but it had to be done. A blow that missed the drill head would find his hands or face. But of that neither thought. Jim tapped the drill lightly until Jake was set and his own muscles were free, and then sent his answer through the stretch of rock to the unknown man above.

When Jim stopped to get his "wind," Jake said: "I wish thicky bloke could see you do un. 'E wouldn' be so proud."

Jim smiled. " 'E's your turn next, comrade."

About midforenoon they heard footsteps approaching and immediately stopped work. Such was the code of the Cornish pits. Had they been sitting when the sounds reached them, they would have remained seated. Captain Chenoweth came in, accompanied by the shift boss. He greeted the men, found a place to sit, and lighted his pipe. Jake joined him. Between words the captain's eyes wandered around to appraise what these new men had produced.

"Do e 'ave a comfortable place t' live, boays? An' 'aouw do e find the men? The weather is some diff'runt 'ere, I dare say. 'Aouw are e fixed for clo'es? You seem t' be gettin' along all right."

These questions answered, the captain arose, put his pipe into his pocket, and left.

" 'E seem like a nice anough man," Jake remarked.

"America 'ave n' altered un none, 'nother," Jim replied.

"I wouldn' say that, comrade, but I dawn't b'lieve it have done un damage."

They returned to their tools, and by noon were ready to eat. They went back to the puffer room again and were soon joined by the pair from the main drift.

These were the same men who had eaten, had grunted a word or two between bites, had slept the rest of the hour, the night of the boys' first shift. They looked ten years younger, Jim thought—the effect of being day shift.

On Sunday, Jake had told a boarder where he worked. "Oh! You're down with Sailor Lobb an' Johns!" he exclaimed. "The Sailor have seen the world, 'e 'ave. Dawn't cross un, my son! 'E's some savage if 'e's crossed."

"Dawn't e have a word for Johns?" asked Jake, amused at the boarder's awed respect for Lobb. "Pity t' slight 'e."

"Oh, 'e! 'E's awnly a cheap-Jack—a cheel out of 'is mother's sight a-makin' free."

So, when the two entered the puffer room, Jake was alert and, as he conceded, a bit curious. Johns was talking and laughing at his own tale. Lobb might not have been listening. They made themselves comfortable and opened their buckets. While he ate, Johns talked of his Sunday's experiences in Calumet. Strange hearers did not restrain him. He exposed himself with childish abandon. He appeared to believe all he said was enlightening and amusing.

"Maybe the strangers would like t' talk, Johns," said Lobb.

"Blaze away," said Johns unabashed, looking from Jim to Jake. "Blaze away."

"My crake bayn't moosic t' me nor nobody helse that I knaw by," said Jake.

Lobb's lips spread slowly into a smile. "There you be, Johns," he said. "Lashed to the mast."

Jim and Jake were amazed at Lobb's disdain of any offense to his mate. As he shoved his bucket aside, he turned his head and revealed a scar across his cheek that they could tell was not a mine scar. He stretched out on the floor—a good six feet, Jake thought, an' rawboned. Belike 'e could brawl or do a good shif's work. 'E seem peaceful anough, but no doubt 'e be well armed with awnly 'is fists.

Seeking to be sociable, Jake asked the usual question: "W're did e come from, Lobb—yer 'ome, that is?"

"Home?" he asked as if the word were new to him. "Never 'ad one. Orphan. No place for me on land, so I went t' sea. Name any port in the world, an' I come from there."

"You've lost yer Cornish spaych, almos'," said Jim.

"Iss, you," answered Lobb, smiling at his conscious reversion. "Cornish was fit only to be laughed at, so I bundled un up with the ghosts an' gods of Cornwall an' chucked un overboard." He scrambled to his feet and led the way back to work.

Back among their tools again, Jim said: "Hi do envy men like they sometimes. They dawn't seem t' have a care. An' the 'omeless boay runnin' off t' say! There be courage in that most of us dawn't have."

"You'm right, my son," Jake replied. "Most of us like a open road. Us dawn't like strange ways." He hung up his coat and adjusted his candle for convenience.

"They strange ways made a strange man out of Lobb. I wonder if they'd 'a' done the same for we."

Jake did not answer, but spat into his palms and picked up the hammer. While Jim chose a drill and selected the most comfortable position for twisting it, Jake continued:

"Thicky gabby Johns talked me tired. Lobb said nothin' an' filled me with questions I wanted t' ask, but I knawed better." He shook his head. " 'E make the second interestin' man us 'ave met. Us sh'll 'ear from 'e again."

Again the drill was raised, turned and rang, was raised, turned and sank under the hammer. There was something satisfying in the flushness and certainty of its blow—music in its ring on the steel. These men knew the pride of the frontier marksman, of the woodsman with his ax. Between spells they planned the succeeding steps of their program, ways and means to ease as well as speed the yardage they needed.

The afternoon wore on. Jim went to his coat where he kept his watch, to see the time.

From the drift a footfall splashed to their ears; a light blinked into view, and a stranger entered the place.

"Is Jake Collins here?"

"Aas, my son, I be 'e."

"Your brother's partner is hurt, hurt bad, and Tom wants you to come up."

Without a word Jake went out of the drift to the shaft.

Jim stayed to collect the tools and to sort the drills that had lost their edge, and then followed Jake and the messenger. The shift was not ended by two hours; but a man could do little singlehanded underground if he would, and besides, for obvious reasons, a man did not work alone in the mine.

At the surface Jake found Tom waiting by the shaft gate, his face pale and his eyes still wide with fright.

"W'at's 'appened, Tom?"

"Walters be 'urted. 'E's in the bosses' dry. The doctor be there now."

They went to the dry and saw the injured boy lying unconscious, the physician holding his wrist. A bandage hid his face almost completely, and his right arm was bound rigidly to a strip of board.

"That's all that can be done now," the physician said. "He may be taken home. Somebody must go to his house to break the news and make preparations."

Jake said, "I'll go," and left.

Tom waited until the stretcher with its covered burden was taken away and then went to the doctor.

"W'at can us 'ope for?" Tom asked. "I be 'is comrade."

"Well, my boy, I am afraid he will never work with you again. If he lives, he might not— Perhaps it would be better—" With his observant eyes on Tom's face he broke off whatever he had in mind to say. "You had better go home and lie down for an hour. Take this!" He reached into his case and gave the boy a small envelope. "Put the powder on your tongue and take a drink of water."

Tom walked away. He did not see the boarding house when he passed it. Through the village he went, unaware of his direction and oblivious to his underground clothes. His head was bent to the wind he did not feel. His boots grew heavier with the wet clinging snow. Onward he went until the trees overhung his way and the gloom of the forest hastened the end of the day. His mind was focused on one idea: Only God could save his partner's life! Vaguely he recalled an assurance for such a petition as his, and he repeated it as he prayed. "Whatsoever ye shall ask in prayer, believing, ye shall receive." At last he sank in the snow beside the road, worn out.

A southbound stage brought him to the house. It was dark when the driver steadied him to the door. The house was only half alight. Mrs. Uren came to the knock, and, as the door opened, two pennants, one black, one white, fluttered from the door side into the light.

Jake met him and led him into the washroom to change his clothes. A rope had been placed across the end of the room, and blankets hung from it to the floor. Jake with a father's solicitude helped Tom as if he had been a child. He opened Tom's hand to wash it and found the small envelope. When they came out Mrs. Uren had prepared hot tea which she persuaded the boy to drink. Jake then led him to bed and sat beside him, applying heated bricks wrapped in towels and bottles of hot water to Tom's legs and body long after he had fallen asleep.

Tom did not open his eyes until it was well toward midnight. The men came in quietly and slipped into bed. Jake still sat beside him.

" 'Ow be e, boay?" he asked.

"I be all right," Tom answered.

"Brave. I'll sleep beside e for comp'ny an' if you need somethin'." And Jake removed the bricks and bottles and began to undress.

"Jake," Tom said in a low voice, " 'ow izza, Walters?"

" 'E's gone, my son!"

Tom's face whitened in the candlelight, and a strange look came into his eyes. Jake tried to define it but could not make it out. The awnly thing that come to me is hate, he thought. He wondered what Tom hated.

In the morning Jake said: "You stay abed t'day. I'll fetch yer meals an' take care of e." After breakfast he ordered Tom to sleep and went downstairs. Jim and Spargo and Jenkins were sitting in the middle room in silence. They looked questioningly at Jake, and he said, " 'E's better." The mine would not work today as a token of respect to the departed, which explained why Spargo and Jenkins were at home. The rest had gone out. Jake sat down and lighted his pipe. For minutes each man sat as if alone. Then Jake spoke. "They'd come t' be like David an' Jonathan in three days."

A knock on the door was followed by a voice asking if any of the men were at home. Mrs. Uren brought the man in. He looked at the four and said: "I want two to help me with the grave. There's a boulder in one end too big t' move."

Jim volunteered, but Spargo said, "No, you stay with Jake"; so he and Jenkins left with the gravedigger. An hour later the stillness of the day was broken by two explosions —a miner's salute to the departed musician.

"They 'ave blowed un out, comrade," Jake said, "but us mustn' tell Tom w'at 'appened."

Jim nodded in understanding, and shortly Jake went upstairs again.

Piece by piece, interrupted by admonitions from Jake not to talk and to think of something else, Tom told how the accident occurred.

"Us was ordered t' do a job of timberin' seventy t' eighty feet up an' all hopen below. Us 'ad the job finished. 'E said, 'The job look as good as can be t' my eye.' That was praisin' me because he said I was the miner. Then 'e looked back to the ladder an' the laggin' footpath leadin' to un and said, 'Think of a man in a place like this all 'e's life! Danger be reachin' for un from ev'ry chink! Not me!'

"Then 'e started ahead of me t' walk they laggin'. I seed they laggin' roll under 'e's feet, seed un reachin' for a holt, 'e's hat come off, an' 'e's light go out; and 'e was gone."

"There, there, chul, that's anough. Bes' try forgit now. Bes' forgit," persuaded Jake.

After a long silence Tom spoke again. His voice was lowered as if revealing a secret. "Jake, I prayed, prayed till my heart 'urted an' the inside of my head. Dawn't the Book say 'W'atever you ask in faith, in faith, b'lievin',' or somethin' like that, 'shall be done'?"

"Somethin' like un, seem t' me like," said Jake, wishing Tom would stop and knowing well enough what Tom was driving at.

"See what 'appened!" continued Tom. "See w'at 'appened! Jake, I shan't b'lieve again, I shan't pray again."

Before Jake could determine what to say, Tom was off once more.

"Jake, lettin' Walters be killed be like a man makin' a fine machine an' then puttin' dynamite in un. 'E's maze."

"Hold on a minute, boay," said Jake, aghast in spite of himself. " 'Old on a minute! They be big questions, my son, too big t' be answered in a minute. Awnly Time can answer questions like they. No tellin', maybe some day somethin' will 'appen that will given a hanswer that will be like a light in the dark. If you want a hanswer, wait a bit an' keep yer mind open."

Jake got up and bent over his brother. "Hast thee forgot Ol' Parent? Write un yer tale, my son. Tell un w'at you've told me. 'E's old, an' 'e's wiser than most. 'E dawn't mince words or run away from facts. Try 'e."

Jake arose, patted Tom on the shoulder, and left. On the stairs he stopped. A sound of surprise came involuntarily from his throat. "That look!" he muttered. "That look's explained. 'E was close t' hate, I fancy."

That afternoon Walters' body was laid to rest. While the small group stood around the grave and the service was read, snow was falling in large feathery flakes. Jim and Spargo stood at the foot of the grave close to the man who had dug it. "The Lord giveth, and the Lord taketh away," the preacher said. "Ashes to ashes and dust to dust."

Jim looked at the sexton, but he made no move to sprinkle earth upon the casket. That's better, Jim thought; I hate the sound of the groot on the lid. His eyes followed some large flakes that came to rest in silence on the coffin. "That's better," he repeated.

The three men walked back to the house in silence. Jim was thinking of the dreams Walters had described to Tom, his own and his father's. They had fashioned a future in vain. The grave had now hidden the boy and his ambitions in its fastness as the blackness had swallowed him when he fell.

A dozen men were gathered in the middle room when Jim and his companions got back. Comments of all sorts were passing around, the commonest, the oftenest repeated being, "They 'ad no business t' put two boays in a place like that there."

"You say the pit be dang'rous, William." Allen addressed Penglaze but was speaking to the group. "But 'ark t' me! If the miners had spiked they laggin' as they should be, they wouldn' 'a' slipped hunder 'is feet. An' if the bosses had hordered hev'ry set covered back t' the ladder—covered from side t' side instid of allowin' a 'alf-dozen or less for a path— the thing wouldn' 'a' 'appened. An' if the poor boay 'ad stopped a minute t' try they poles—" Allen shook his head. "We do blame the pit, but the blame ain't there altogether. Some day inspectors will be paid to see after things like that."

"An' interfere with the miner?" asked one rebelliously.

"Iss, my son, an' horder un t' do w'at 'e want un t' do. A miner dawn't 'ave heyes in the back of 'e's head t' see everything; an', like others, he will take risks. Miners as good as you or me 'ave got killed takin' a chance—forgettin' or hurryin'; an' a lot more will be. Pride ain't half as important as life, my son. The inspector will be here some day, shore's you live."

Jake was sitting with his back to the stairway door. Suddenly he felt a hand on his shoulder and looked up at Tom. "W'at be you doin' 'ere? I thought I told e t' stay in bed."

"You did," answered Tom; "but I bayn't sick. I feel fitty. I'm leavin', Jake." Together they went upstairs again. "I can't stay 'ere, Jake," Tom went on. "I'm goin' t' Central. I'm goin' now."

Jake looked at the boy steadily as he spoke, and was assured that argument would not avail. Besides, he thought, I b'lieve I understan'. He saw Tom's bag on the bed and said, " 'E's fuller now than w'en you come."

Tom said, " 'E'll be full w'en my diggin' clo'es be packed, shore 'nough."

They went downstairs and got the mine clothes, wrapped them and packed them. Tom was right: the bag was full. For a few minutes they sat on a form in the washroom and talked about money, work, and writing home. Not a mention did either make of going or not going. With Tom's announcement, that was settled. Jake looked at his watch. "A 'alf-hour till stage time," he said.

They went into the middle room, and Tom said good-bye to the men sitting there. Jim arose, put on his coat and cap to accompany them.

Outside, Jake said, "Tom, my son, I want t' give e a bit

of advice." He looked at the boy for assurance that his words were welcome.

"Say on," said Tom.

"Well, this. Thee't awnly a boay. Live an' act like one. Get out amongst youngsters of the place, an' mix in their sports. Learn t' do w'at they do: skate, ski, go t'bogganin', sleigh-ridin', even dance a bit if need be. Dawn't grow w'iskers. Be a boay as long as 'e be seemly."

Jake gathered his beard in his mittened hand and stroked it, looking at Jim, his plaguing twinkle returning to his eyes for a moment. "W'iskers be very well for me an' 'e. Hi was borned t' be a bachelor, an' that one 'ave always been staid. The Cousin Jacks make a mistake clubbin' t'gether too much. Dawn't mind if they laugh at e. Grizzlin' dawn't 'urt. Git rid of yer brogue so you won't be a spotted bird. Be a boay with boays."

The stage drew up to the office stoop, and Tom got aboard. The three shook hands in silence.

Walking back to the "house," Jim said, "Well, comrade, that put a drop more in our cup than the rest 'ave 'ad this day."

Chapter Eight

JIM WANTED TO BE ALONE. He looked around the room, at the faces of Penglaze, Spargo, Jenkins, and others, listened half-heartedly to their remarks, and wished they would all leave him. His selfishness almost brought a smile to his lips. Why should they go out into the cold to accommodate him? Even if they went, he would not be alone. There were Mrs. Uren and the children. He couldn't be alone in the house. He thought of the bedrooms, but they were uninhabitable except when one was under covers. He put on his cap, overcoat, and rubbers and left the house.

A full moon held all but full possession of the sky. The stars that had seemed so close, so cold, so ready to fall the night of his first shift were dimmed now, distant, small. The path through the forest beyond the village was almost as distinct as on a clouded day. Shadows were definite, clean-cut. A half-dozen blocks, and the last house was behind him. He was not afraid; fear did not come to his mind. The snow overspread the world with innocence. He was, as he wished to be, alone with his new possessions.

Jim's ledger was filling fast, too fast for his ability to add, subtract, and equalize. As soon as he neared the solution of one difficulty, another arrived. He was so sensitized to his new environment that his mind ran hither and yon, uncontrolled.

"I dawn't want t' miss nothin' that will 'elp me hup or fit me for w'at be ahead." If the new land would take him in its arms, he would try to take it to his heart. "I want my life t' mean more'n jus' work an' pay an' meat," he said. It was worth while to see the meaning of events, to analyze and interpret conditions as they changed. Life must have a meaning. What did it mean?

For a while the whole episode of Walters' death had occupied his mind. The sensations, the questions, the applications of it still came with chilling poignancy. The threat of a similar end hung over all of them! He had looked at the men around the table on Sunday and when they gathered in the middle room: It might 'ave 'appened t' any of they! he thought. And then, as though the thought had shape and substance and could be felt, he saw wives in England bereft, widowed, their children fatherless. A flash, and it was himself! Pol was alone, save for her babe! His Pol a widow! He shuddered as if with ague. "W'at courage they women had!" They knew that work in the mines meant all this, and that such accidents happened distressingly often!

A few days ago religion had been more than half of his concern, and then Allen came to upset or to substitute something else for the forms he had known. How easy and clear the man's explanations were! How terse were his statements! He seemed friendly with big questions; he treated the biggest of them, Jim thought, almost lightly, handled them with the common phrases of everyday speech. He made religion a thing of the open fields, the woods, the seasons, a thing to which a house, a ceremony, bells were not essential. Religion was a garment of happiness to wrap about duty, justice, honor. To Jim, religion was these things unwrapped, stark, austere. How he coveted Allen's incisive speech and fearless reasonableness.

And citizenship! That had been outside his experience. It came to him like something newborn. By heritage he was a pauper in his own land. Like the rest of the village, he was indigenous to the soil—to the rock under the soil. Then came his uprooting by an uncontrollable upheaval. He had no choice in the transplantation. His rootage there was a matter of birth, friends, livelihood, and his four-walled home. "Citizenship" was a new word to him. It startled him. "A citizen do take part in the management of the village 'e live in," he said. "An' the state too, an' the United States!" He pictured again the far-spaced hamlets he had seen as he came northward. How did they maintain their kinship? How did the government protect them? Citizenship bridged the distances between them, maintained the family ties of these scattered places! "As a citizen a man do mean somethin'," he said aloud. He felt himself take on importance, rise in consequence. "Hi see 'ow 'e might be proud," he continued, and after a pause, "or 'shamed of 'isself." Again he saw so plainly —so plainly that it hurt his eyes—that to make use of his privilege, if it came to that, he must read; he must know. Like a living echo the words of the schoolmaster set for him again the little scene in England, and the voice said, "For the man who is not afraid of work, the man who invests himself, the intelligent . . ." He was beginning to understand; the teacher's meaning became clearer daily.

Not the least of the items he pondered was the strange but attractive man who had disturbed his Sabbath composure but excited a new meaning in an old subject—Allen. He came into the group at the house as no other did. Jim thought of Penglaze and Spargo and Jenkins—good men, all of them —but different. When he entered the room where these were sitting and talking, they would suppress their discussion, whatever the subject. Should any of them continue, it was in a sort of belligerent self-defense, a false self-assertiveness. It was clear to Jim that Allen was not liked by the men generally, and Sims declared war the moment Allen appeared. Allen was separate from them. They felt the distance but did not understand it. Matters that excited them seemed never to disturb him. A question, and he scattered their arguments like thistledown. The usual affairs of the day he assorted as a miner assorts rock from ore; he assayed them. Circumstances did not rattle him. Men, no matter what their position or authority, were only men to him. There were no supermen in his world. Jim wondered if education caused the difference, made a man so.

Jim recalled an argument that had stirred all the men in the room to take part. The last word had been spoken by Penglaze. He settled the matter or, at least, stopped the discussion of it as Jim had heard it done before. Penglaze was "full t' the guzzle" of old sayings and mottoes. "Ain't that so, Allen?" he asked as Allen came into the room. Penglaze repeated what some of the others had said and repeated his own retort. Allen did not answer directly but with a few clear statements showed that what Penglaze thought had been proved, was not so, could not be so. He did it quietly and, Jim thought, inoffensively; but Penglaze's face took on a disturbing look. Allen put on no airs; he did not boast; in fact, he did not talk much in the house; but when he did speak, "Hi feel as though somethin' be goin' t' happen; a prop fall out somew'ere." Jim talked to his own heart, to the sound of his feet on the snow, to the trees standing in priestly silence about him, to the men scattered to their haunts about town, to the men in the pit. "Shore 'nough, Allen must be edicated," Jim muttered. "Hi never seed 'e's like afore in a mine."

Back again his mind turned to the accident that had frightened Tom away. For a brief moment everything gave way to it. The mine closed in respect to it, the men forgot their casual tastes and distastes, their rancors and boastings. They became docile, passive, silent. The mood lasted noticeably for days. How planless death was in its selection of victims! Jim recalled the story Tom had told of Walters' ambition. Death struck and, ambition or none, gave it no concern; fitness or unfitness aroused no question. Death struck, that was all. "W'at is the use of a man tryin' t' improve 'isself if—" That *if* brought back Allen's series of *if*'s: if the bosses—if the miners—if the boys! "A man is give sense, sense to fight death with," Jim said aloud. With this he stopped as if a hand had touched him. "The Lord giveth, and the Lord taketh away," the preacher said! Before he was aware of it Jim said, "Tedn' so!" And then he was aghast at what he had done. He was not sure where the quotation came from. "S'pose 'tis in the Book!" "Tedn' so, any'ow." And then, to soothe his anxiety, he added, "It shorely be awnly a church sayin' an' not in the Book."

Once more Jim realized his need; it was as recurrent as a throb of pain. How could a man be pious, a Christian, a good citizen, be able to think for himself without fear, trust himself with the problems Life threw into his lap unless he could read? The minister was not always near, nor was he always to be trusted. A man did not want to be running to some one else with his questions his whole life through. Aloud he said, "Jim, my son, you've got t' read—aas, you've got to, an' no mistake."

He was back on Main Street again, and he felt a sense of relief when the shop windows drew his attention away from himself. People passed without noticing him, and stray sentences or phrases or words came to his ears. He smiled at the uses his own brain made of them. Others approached without talk, but, almost without fail, when they came abreast with him, one or both would burst into speech as if to demand recognition, if not of their persons, of their presence. That too amused him. "People like t' be seen an' 'eard if 'e be awnly me t' see an' listen." Suddenly he became aware of two men immediately ahead of him. A familiar voice came to his ear. He looked again; he was right; it was Allen. But Allen's words were different; they didn't have the twang of West Cornwall, the half-words, the slurred word groups. Jim

could not say he was talking good English; Jim didn't know
what good English was. He called it American.

A small worry fluttered through Jim's mind. And yet, one
of his questions appeared to be answered. Allen was an edu-
cated man. Jim felt sure of it. But why should he talk one
way at the house and another way on the street to the
stranger? Izza 'shamed of 'e's tongue? And then, because he
liked the man, he said, "There be no reason w'y 'e should
talk Cousin Jack to a stranger, an' none w'y 'e shouldn' talk
un at home." But in spite of his good intention Jim was
troubled by his discovery. He passed the two, he thought un-
noticed and stopped to look at a display in Marx's window.
As he started on again a friendly Cornish tongue said, "Thou
shalt not covet, my son," and chuckled. Jim turned around,
and Allen was alone.

In spite of Bob's jovial greeting Jim became silent as soon
as they began their journey home. He was not ready to talk.
Allen also seemed to have something on his mind. Jim was
certain Bob would advise him readily enough—he might even
consent to instruct Jim himself; but to ask or even to mention
his problem took more courage than Jim could muster just
yet. They found the kitchen and middle room empty, and as
they had to go to work in the morning they bade each other
good night.

As soon as he was abed, Jim reviewed the journey he had
taken and apportioned it according to the subjects he had
pondered as he walked. A text a village youngster had used
for his trial sermon came to his mind: "And there were giants
in that land." Jim smiled to himself in the darkness: 'E dedn'
say 'e was talkin' about America. But while he strove with the
monstrous forms that loomed around him and coveted from
a distance the fruit of his promised land, while he envied such
men as Allen and the old schoolmaster their sharp-edged
minds, he wished still more to share his dreams, the day's
events with his wife: Half—aas, all of it belong to she.

A few days after his walk, Jim was alone one evening in the dining room. A book was lying on a chair, put there evidently by one of the children. He picked it up and turned his back to the door that Mrs. Uren or a passing boarder might not see. On the first page was a picture of a dog, and underneath it a short word. He assumed the word to be the name of the animal. He examined it closely for minutes and then spied it in the line at the bottom of the page. Immediately he wondered if it might be in each of the other lines. If so, could he find it? He did in every line. On the next page was a cat. He repeated the process and found his word as before. At this point the door opened and two boarders came in. Jim put the book where he had found it and assumed a show of interest in what was to be seen outdoors. He was conscious the while of a new sensation, a glow, a great happiness. He had taken a step toward the biggest accomplishment of his life. He could read two words!

The second lesson came a few days later. He was night shift and had left his bed earlier than the other men to gain another few minutes with the primer. The children came in from school and put their books on the form where he was sitting. He picked up the little volume and, when sure no one was looking, found the dog and cat again. The two words still stood out in the lines as if beckoning to him. "I shall always like they beasts from now on," he muttered to himself.

While he was still enjoying the pleasure his accomplishment gave him the owner of the book came bounding in for something she had forgotten and seeing the man with the book ran to him saying: "That's my book! I am in the first grade. Let me read. I can read." She took the book and turned to the page where evidently her last lesson had been and began jerkily, her small finger pointing out the words while she held the book close to her face. She was uncertain, and Jim saw danger. She might ask him what the next word was. "Let's begin at the fust page, my dear, an' see 'ow far us can go." He was sure enough she could read the early pages without help. The child was willing and read eagerly, while Jim watched closely. She read two lessons, and her zeal was spent. She ran out of the room to her play again, but Jim had learned a half-dozen words more. "My fust lesson," he said, "and my fust teacher."

At work, Jim was unusually silent. Jake noticed it but asked no questions. One night of that memorable week, while the two were resting on their shovels, Jim was as wordless as the timber about him and Jake appeared absorbed with the smoke from his pipe. Suddenly Jake said, "W'at did you say, comrade?"

"Hi dedn' say nothin'," said Jim, embarrassed. He saw Jake's eyes sparkle with the drollery that prompted the question but realized, none the less, that he had not been fair to his partner.

"Bayn't e goin' to then?" Jake asked.

"Hi been thoughtless of e, Jake. You'll forgive me, but I been worried since Tom left about writin' 'ome."

Jake did not answer, but Jim's seriousness did not dissipate his humor. Both of them should not be too grave at the same time. He continued to look at Jim expectantly.

"Say on, comrade," he said at last.

"I've got t' learn t' write," Jim answered, "an' I dawn't knaw how t' begin." His lips quivered.

"Now, now!" said Jake. "Let's take un aysy, slow like. W'at can't be coored, must be endoored. The writin' can be coored. W'at can't be, be the time 'e take. You can make that as short as possible by doin' yer best."

Jim got up and walked out to the drift and stood there in the dark. Jake waited.

'E's awnly a boay, thought Jake, looking from the height of ten more years. T' leave father an' mother an' a maid of 'e's awn be a heavy dose for a boay t' take. Jake shook his head understandingly. But 'e'll come through.

Jim came back in a few minutes, composed again. Jake got up thinking he would say nothing more but would go immediately to work, change Jim's mind by making him busy and perhaps a word or two here and there between shovelfuls. But Jim halted him.

"Jake, tedn' awnly that I want t' write the maid, bad as I do. There be other things that say I mus'."

He looked steadily at Jake as though Jake should read his mind. Unconsciously he tried to compress into a sentence the issues that had assailed him and had converged at a common point. They all lay back of his next words:

"There be somethin' that say I be 'ere t' stay—I'll never go back again. That somethin' say I must. Hi never feeled thicky way afore."

"Brave, my son," complimented Jake, proud of the boy's recovery and control. "Brave! But one thing at a time. T' write the maid be foremos' now. Be cose, you must learn t' read an' you will. Somethin' will turn up to make the way."

Jake moistened his hands, but he only swung his shovel idly before him.

"Now for the second point. That be a long-distance worry —the foolishest kind of a worry t' my mind. I bayn't scoldin', mind e! A man may be forgive' fur worryin' about tomorra or maybe for a week a'ead, but there bayn't no pardon for a man 'oo worry a year or two a'ead. A lot of things can 'appen afore you git yer citizenship papers." Jake's trouble-dispelling smile appeared, and he turned to work.

They loaded three cars and pushed them to the switch before they took another rest.

"They cars 'old a lot of dirt," muttered Jake as he put on his coat.

"They be big," agreed Jim.

They sat in silence while rest soothed body and mind and their pores closed. Jake blew smoke toward the open drift and Jim toyed with a bit of soft grease squeezed from the flame end of his candle.

Together they rose and turned to the dirt pile again.

"I 'ave a s'prise for e, comrade," announced Jim.

Jake looked and waited.

"I've 'ad one lesson," continued Jim. And he told of the little child reading for him and the ruse he had adopted to save himself embarrassment. They laughed together at the experience.

" 'Out of the mouths of babes,' " Jake quoted.

Jim finished the quotation ending it with, "an' shame."

"Shame that you c'n laugh at edn' 'ard t' bear," added Jake.

Jim's next step was to buy a book such as the little girl used, for himself. He carried it with him and studied it as he could. He took it underground and stayed in his place during dinner or supper hour. Jake made no objection. The first night Jim said he would not go out to the shaft. Jake threw him his own coat saying, " 'E'll be cold for e sittin' 'ere." Jim said nothing, but he swallowed hard as he watched Jake go out the drift. "There be foo like 'e," he said.

Jim was not deceived by the success of his first lessons. Capitals and small letters confused him, and he did not know the sounds given to them. The printed words were just "other" pictures of the creatures they represented. He copied whole lines, but when they were done he was helpless to explain their parts. He would have to divulge his secret to somebody, confess his inability—his ignorance, he called it— and ask for help.

One afternoon he sat alone pondering his problem when the boarding missus came in. She caught the look on Jim's face and asked, "Be e sick, Jim?"

"No, missus, I bayn't sick," he replied. "I bayn't sick."

" 'Omesick, maybe, which be worse. W'y dawn't e go down t' the store with the boays?"

Jim did not answer but wished she would leave.

"If you be 'omesick, my son, if you'd write a bit t' the maid, it might make e feel better."

Thus she tore the cover from Jim's trouble without knowing it. He remained silent for a moment and then said, "That's it, missus; that's it. I can't write."

"That's a small matter," she said promptly. "W'y dawn't e ask one of the men t' write for e? Spargo can write a bit. 'E couldn' spell big words—but anough. An' Allen can write, if so be 'e bayn't too praoud t' 'ave anything t' do with e. They do say 'e spen' 'is time with the schoolteacher an' the mine doctor. Hi wonder 'e do mine, I do!"

Mrs. Uren seemed to get more enjoyment from her criticism of Allen than from her effort to help Jim get a letter written. Her remark was just a trickle from the undercurrent of dislike for Bob that ran through the house.

Jim wanted to reply but could see no gain for Allen or himself. He was not surprised that Bob had been discussed. Jim remembered his own thought when he first heard Allen talking to the teacher. Most of the boarders would have less reason for thinking charitably of Bob's differences than he had.

"An' my oldest, the boay, can write," she continued, "but 'e wouldn' leave 'is play."

With no thought of discourtesy, Jim arose and went for his outdoor things and left the house. "I can't blame 'er. I let the cat out of the bag. 'Er run the scale from Spargo to the boay thinkin' more t' praise 'er fambly than t' lower me."

He knew he could not go far—it was too near suppertime; so he chose streets that he had not traveled before, around the outskirts of the place. He walked briskly and soon found that such air as he was breathing was an elixir for his ills. It reached beyond his flesh into the innermost recesses of his spirit. Soon he possessed a new sense of freedom, and hope bordering upon certainty filled him. Of course he could do it! The missus had helped him more than she knew. Spargo can read and write! And Allen! He would not compare himself with Allen, but the thought pleased him that he understood all Allen had said to him. That signified something. And then the children! If they could! He did not believe he was naturally dull, a dunce. All he needed was patience, perseverance and some one to guide him. He had the first and second; he might find the third. Before he was aware of it he was on Main Street again.

"Hi must learn t' take the air for medicine, times like this," he said.

Again he saw Allen walking with the stranger and wondered if he was speaking Cornish or American. Again Mrs. Uren's words came to his mind. He was not surprised by what she had said, but that she had said it. She seemed far separated from the men as she plied her drudgery, but evidently the gossip that suited their tastes was spice to her tongue too.

Jim stepped into the post office to ask if a letter had come for him. It was his first time. He thought Mary Ann might have written as soon as she heard through Grace from Tom. By counting the days he concluded that a letter had had time to make the journey.

With a strange mixture of hope and doubt he mentioned his name at the wicket and to his delight received his first message: his first letter from Pol, the first letter she had ever written him, the first letter he had ever received. "The maid was quick," he murmured. His hand shook as he took it from the clerk, and he fumblingly let it fall. The clerk picked it up and put it into his hand again. It became strangely indistinct. The walls, the door, the people on the street were not clear. He stumbled when he stepped down to the walk. He put the letter into his pocket but kept his hand on it, securing and in a way caressing it. In fancy he saw Pol at her snow-white deal table writing it, her head bowed over it, her black hair glistening in the candlelight. He followed it from Plymouth to Southampton and pictured it, one among thousands, perhaps, in the dark hull of the ship. In New York it would be in greatest danger as he had felt himself to be, danger of being lost. And then, journeying day and night across the great distances of this new world he followed it. What a piece of luck it was that it had got to him! "From 'er 'and to mine," he said. "The day of miracles bayn't past."

Jim told himself what it would say. It would tell him that Grace had called with the word he had given Tom. Pol was well—or ill! lonesome for him or hopeful and brave as on the night she bade him go. Those who had called on her, she would name; and those who had forgotten or overlooked the demands of her loneliness, she would not name. Who else in the village had left for foreign lands, who had died and to whom life had come, frail and weeping out of the deep. All of these things it kept in silence in his pocket, hid in its enigmatic lines. Who would release them from him?

Suppose it was not from Pol! Jim stopped like a man turned to stone at the thought. Suppose S. P. R. had written him, getting word from Grace too and beating Pol to the pen! Or Cap'n Harry! Or the schoolmaster! With an effort Jim made himself go on. Nothing about the letter that he could see told who wrote it. But they would have no reason for writing to him. It was from Pol! Jim took the letter from his pocket again and looked at it.

"If the clerk dedn' give un to me, I wouldn' knaw 'e was mine! I can't read my awn name!"

There was no quiver in his voice as he spoke. Moisture had gone from his eyes. There was no curse in his heart for the land that had kept him in ignorance. A new passion took hold of him, a passion of determination. From that moment Jim knew that he would read and write.

Three days later the letter was still unread. He carried it wherever he went. In his room he had scanned its lines and, once, traced them with a pencil as though that might bring their significance to him but more to feel that his fingers moved where hers had moved before. He leaned back in his chair, defeated. " 'Er be speakin' to me," he said, "an I can't 'ear 'er voice."

In their place at the bottom of the mine on that third night the partners found that in two hours or less they would need timber. As a consequence Jim went to the level above to find the timbermen. He found them, detailed his needs, and was returning to the shaft. Coming toward him was a light apparently as remote as the farthest stars. At times it disappeared and then flickered again as the hand of the bearer hid and uncovered it. Slowly it took on size and color until a faint glow spread around it. The miner was shading his light with his hand that he might see better where he stepped as well as to protect it against drafts and dripping water. Soon the two were close enough for their lights to fuse; each raised his candle to illuminate the other's face and stopped.

"It's you, Jim!"

"Aas, Bob. Come up for timber."

"That's w'at I'm after."

Jim told him where the timbermen were.

" 'Ave e 'eard from 'ome yet, Jim?" asked Allen.

"Aas," Jim replied. "Word come three days ago."

" 'Aow is the maid, my son?"

Quietly but without shame, he said, "I dawn't knaw—I can't read un." The determination that had come to him steadied him, exalted him, made him feel that he already was what in time—a short time—he knew he would be.

Allen did not speak immediately. He studied the boy's face, the while trying to decide what his course should be. To read Jim's letter was to step into the innermost precincts of Jim's life. He wondered if he dared to volunteer. A deep pity for the boy before him and the girl across the seas swept over him. Somebody must help them, he thought.

"Jim, if you can trus' me, I shall be glad t' read un for e."

Without a word, Jim drew the letter from his pocket and handed it to Allen.

Before the bit of paper was unfolded, Jim's anxious mind ran the entire gamut of its possible content. He felt perspiration come to his forehead, and his hands became damp from his inner tension. Before Bob began to read, Jim spoke. " 'Er might say somethin' about—"

"Never mind, my son, I understand. An', Jim, w'atever she say will be the same's if I 'ad never seen un."

And then, in the little island of light in the underground blackness, he read Jim's first letter from Mary Ann:

"Dear Jim:

"Grace brought Tom's letter this morning and read your words to me. Her read the whole letter. I copied the address and put un in the clock to be safe. Not that I'll forget un.

"I be as well as can be expected. Better than most in my condition, so Mother say and Lizzie Ann.

"S. P. R. come to the door once to ask for you afore the letter come. So did Captain Harry and the schoolmaster. He preached last Sunday and stopped on his way.

"Tom Harvey have gone to Africa—a onhealthy place, I'm told. I be glad you ben't there. Mary Ellen have gone to her mother.

"Everybody, seems like, be kind to me, drop in for a cup of tea, bring their knitting or sewing and stay a hour or the evening.

"I almost forgot Dr. Davey. He called too, said I shouldn't worry. Everything is well.

"I miss you, Jim. I look down the road for you, the time you used to come home from work. I think I'll get supper, Jim will be here in a minnit. I am on the floor sometimes to get breakfast afore I come to and see you ben't in the bed.

"Be careful in the mine, Jim. Tell me everything you can.

"I pray every day for you, and it look like my prayers be answered so far.

"I love you.

"Your wife

"POL"

When Allen was done, Jim, his voice sounding as though it came from the lips of another, said, "Read un once more, Bob, playse," and Bob read it again.

"Thank e, Bob," said Jim simply, and both turned to go.

"Jim!"

"Aas, Bob."

"Dawn't think I be nosy or interferin', but I been talkin' with Jake. He told me some things you be tryin' t' do. 'E's awful 'ard, my son. You'll need 'elp w'ere you won't feel ashamed. Hi spawk t' Mr. Frost, the schoolmaster, for e. He'll be glad t' help e, Jim. A fine man that. I'll take e up t' see un."

"Thank e, Bob."

"If I can 'elp e at any time, jus' give me the wink."

"Aas, Bob."

"I'd do the job myself, Jim, but the other is better—more fitty."

"I see," said Jim.

"So long."

"So long."

Again the two separated, and this time Jim called to Allen. Allen retraced the steps he had taken.

"W'en you talk to me, will e speak the same as you do to he?"

Allen looked puzzled for a moment, and Jim explained. "Hi 'eard e speak that night with un."

Allen smiled. "Keyholes have eyes, and walls have ears," he said. "Yes, my son, I will speak to you as I do to him."

"Thank e, Bob."

"So long, Jim."

As Jim descended the ladder to the bottom, Jake's words came back: "Somethin' will turn up to make the way." He felt something inside himself like "quiet singin'." Then to the bars of the ladder he was climbing he said aloud, "Nobody knaw better than Jake that things turn up faster if they be 'elped."

Chapter Nine

THE OLD-TIMERS SAID this was the worst November they had ever seen. Snow piled to door and window tops, and blew away to be repiled. Passages had to be cut from door to gate and from gate to road. Not much use trying to keep sidewalks open. Woodpiles that stood in provident ricks shrank at an alarming rate, such was the persistence and intensity of the fires inside. Between falls of snow, with the opening of the roads, loads of wood in cord lengths or uncut poles screeched and crunched their way along the streets. The men took a hand in helping the boarding boss to sate the appetites of the reddening and dulling stoves. To be out of wood meant distress and a test of neighborliness. "As soon as the roads are broke again," was a frequent answer to the call for fuel. The Bay was frozen over, and loggers crossed from Baraga to L'Anse on the ice. As far as eye could see, it was said, Superior was roofed with ice.

The nights were uniformly bitter, the days seldom brought relief. The thermometers on the bosses' dry and at the company store told the slight variation of four or five degrees from night to night. Daily the mercury scale was discussed; the boarding house never quieted to pipes and easy conversation until some one "stepped over an' made shore." Not to know the temperature had the effect of a splinter in the skin.

The weather was the headline interest of the boarders' day, persistent, undeniable, the substratum of their peace of mind.

Day and night, the cold clawed at their dwellings that creaked and cracked with pain. Sharp reports came from the walls.

"W'at's that?" a newcomer asked.

"A nail breakin' from the cold."

"Dawn't 'aouses ever fall t' pieces?"

"Too many nails in mun." And the old-timers laughed at the annual joke.

Jim stood at the window, looking toward the mine and the forest beyond. He was thinking of the vast silence, the stiff and naked trees, the desolation, when suddenly he spoke aloud to himself. " 'E must be hawful out there."

"W'at's that, Jim?" asked Spargo.

Jim blushed with embarrassment at his involuntary speech.

"I was thinkin' of they animals in the woods a time like this—deers an' squirrels an' the rest."

"A lot of mun freeze t' death, I fancy," said Jack seriously.

Jim came away from the window glad to escape the laugh that might have arisen. His sympathy for the starving, unsheltered beasts struck first and saved him before his "talking to himself" could stir ridicule.

The same cold that moved Jim to pity for the wild things of the woods had preyed upon the life of the mine as well.

One night a trammer who had been reprimanded the night before for being late, ran past the night boss who had rebuked him, saying, "Me no late tonight, Cap," stepped into the thick fog that hid the mouth of the pit, opened the gate and rushed into the open shaft. He struck the top of the cage resting on the bottom and bounced into the plat. He was found lying there, his face upturned as though unhurt; but to the hands that lifted him, he was invertebrate. He was taken to his boarding house; the mine stopped for his funeral; that was all. The grief caused at the boarding house by his death would be assuaged by the coming of a new boarder. The other groups never missed him. No one from Uren's house attended his last rites. " 'E was a Finn," some one said—and then silence.

The men did nothing between sleep and work except when emergency arose, and the one emergency in wintertime was more wood. Otherwise they sat about, paperless, bookless, smoked and talked, or—smoked and dreamed. They discussed the superiority of the English lever to Swiss watches; how best and quickest to color a meerschaum or a common clay pipe, and the brand of tobacco to do it with; Cornish wrasslin', the Cornish pasty and Cornish cream. Some man who had gone to another camp left a glamour to be redescribed. He might have been a drinker, fighter, wrestler, or daredevil at a hoist like Hell-Fire Jack Chubb. "Some man, 'e was!" Some had left a shame or a folly or a disgrace even, which always made good talk. Northy liked dogs. He was sure a dog could think— hunt dogs and sheep dogs anyway. When talk lagged and dreams wore thin, the talkers straggled out to find at the stores and saloons new participants who would freshen the subjects that had dulled at home. They lounged around Tophet-like stoves in close proximity to the poor box, took new "holts" on old handles, inspired by the change in person and place. They lived in a stove-centered world.

Sunday was their hard day. Then the stores were closed, and the favorite corners, snowbound and wind-swept. The outdoors was uninviting, but the indoors was a stuffy prison. Now and then a pair would take a turn around the block, but they hastened back to the warmth they had left. The day was endless. "Strike up a tune, somebody!" was a standard remedy for dullness. For an hour the meters of the stone chapels "back 'ome" stirred the dead boarding-house air. They seldom knew more than a verse of any hymn they tried.

"A purty tune, that! Let's 'ave un awver again."

But the hymns had a way of leaving the atmosphere heavier

rather than lighter, and an ache followed them that was plainly observable. Arguments ended in bitterness. Ill feelings were stirred that lasted for days, and bedmates would sit together at mealtime without a word.

Jim had had experience with the lift that a chestful of fresh air gave a man, and he made use of it.

"Let's go out," he said to Jake. "I can feel myself goin' down."

Jake agreed, and together they went to save themselves from depression and to make a long evening easier to endure. "From seven to ten of a Sunday night be the longest three hours in the week," Jake said.

A time or two Jake stopped, his face upturned as if looking for a lost star.

"W'at be e seein', comrade?"

"Look for yerself, my son," he said.

Jim looked. The stars, like bits of ice, gleamed and winked in their frozen distances. They added only coldness, a silvery chill to the already frozen earth. And yet they shone from a blue that only favored eyes may see, such a clear, fleckless deep of it as well became the floor of the mystic's heaven. It was too cold for them to stand long looking at the pageantry of a boasting deity: the worshipers would freeze at their worship. So the two moved on.

"One night they was so low an' quavery they was ready t' fall. Now—somebody must 'a' ringed, 'Hoist hup!' W'at was flames be awnly sparks."

Jim said nothing. Jake's voice sounded different to Jim. He did not whisper, but it had a hush in it, something like reverence. It was new—strange to Jim.

"Spayk on, comrade," Jim said quietly.

"There edn' much t' say," Jake answered, and his voice was natural again. "Maybe I 'ave missed a lot of chances, but I never seed skies like us 'ave 'ere afore." He stopped, as was his wont, as if afraid of too many words at a time. "I dawn't

knaw no words for w'at's up there, nor for w'at's in 'ere"—
Jake touched his breast. "I awnly knaw I want t' stand an'
look."

Jim looked at his tall, gaunt, bearded partner in silence and
awe. I discover somethin' new in un every day, he thought.

The last week in November, Jim began his visits to the
schoolmaster's home and to the school. The former he made
when he was day shift, after supper, and the latter when he
was night shift, between four and six. He found three others
availing themselves of the teacher's kindness. They were not
Cornishmen, he knew, and they differed from him in that
they could read and write their own language.

The night of the second study period, he arrived early and
sat within hearing of teacher and pupil. Mr. Frost was trying
to correct and direct the pronunciation of an English word.
The word was "crucible," which the man repeated with a
strange gutturalness that was amusing to Jim. He wondered
why a man could not make his throat and tongue do what he
wanted to do.

When the lesson was done the teacher introduced the two
and excused himself for an intermission.

"Hi dedn' get your name," Jim said.

"Charasch—Lazarus Charasch," said the man. "What is
your nem?"

"Holman," said Jim. "James Holman."

"You are English," said Charasch.

"Yes, Cornish," explained Jim.

"I am a Jew," Charasch said simply. And then, nodding
after the teacher: "He is a nize man."

Many times Jim tried to pronounce the Jew's name as the
Jew had done it and failed. He wondered if the teacher could
do it. Lazarus, too, was strange to his ears as an everyday
name. He knew the tale of the Lazarus who was raised from
the dead, and of the one who had sat at the rich man's gate
with dogs for comforters. This was really the first Jew he had

ever met. When he had purchased his clothes from Marx, the day he arrived in Allouez, he was unsuspicious of the man's extraction. Marx spoke without accent, and Jim was not versed in facial characteristics. This man said he was a Jew. He must be fresh from Jerusalem or Nazareth maybe, or Emmaus. Jim could scarcely listen to the teacher for thinking of the man. He went from story to story, from miracle to miracle, from gospel city to gospel village in fancy, and thought of this man as recent from any one that came to his mind. What a fascinating man he would be! He was a descendant of the patriarchs and prophets, one of the Chosen People! He would talk to the man again some day.

One afternoon when all the men had gone out, he sat with his little book in his hand trying to unite the significances of its lined words and to commit their spelling to memory, when Allen came in.

"Studyin', I see, Jim. You'll be able to write that letter soon, my son."

"Hi be afeared 'e is a long way off," said Jim, grateful for Allen's encouragement. "Hi keep thinkin' about that Jew." He mentioned the connotations that had come to his mind.

Allen laughed at the boy's seriousness.

"Forgive me, Jim. I was thinking that that Jew, very likely, never saw Palestine. He probably came from Russia. And you might know more biblical history than he does; certain it is, you know more New Testament history than he knows."

Allen could not help laughing again at Jim's look. "You told me there was an Italian and a Swede in the class. Don't you wonder about them?"

"I never thought about they," was Jim's frank answer.

"The chapel has made you one-sided, I'm afraid—a bit prejudiced in favor of the Jew."

"I dawn't knaw nothin' about Italy 'cept that's w'ere Rome be, an' Paul went there."

"Exactly. And since Paul never went to Sweden, you slight

the Swedes. Fair enough. That proves my point. The chapels have prejudiced you."

Allen's eyes twinkled as he spoke, and Jim enjoyed his humor.

"Italy is a fair land, Jim, and its people have produced prophets and statesmen who have bettered the world. Some of the best music you will ever hear, some of the best writing you will ever read, and paintings I can't describe came out of Italy. Once it was the seat of the world's greatest empire and gave us, and other peoples too, a heritage of language and law."

"Language?" said Jim, not understanding.

"You will learn about that, my son," Allen continued. "And the Swedes too are 'no mean' people. All of these peoples have suffered and sung, have known oppression and struggled for liberty, helping the world upward."

Allen struck a match and held it to lifeless dottle more for the sake of the words he had spoken than for the smoke left to him in the bowl.

"They, Italians and Swedes, have their great names that will live as long as the biblical prophets. All of them deserve a word of praise. And don't forget, my son, when you see them and hear them, that they, like you, are fighting the age-old fight for better things for themselves and their families. Many of them are bringing their best to America, where time will wash out the surface markings of the old and make of them something new—Americans."

For a few minutes Jim was wrapped in reverie. As so many times before, Allen had again opened new vistas before his eyes. He felt an eagerness that was almost a pain to begin the journeys he wanted to take by way of the printed page. Life was worth living to the man who could read!

"Hi've been wonderin', Bob, w'y more of the men dawn't take advantage of the schoolmaster's kindness. 'E could teach a dozen as well as three or four."

"They don't all have wives to write to, Jim."

"For their awn sakes, then! See w'at thicky Jew be tryin' t' do."

"The Jew is not interested in English for the sake of its literature. He is a business man. He probably speaks a half-dozen languages now and is adding English, as you see. In these camps a dozen nations are represented, and he wants to see to as many as he can in their own tongues. English, of course, he must know. Business is the big word with him."

"W'at is the word with the other two?"

"I don't know, Jim. Talk to them a little some day, and very likely they will tell you."

"You dedn' answer my fust question, Bob."

Allen smiled indulgently as he said: "I did not, Jim; I think you can answer it in part yourself. Is it always easy for you to go to your classes or to puzzle over your lessons as you were doing when I came in? Is it always pleasant? Are there not times when you would rather do something else? And I know it is embarrassing for you occasionally. You have seen times when you could tackle a cut of dirt with a short-handle easier than you could make yourself study."

"I 'ave that," said Jim earnestly.

"Most of us are naturally brain-lazy, I guess, Jim. It is easier to take things as they come, without question, than it is to put our brains to work."

Both were silent for a time, Allen apparently voyaging into the past and looking as though the seas he sailed were troubled. Suddenly he said:

"Men cared for their bodies—fed them, wrapped them, rested them—a long time before their brains put in their claim. They haven't recognized it with the same horse sense that they do their bodies. They can work their carcasses all day, but a half-hour of mental strain is twenty-nine minutes too much. A half-hour of thinking fags them, puts them to sleep, or makes them want to fight. Yes, their brains are new to them."

Allen seemed to be talking to himself—to be lost in a soliloquy. Jim felt himself outside the enclosure of his friend's thinking and remained silent. He was sure Allen was not talking to the moment only, that somewhere in his past was the real explanation of his words. It was merely incidental that what he said might be applicable to Jim's own case. When Bob did not continue the boy ventured his query.

"W'at do e mean?"

Allen arose and went to the window, his face unmistakably troubled. He looked out, but Jim was certain he was not seeing what was within range of his sight. A faint smile passed over his features as he said without turning, "Did you ever hear of Darwin or Huxley, my son?"

"No, Bob. 'Oo be they?"

"Two English prophets whose names will be known to the end of time. You will know some day, Jim, unless—unless you, too, become afraid to think for yourself, afraid to change your mind. They are still alive, I believe," said Allen reverently.

"Tell me w'at you mean."

"Do you know the shape of the earth, Jim?"

"I've 'eard 'e's round."

"Right. But the man who first said so was regarded as crazy —maze," said Allen. "Do you know that the earth moves around the sun, and not the sun around the earth?"

"Hi never 'eard of that," was the honest reply.

"The man who gave that idea to the world was persecuted for his gift."

" 'Oo by?"

"The church."

Allen watched the boy's face to note the effect of his answer, but Jim's look was still that of one deeply interested and not yet disturbed.

"W'at be you drivin' at?" asked Jim.

"This, Jim. Men will often stand to have their money stolen or their honor doubted more readily than for a new idea, a truth that contradicts some favorite belief. How would you feel if some one tried to show you the earth was not made in six twenty-four-hour days? Suppose a minister showed you that the Genesis story was an allegory. What would you say?"

"Hi dawn't knaw. Do anybody think that?"

"A few," smiled Allen. "Most people find it so comfortable to rest on the traditions they have inherited, to soothe themselves with 'old wives' fables,' to cling to jingling words and apt phrases, that they regard question of their truth as a personal affront, and they can condemn and kill with religious fervor any one who disturbs them. Remember Penglaze? Those fellows don't want to be worried with ideas; facts are only troublemakers to them. They want only to eat and sleep in comfort; a job, to give them promise of these two items, begins and ends their concern."

Jim was ready to stop. He felt himself proving Allen's thesis; his mind was getting tired. He could still work all day and come home feeling vigorous; but ten minutes of Allen's talk and he was tired!

"Bob! W'y do you talk one way with they an' another with the taycher? If I could talk—" Jim stopped, aghast. He was accusing, and that he did not mean to do. His question was asked to satisfy a curiosity and, he thought, to change the subject.

Allen saw Jim's predicament and smiled. Dismay lifted from Jim's heart and face and left him wondering still more about this strange understanding man.

"I am a Cornishman, Jim. I was born 'down west' as we say, and that lingo is natural to me. My father was fairly well to do. He made some money prospecting in old Dolcoath and was quite comfortable although not rich—a long way from that. I had one brother ten years older than I. He went to Australia. There he made some money—we never knew how

—died of lung fever, and left the money to Father. Then Father moved to Plymouth.

"From my childhood my parents had me consecrated to the ministry. You know the Cousin Jack's ideas on that subject and how he got it. Scores of boys have seen the steps to the pulpit as a ladder leading out of the mines. I have known some to get on the plan without being able to read. To be free of speech and stocked with the usual phrases of the pulpit did the trick. You know how it is done. They come to America and become pastors in places like this. The man who preaches here is a Cornishman of that very sort, I am told. I have not seen him."

"Hi noticed 'e 'ad a brogue."

"Father decided the issue. He sent me to school."

"Was e converted?" asked Jim.

"I went into the church during a revival when I was ten," smiled Allen; "and, as I was a timid sort of a youngster I never strained my probation very hard, I guess, so that part didn't matter. With me in school Father saw his own name in little bigger letters.

"I was happy enough in going to school because I thought many things could happen before I should have to take theology. And they did, but my first work there fascinated me.

"While there I first heard of Darwin, Wallace, and Huxley. Soon the college was divided into warring camps. The authorities ordered the new teachings suppressed."

"W'at did they men teach?" asked Jim, his interest stirred by Allen's tale.

Allen tried to explain in simple words what the teachings were, and how, to the minds of the clergy, the new ideas contradicted the Bible.

"Did they say man come in that way too?"

"Yes, Jim. And that seemed to be the thing that hurt some

people most. They seemed to think there was a sort of degradation about it. They had all seen men make beasts of themselves, but they resented the idea of a physical likeness and relationship."

"But dawn't the Book say—"

"Yes, Jim. That is the next, or perhaps that should be called the first, affront the clergy felt. You see, my son, that proposition laid the Bible open to question like any other history. It demanded that one should read it with the same analysis that readers brought to other books—read it intelligently and not blindly. It made the Bible everybody's book, put a premium on freedom of thought."

Allen began to fear that he was saying too much, was giving the boy too large a dose for the first treatment. He had not expected to say anything about the subject at all, but it all seemed to come in a natural sequence somehow. Again he studied Jim's face. Interest was there, but no dismay. Allen was glad.

"Did e hever see they men, Bob?"

"Only Huxley. While I was in Bristol he came to Birmingham, and I went to hear him. I went back with a profound reverence for him and complete confidence in him. After that, I knew that trying to stop their influence was like trying to shut out the night air."

Allen was moved strongly by his own review. At times his eyes filled, and his voice was hoarse. He still felt the old pain in spite of the years that had passed. Jim hesitated to break the silences that divided Allen's tale. He had two questions he wanted to ask, and debated which to ask first.

"Do edication make a man a onb'liever?"

"That depends on many things, my son; but not necessarily so. Religious men seem to think so, and many say so. My father thought so. But I heard Drummond, too, while I was in school. He was a brilliant scholar, eloquent and a thorough Christian. He answered your question for me."

"W'at did yer father do?"

"That is hard to tell, Jim; hard to tell." Allen's words quieted to the memory of what his father had done.

"You see, all the churches in England were seething with a sort of fear, an uneasiness. Soon, every church meeting was disciplinary. We students were watched and reported. Word was sent to Father that I was an agnostic. I who was to be his pride became his shame."

"W'at is 'agnostic'?"

"An agnostic is a person who has the courage to say, 'I don't know.' That is the meaning of the word, Jim."

"Hi dawn't see nothin' hawful in that!"

"I don't blame Father overmuch. He was set in the way he had been brought up. Look at Penglaze again. Hard, honest, unchangeable. Stubbornness in what he believes, he regards a virtue. So with Father. The Bible was infallible—couldn't be wrong. 'Science' was a new word to him, was upstart in spirit, the scarlet woman and so on."

"Did e try to hexplain to Father?"

"Yes. I tried to show him that science was simply the reading of another Book that God had written, written with His own hand without prophet or scribe as a go-between. But he would not hear me. Who was I to question God's word? He told me to go, that he disowned me, that I would bring his gray hairs in sorrow to the grave."

Again Allen was silent. In his mind while he talked was the question of what he was doing for this boy. He smiled at Jim as if to show that he had recovered from his own grief.

Jim did not smile. Allen had put too many weights on his mind and spirit. "Is thy father livin'?" he asked.

"I don't know. I have heard no word from him since I left home."

"W'at did thy mother do?"

"What do mothers mean in a Cornish miner's house?" Allen asked bitterly. "Father's word was law always."

"Bob!"

"Speak on, Jim."

"Be you sorry you went t' school?"

Allen's expression changed as his mind came back in a bound from across the sea to meet the question before him. Jim's words seemed crammed with significance, and Allen was startled by the possibilities he had turned loose. He looked straight into Jim's questioning eyes and smiled.

"No, my son, I am not. Truth must always be a man's best friend. Truth can never hurt God. However God may have created the world and man, the facts discovered by any means will agree. You say God is truth. Then all truth is a part of Him. Errors and mere traditional beliefs will drop by the way. Do you want to know God, Jim? Then you've got to know truth. Without it you will be seeing 'through a glass darkly' or not at all. Understand, Jim?"

"Hi b'lieve so."

Again silence held the pair softly, tenderly. Allen's fear of hurt to his friend had loosened its hold.

"Jim!"

"Say on."

"Should I talk before the men as I have talked to you and the teacher?"

"No, Bob. They would hate e more'n they do now."

"Yes, my son, they would. They are coming, and it is almost time for supper."

Jim rose and went upstairs. "W'at a praycher 'e would 'a' made!" he murmured. It was the highest tribute he could think of at the moment.

Chapter Ten

WHEN CHRISTMAS WAS TWO WEEKS AWAY the boarding boss lighted the fire in the front-room stove, or had it done, each afternoon so that the men might have access to the organ. That the season was having its effects on the boarders was evident. They hummed carols or whistled them; they sat around in silence with far-away looks in their eyes. Being away from home at this time was telling on them. Christmases past were crowding other things from their minds. This season so fragrant of home and children filled them with melancholy. When several of them happened to be together they fought off the gloom that assailed them, with laughable jokes and tales of Christmas times in the old land.

"Hi remember the first time I went currol-singing," said Spargo. "Hi was seven year old. Hi singed alto. I was the praoudest cheel in the village because the older chaps took me along. Us traveled a long way that night, an' the chaps carried me on their backs w'en I got tired. A lot of times they 'ad t' wake me up t' sing. W'en us got 'ome us divided up, an' we 'ad five bob nine apiece: the first money I ever hearned."

"W'at did e do with un, my son?" some one asked.

"Iss, you, tell us w'at you done with un."

Everybody laughed at that because everybody knew the answer.

139

"Hi never seed un no more after Mother caounted un," said Spargo.

"Currol-singin' with we was a bit of a lark," said Northy. "I couldn' sing then more'n now, but I always went. Us singed currols sometimes, and sometimes us dedn'; an' sometimes us come 'ome tipsy. One time I got too tipsy t' travel, an' the boays left me t' sleep in a linhay with the cows."

"Hi remember 'aow onaysy I was in the front room of some tony one, especially w'en the maid come 'raoun' with the cider an' cake. The toniest of mun would be sociable then, though they wouldn' spayk to us any other time. Christmas do change folks, an' no mistake."

"Do e mean the maid or the maister an' missus, Northy?"

"Hi mean the maister an' missus," said Northy. "But 'e was laughable t' call the maid Miss in 'er service w'en us called 'er Liz or Soos if us met 'er in a lane."

"Did 'e ever 'ang up your stockin', anybody?" asked another.

Everybody laughed at that—everybody except Penglaze.

"Gran'father Christmas never come daown a miner's chimley, an' besides, that stockin' 'angin' be a Yankee idee," he said.

"You'm wrong there, William, my son," said Jake. "I 'anged up mine once. Mother tooked me t' town—Callington —t' spen' Christmas with 'er huncle. Christmas Eve, Uncle told me about Gran'father Christmas an' showed me w'ere to 'ang my stockin'. I did w'at he said.

"I can see the ol' man yet. 'E 'ad one heye—lost tother in the bal. 'E 'ad a red cut w'ere 'is eye used t' be.

"In the mornin' my stockin' was full. I remember w'at was in un. On top, a horange; down under was raisins, a brass snuffbox, a pocketknife, an' some marbles that 'ad been played with.

"Durin' the day I missed the snuffbox an' knife, an' I cried. The ol' man looked at me with 'is blank eye an' said, 'I'll war-

rant thee's done somethin' bad, told a lie or somethin', an'
Grandfer Christmas 'ave tooked mun away from e.' I'd never
go t' Uncle's 'ouse again."

Several of the men expressed their opinions of Jake's uncle.
"Ought t' 'ave los' both heyes" got the most approval.

"Hi dawn't b'lieve in un," said Penglaze. "Chuldern w'at
be borned t' the poor shouldn' be pampered. W'at they dawn't
knaw abaout won't grieve mun."

"Once more, my son, I dawn't agree with e," said Jake.
"A bit of 'appiness, if 'e 'appen awnly once, dawn't 'urt no
cheel's mem'ry."

" 'Ear, 'ear!" went around the room.

Spargo was sitting with his chair tilted against the wall
until Jake spoke. Then he swung the chair to its four feet
and said, " 'Ark to me! I 'ave a idee!" And he looked from
face to face for permission to express it.

"Let 'er go!"

"Fire away!"

"Spayk up!"

"There be two chuldern 'ere, a boay an' a little maid.
They've never 'ad a Santy Claus Christmas. Let's give um
one!"

Again he searched the faces about him.

" 'Aow?" came voices together.

"Ev'ry man 'ere give a dime or a quarter or w'at 'e like for
the presents, an' somebody see that the stockin's be hup!"

" 'Ear, 'ear!" and "Brave!" sounded from the group.

"W'at abaout the other men?" asked Northy.

"Pass the word along. W'isper like, an' say if they dawn't
want t' give t' keep still."

"Judgin' by what I've seen, you be the boay t' plan with
the chuldern," said Jenkins. "Iss, you, an' buy the presents
too."

"You'm givin' me all the fun, my son," answered Jack.
"Dawn't somebody helse want t' play with me?"

"I'll play with e," said Jake, "an' 'ere's a quarter t' begin the game."

"Remember naow, no talk w'ere the chuldern can 'ear," ordered Jack, "an' no questions. Jus' hand awver your money an' keep still till Christmas mornin'."

" 'Ere come bad news," said a man who had taken no part in the Christmas planning, and he nodded toward the street. All eyes followed his nod to see the captain turning in at the gate.

"W'at do 'e want, Hi wonder?" asked another. To which came a fusillade of replies, some of them pessimistic enough to suggest "sack" for one or all or the closing of the mine.

"If we do wait a minute, Hi spect we'll knaw," volunteered Penglaze.

The captain was stamping the snow from his feet on the porch. Mrs. Uren admitted him, and after a "Merry Christmas!" to her he came directly into the dining room where the men were sitting.

"Good afternoon, Cap'n," came in a choral greeting, and half of the chairs in the room were offered him. Some were stolidly retained.

The captain straddled a chair and rested his hands on its back. He looked around the group, smiling in a friendly way toward every man there.

"Hi 'eard singin' the other night w'en I was passin'," he said, "an' 'e made me think of the old country. Hi thought 'e would be nice—a bit like 'ome—t' 'ave some singin' Christmas. Hi talked to my missus, an' us determined t' ask e awver Christmas Eve. Will e come, all of e that can? Abaout seven-thirty. Come as you be—all of e come."

"Thank e, Cap'n," came in a sizable ensemble.

"Hinvite w'at men bayn't 'ere," he continued. As if a new idea came to his mind he added: "I'll make another call or two. We shall 'ave a good time, I 'ope."

Mrs. Uren, eager to learn the captain's errand, had stood in the door. When he turned to go she said, "Will e 'ave a cup of tea, Cap'n?"

He thanked her and spoke again of other calls to make before supper.

As soon as the door closed behind him his mission and motive were discussed. Some declared that it was "fitty an' proper," the thing he did, that he had an English heart and was one with his men. Some suspected a hidden purpose but could not name it. They did not propose to be "beholden to nobody" and would not go.

Jim had not spoken during the entire conversation. He had sung with many carol groups, but he had no story to tell. He had never hung up a stocking or received a present. Christmas had meant a few timely hymns in the chapel but not an extra potato in the pot. The day was most like another Sabbath to him—scarcely more. But here it meant homecoming, a little added consideration in the family group, more warmheartedness between friends. It was a spirit easy to catch. "If I 'ad thought of un afore, I'd 'a' sent 'er a gift," he murmured.

It was at this point that suspicion of the captain's motive was expressed. The idea grated him. He leaned forward in his chair.

"I be new in the 'ouse an' in the mine," he said. "I dawn't knaw the cap'n, like you do. I was wonderin' if 'e ever spent many Christmases in a boardin' house. If 'e did, that might explain."

Spargo's " 'Ear, 'ear!" sounded through the suspicious voices asking. "Wha's tha mean?"

Jim sank back into his chair as if a little frightened at his own rashness; but Spargo took the cudgel from his hands.

"A blind man with a stick could see the point of that," he said, his laugh easing the taunt of his words. "And you boays

knaw w'at Jim mean withaout tellin'. I fancy the cap'n dawn't
'ave t' beat araoun' the bush. 'E's askin' of e t' come because
'e want e."

As Jenkins suggested, Spargo agreed to talk with the children when he and Jake had drawn up their plans. Jack had no
trouble getting them around him. He alone of all the men
gave the little ones any attention. Mrs. Uren kept the boy
and girl "from under the men's feet," as she said, and the
men seldom spoke to them. Frequently Jack joined them in
their play indoors and out. He tumbled them from their sleds
when he took them for a pull and laughed at them for falling
off. " 'Old tight," he would say. " 'Ere's a bad place." And the
sled would swerve suddenly or leap forward, usually empty.
He would stumble intentionally to give them a chance to
even the score, letting them bury him while he futilely struggled to get up. He would challenge the two to snowball wars,
and in time would flee from the field in defeat.

"You'll be the ruin of they chuldern, Jack Spargo," Mrs.
Uren would say. But she put a few extra bits of meat into
Jack's pasty or a cooky in his crib bag. Her voice reproved
him, but her eyes beamed a mother's pleasure none the
less.

By the kitchen stove he talked to the children about Santa
Claus.

"W'y dawn't Santy visit more folks 'ere? The chimbleys
be small, and they lock their doors! 'E dawn't carry keys, you
know."

The boy was a bit skeptical about it all, but Jack was
amazed at his unbelief. "I'm a firm b'liever in un," he argued.
"If the boays wouldn' laugh at me, an' if Mother dedn' lock
the door, I'd hang up my stockin' shore!"

"An 'ere's another thing. Santy would get 'ere early, afore
'is pack was forked, an' you ought t' get some purty presents.
You see, 'e do live up North an' there bayn't many people
atween 'ere an' the North Pole. That's a fact. W'at do e say?"

The little girl agreed, and the boy consented.

"Remember naow, they stockin's must be hup early Christmas Eve, an' you must be early t' bed."

"The boay was a bit 'ard t' convince," Jack told Jake. "I 'ope the recordin' angel wadn' list'nin' to the plod I told the boay."

"The recordin' hangel 'ave thrawed thee out for addle long since, my son," laughed Jake.

After supper on Christmas Eve, when the men had all cleared out, Jack led the children into the front room.

"You see, my sons, us dawn't 'ave no chimbley 'ere, so I scat this thing t'gether t' make b'lieve 'e's a chimbley. Us'll fix they stockin's t' the top of un, this way." He took a stocking and tacked it to the top of the little frame he had made. Then another and then another.

"Santy will see they all right, an' that's all us want. Naow, hoff t' bed with e! Begone! An' dawn't let me see e till after breakfas' t'morra!"

Mrs. Uren had been a witness to all that Spargo did. Her eyes were full when Jack turned from his job. "Naow, missus, you git, too. Run along with e! Nobody come in 'ere but Santy Claus till t'morra mornin'!" And then in a raised voice he added, "An dawn't forget t' leave the door unlocked!"

Obediently Mrs. Uren went back to her work.

At the captain's house with Jake, Jim saw a few men from other places, some of whom he knew by name and some he had never seen before. He counted thirty in all. Extra chairs had been provided. Two rooms with a double doorway between them accommodated the guests comfortably.

"Make yourselfs at 'ome, boays," the captain ordered. "We be all Cornishmen—Englishmen, that is," he corrected, seeing a Yorkshireman present. "Hi want e t' sing, an' after a bit us will 'ave a trifle of somethin' t' eat an' drink."

Seeing that the men were somewhat strained and ill at ease, he said: "Talk a bit together first if you like, but dawn't forget t' sing. My missus be 'omesick for a currol. W'at shall a be?"

Two or three attempted to "strike up" one too high and one too low. Another was unable to set his melody to his own key. Finally Jake said, "Jim, boay, show mun 'ow we pitch a tune w'ere us come from."

Jake's taunting humor brought a laugh that broke the ice. "Let's 'ave ' 'Ark, 'Ark, ' " some one said.

Jim started it:

> "Hark, hark, what news the angels bring!
> Glad tidings of a newborn king."

By the time the third word was reached every voice in the room had joined in. Soon they sang with freedom and athomeness. The captain and his wife were delighted with their own undertaking.

"W'y ded'n us think of it before, husband?" she asked.

"It was your 'omesickness an' my 'earin' the boays at Uren's, I guess," the captain said frankly.

"I wasn' more 'omesick than you," she parried. "W'en I mentioned currols an' you 'eard the boays, you be'aved like a cheel. I was 'shamed of e—the way you carried on."

Everybody laughed at her retort.

" 'Ave your awn way, maid," said the captain. "Sing some more, boays."

Again they sang, forgetting completely the novelty and strangeness of their surroundings.

They were beginning to run low on carols well enough known for all to sing, when Mrs. Chenoweth and two other women she had asked to help brought in food and drink.

"They be store cookies," said Mrs. Chenoweth, "an' these I made myself. Take some of both an' see 'oo's the bes' cook, me or the baker."

Gallantly the men took some of each.

It was still early when the food was disposed of and conversation began again.

"Cap'n!" said a voice from the group.

"Say on, my son," said the captain.

Jim turned to Jake and said: "That's Allen. 'Ark for somethin' now."

" 'Aow would a foo Christmas plods be? Currol-singin' plods? Everybody 'ere 'ave been a currol singer. True plods, though, mind."

The captain hesitated, and Allen went on, satisfied that his idea would add fun to the evening.

"Hi sugges' that Northy tell the tale 'e told this afternoon, t' give the idea."

" 'Ear, 'ear! Northy!" came from the Uren men. And the captain said, "Iss, you, come on with e, Northy."

Northy told his tale, and the men understood.

"Naow, Collins," said Allen.

"Speak on, Jake," came encouragingly from his fellow boarders.

Jake followed with the same story he had told before to prove the stocking-hanging at Christmas time in parts of Cornwall, at least.

The men got the idea and several humorous, happy yarns went round. When no one else seemed to have anything to say, the captain spoke.

"Thank e, Allen, for the idee," he said. "Naow I'll tell one. Some folks will say 'e ain't true, but I 'ave the proof— a good one.

"I went currol-singin' once daown Carn Brea way. Us singed for the big landawner of the place, an' 'e invited us in. Us went into the kitchen and singed some more. After the singin' the missus asked the maidens, two of um, t' serve the victuals, an' then with 'er man went aout. The maid w'at served me put two spoons of cream in my cup. I watched 'er t' see 'aouw she served the others. They all got one. W'en 'er come with the cakes, 'er said, 'I made they,' an' pointed to the saffern. 'See 'oo's the best, me or the baker.' Then I took two of they. Finally at last we got ready to go. Us 'ad t' go

through a long hall to the door. I managed to be last t' reach
the door. W'en us got there I dedn' go aout. I closed the door
an' stayed be'ind. I dawn't know 'aow far the boays went
afore they missed me. I bayn't much of a singer, so they
dedn' come back. I felt my way back to the kitchen door an'
knocked. The maid w'at gived me the two spoons of cream
opened un. 'Er dedn' seem surprised, but 'er said, 'W'at be
you doin' 'ere?' I said, 'I come back for another spoon of
cream.' She laughed, an' I went in the kitchen again. The
tother maid was gone. Soon us was settin' on the settle close
t'gether like, an' before midnight us 'ad said a lot of things
pleasant t' say an' 'ear. I told 'er I was goin' to America an'
asked 'er if 'er would come. W'at do e s'pose 'er said?"

All eyes were on Mrs. Chenoweth. Her face was crimson.
Her two friends were enjoying her confusion.

"Charles!" she cried. "Mr. Allen said you was t' tell true
stories!"

Captain Chenoweth looked at her with sparkling eyes.
"You men 'ave the proof," he said. "You 'eard 'er say like
'er did then: 'I made they. Take one of each an' see 'oo's the
best, me or the baker.' "

The men had caught the captain's spirit and laughed with
him.

" 'Er still give me two 'elpin's of cream w'en us 'ave scalded
cream," he said. "Dawn't e, maid?"

"Iss, but you dawn't deserve it," she retorted.

"An' naow you know 'oo got 'omesick for currol-singin'
—an' why."

The men applauded the story and began to get up to go.

"You'll sing a good-night number for the missus, won't
e?" the captain said. " 'Er do love currols."

"Let's 'ave 'Rule Britannia,' " somebody said, and started
it.

One by one the voices swelled the anthem until all seemed
to be singing. They sang with the gusto of patriots who had

been better treated by their native land. The thing was done so suddenly no one had a chance to object if any one wished to.

Outside, Jake said, "I dedn' enjoy singin' that last one like I should, comrade."

" 'E wadn' proper, shore 'nough," answered Jim. "I felt that."

" 'E'd 'a' been all right t' sing fust if us 'ad a 'Merican tune t' follow with. W'en us put up the flag of our 'ome, the 'Merican flag should go with un—on top. But us mustn' blame mun too much," continued Jake. "They've been transplanted but 'aven't took root. So far, they awnly 'ave a job. That bayn't anough to give a man a feelin' for a place."

As the men came in, they went upstairs to bed, all but Jake. He bade Jim good night, saying, "I be night core,* " and continued into the front room, where he found Spargo at work over a small conical evergreen tree that he had smuggled into the house. Already he had draped festoons of threaded cranberries and popcorn over its branches.

"W'ere did e get they, Jack?" asked Jake.

"The church folks 'ave been workin' at a job like this for days an' I hoffered t' buy a foo yards. They wouldn' take no money; they gived mun to me."

" 'E make a purty show," said Jake admiringly.

This done they clipped small candle holders to the branches and affixed the candles. "I seed they in Marx's winda," explained Jack. Candy crooks were then dangled from the limbs.

Filling the stockings came next. To Jake's surprise a third hung from Jack's frame, a large, long one.

"You been keepin' a secret from me," he accused.

Jack laughed. "My little joke on all of e, my son. I couldn' 'elp un." And then seriously: "Christmas be Mother's Day

---

* Shift.

too, you knaw. Couldn' 'ave Christmas withaout a mother."
And the big stocking was filled.

Jack looked sheepishly at Jake. "Hi tooked un off the
clo'es line Monday. 'E 'aven't been missed. I misused funds
for that shore 'nough. Thee's 'ave t' bear the blame with me,"
he said.

"I volunteered t' work with e for better or for worse,"
said Jake.

Under each bit of hosiery was stocked an assortment of
things suited to the age and sex of the wearers. To the large
stockings were assigned two pairs of gloves, one for Sabbath
wear and one adapted to the cold hurried trips to the hydrant.

"Did e 'ave money anough for all this?" asked Jake.

"Ev'ry man gived but one. He said such things took folks'
minds off the message of Christmas."

"No need mentionin' names," said Jake, "but still—"

"I w'ispered t' old Gornell the candy man, an' 'e was
gen'rous. To Marx, too, an' 'e dedn' want t' take nothin'."

A festoon of paper bearing the words, "Merry Christmas"
was stretched over the improvised chimney, and as Jack
pressed tacks through it he said, "Marx gived that."

The two stepped back to look their work over.

"A brave sight, shore 'nough," Jake said, and the workers
went to bed.

After breakfast the family and the men went into the front
room. The little tree glowed and twinkled and the small
heaps of presents radiated greeting. To each stocking was
attached a paper bearing the words, "Who said there ain't
no Santy Claus?" printed simply with a lead pencil.

Mrs. Uren wiped her eyes with her apron, and the little
girl busied herself with her surprises. The boy, with a skate
in each hand, shouted what he believed was his own discovery.

"I know who Santa Claus is. He's Jack! Jack is Santa

Claus." Jack was standing in the doorway looking over the shoulder of another boarder, just a bystander to the scene. The boy ran to him in noisy gratitude. Jack put an arm around his shoulder and said. "Santy be more than that. Some day you'll knaw."

Jake saw the small drama and turned to Jim. "Boay, from now on I b'lieve in Santy Claus. I 'ope they all do."

At ten o'clock a service was held in the church. The choir had been preparing the music for the occasion for weeks. The only other feature was the reading of the Gospel records of the Christ's birth. A tree service was announced for the afternoon. This left the evening free for home entertainment. After the service Uren invited the preacher to the boarding house for dinner.

The minister was a stodgy man of forty. His head was large and square, surmounting an overfed body. His hair was combed rigidly straight, at right angles to the parting— obviously with the use of much water. His full cheeks hung in a sagging curve at the jaws. His eyes were almost black; he wore a large drooping mustache. When he spoke his voice hushed every other and demanded attention.

He sat directly opposite Jim, which made Jim uncomfortable. He had met the minister at a previous service but only formally. He tried hard to discourage a misgiving that he did not like the man. The other men sat around in evident uneasiness. They spoke in subdued tones and looked askance at the clergyman. Their expressions asked, "W'at did they bring 'e 'ere for?"

The meal over, they all went into the front room, but gradually the men slipped away until only four were left.

"Hi should like t' see you a member of my church, Brother Holman—you an' Brother Collins," the minister said, nodding toward Jake.

Neither had given the matter thought, and neither answered.

"An' sing in my choir, too. I 'ear say you sing very well."
Still neither spoke.

"Yes, you ought t' join the church afore temptation do
come. Hamerica is a wicked place. I 'ear temptation is close
to you 'ere. It is rumored you 'ave hinfidels 'ere, hagnostics,
hatheists!" He said the words slowly and with some difficulty.

Jim's suspicions were aroused, and a resentment too, by
the attack. He was certain Allen was meant and the whole
house was assaulted. He was glad for a moment Allen was
not present—but should he be! Allen had left before the
rest of the house were up.

"That I dawn't knaw," said Jim.

"Are you certain you don't know?" asked the minister.

"Hi dawn't tell lies, Brother," said Jim slowly but emphatically.

Unabashed, the preacher continued. "Is there a man live
'ere called Hallen?"

"There is," said Jim.

"I was thinkin' of 'e."

"W'ich is a hinfidel or one of the others?"

" 'E's all three, I 'ave been told."

"Then, sir, I think bes' you should ask Allen straight. I'm
shore 'e'll tell e. 'Oo be the res'?"

" 'E's all I know," said the preacher.

"You said infidels an' all the rest."

Jim was ready to add the last bitter word when Jake spoke.

" 'Oo was the man 'oo spoiled the fust Christmas?" he
asked.

"You bayn't matin' me with Herod!" exclaimed the
preacher.

"Hi was jus' thinkin' the different ways men do the same
thing—kill 'appiness," said Jake.

The preacher arose to go to the church to oversee the
preparations for the tree service. As he left, Mrs. Uren said,
"You'll be 'ere again for supper, Brother Tozer."

"Iss, thank e, sister," he said, and closed the door.

The tree at the church was not an evergreen. Evident enough it was that it had been chosen with a thought to the load it would bear. Its smaller twigs had been stripped off, and the remaining limbs wrapped in cotton. For convenience rather than naturalness the limbs were entirely swathed in the artificial snow. Ropes of cranberries and popped corn sagged from tip to tip of the branches in pleasing arcs. Sparkling ornaments added to the show, and packages chosen for the glare of their wrapping. Around the tree on the floor the large packages were heaped and baskets placed, filled with bulging paper sacks. All of this had been expressed directly from the polar warehouse to arrive before the Christmas saint could get there. But he would come. Assurances had been received and announced, even to the time of his arrival. When he came still more kindliness would pour from his pack.

In due time—when the songs had been sung and the pieces said—bells were heard at the door. Eager expectant eyes were turned to see him enter. Dressed in red trimmed with white, bearded, muffled, and snow-flecked, he came down the aisle. His pack swung awkwardly from side to side as he feigned the prance and vigor of youth. He went directly to the platform and made a short speech, still holding his sack. A skeptic might have discerned a falsity, a strain in the voice, and a suspicious person might have wondered at the accent.

> But Cornishmen are like the turf;
> Cornishmen roam all the earth.

The speech ended, Santa emptied his pack on the rostrum, waved his hand, said he had far to go, and was gone.

The superintendent of the Sunday school took charge again and began the distribution of the gifts. The children marched past to get the little paper sacks. Then came the major interest, the distribution of the boxed and bundled things. Most of these were gracious tokens of the season extended within families and between relatives—classes to teachers and the school to the superintendent. Many members of the church accepted the church tree service in lieu of one at home. Some who were not members accepted the tree as a public institution. Young people showed the world their approval of one another by utilizing it similarly.

Some packages were marked, "To be opened at the tree." The donors of the gifts in them omitted their names from such. A little vanity was apparent in the ruse when the gift was expensive and eye-filling. More often the gifts, marked so, added laughter to the occasion, sometimes derision. Humorous oddments were displayed, something to emphasize an eccentricity or to recall a laughable episode widely known. Taste in such matters frequently overreached itself, and no laugh came. Dislikes or known enmities, at times, prompted humiliating or frankly insulting tokens, and resentments flamed hotly after their exposure. The superintendent tried to suppress such vulgarities; but something was sure to elude him, and his surprise often communicated the character of what he refused to show. So St. Nicholas and St. Valentine met in church at the tree.

The minister came back for supper, but both Jim and Jake avoided him. At five o'clock the coach from Calumet came in, and the post office would be open for a half-hour. Jim was at the office door when the coach drove up.

Jim struggled to suppress the hope that might precede a too bitter disappointment if he gave it wing. He knew himself well enough to foretell the depth of gloom he would reach if he were too expectant of a letter that failed to come. The *thump, thump, thump* of the stamp came to his ears. He counted them, a thump to a letter; one of them was for him —perhaps. By the counting he hoped to dull the edge of his eagerness; and for the same reason he watched the distribution through the small glass squares of the boxes. He was not thinking of the business interests of the letters he counted, but regarded them all as messages of the reason from friend to friend. They might be all akin to the one he expected. He imagined them going to homes and boarding houses— letters from Finland, from Sweden, from Italy, from England, bringing their treasures of memory and affection on this Christmas Day. Different tongues of different lands, but their loves, their hopes, their anxieties the same. The wicket flew open.

Jim brought up the end of the line and mentioned his name, his heart beating in a tumult of expectation in spite of him, expectation and fear.

"Yes, Mr. Holman," said the woman, and slid the letter toward him.

Jim secured his prize and hastened home. "'Ow fitty," he said, "for it t' come t'day! Now, if 'e awnly hold good news, 'e will be Merry Christmas an' no mistake."

He went to his room, lighted a candle and broke the seal. The first words he made out clearly and with exultation. "Dear Jim!" He could hear her say it. And then, word by word he pored over each line, recognizing one and failing with another, but rejoicing that Pol was so close to him. It was like seeing one uncertainly in a dream, the face coming almost to view but receding again. He thought of photographs he had seen that were not clear. So the message eluded him. He tried it again and again but had to give it up. "I am well; I love you, Jim," she said, and that made the rest easy to wait for. He raised his head, and Allen stood in the door.

"You didn't see any of us when you came in," he said. "I thought I'd give you time to see what you could do alone and then, if you needed help, lend a hand."

"Hi couldn't make un all out," said Jim, and handed his friend the letter.

Allen read, transforming Pol's phonetic Devonese into better English.

"Dear Jim:
"Your letter written by your friend came yesterday. I am glad you are well and making friends. Mr. Allen must be a good man. I hope to meet him some day.

"And the money came, too. I shall be as careful as I can, and save some from each note you send.

"It must be bitter cold there with so much snow. I try to fancy how it looks, so deep and white everywhere. How do women walk in it?

"How do you live, so many in one house? What do they do on Sundays when all are at home? Does one woman cook for all of them?

"I know you miss Bill and Joe and Tom. I am glad Jake is with you. How far is Central from where you are? Give Jake my regards. When Grace hears from Tom she comes in.

"Do you think you would like to live in America for good? You did not say.

"Tell me about the work, Jim, if it is as hard there as it is here. I suppose mining is mining the world over.

"I am glad you are going to school. It must be hard after a day's work, or to get out of bed to study; but it will be like talking together when you can write. The schoolmaster must be a good man too.

"I am well, Jim. Don't worry about me, my son. My mother comes in every day. Your mother does almost every day.

"Jim, it is good of your friend to write for you and he makes an interesting letter, but I can't wait till you write yourself.

"I was just thinking this might reach you Christmas. I hope it does.

"Here's a whisper, my dear. We both send our love to you.

"I love you, Jim.
                    "Your wife,

                                        "POL"

Allen handed the letter to Jim. Jim seemed far away to him, and the candle gave a blurry light.

"Now you read it, Jim," he said, "and I will help you along."

Together they sat on the bedside and read the lines again.

"Yes, my son, you will be writing your own for her soon."

" 'Er dedn' mean no offense, Bob."

"Jim, nobody in heaven or on earth could write for her to mean what your first letter will."

"I know, Bob, I know."

Jim folded his letter and put it away. Allen rose to go below. "I hear you had company while I was gone."

" 'Ave you seen un?"

"He was in the front room when I came in and didn't see me. Northy was in the washroom and told me."

" 'E's a Cornishman, shore 'nough," said Jim.

"And, what's more, knows me. He knew my father, too."

A look of disturbance came over Allen's face. He was distressed, and Jim knew it.

"He spoke to you, Northy said—about me. His being here explains some things. No, no, my son, I don't want you to say anything. A time or two, when talking with the men, little hints have come out. You, Jim, are the first man I have talked to about religion; but before you came I heard some things I never told here."

Allen stopped, and his face lightened. "When you were a boy, Jim, did you ever try to run away from your shadow?"

"Aas, I 'ave."

"Hard to do," said Allen. " 'If I take the wings of the morning, and dwell in the uttermost parts of the sea,' it is there. Your shadow, I mean."

Allen laughed at the look on Jim's face when he ended the quotation.

"The one is as true as the other, my son."

Jim nodded and smiled back, relieved that Allen could laugh at his own trouble.

"He calls himself a chosen vessel, Jim. My mother had one once—a chosen vessel, that is—a fancy bit of cloam. She kept it on the mantelpiece. One day she smelled something and went on a still hunt for it. After she turned the parlor over and inside out, she came finally to her chosen vessel, her cloam vase with its pretty handles and flowers on its sides. Lying in the vase was a mouse, dead and worse. Mother clapped a cloth over it and carried it out doors, turned her back to the wind and emptied it. Chosen vessels can't be trusted too far, my son."

Allen laughed heartily at the memory of his mother's find, and to all appearances dismissed his worry with his yarn.

" 'E's back for supper," Jim said.

"Yes, I know," Allen answered, and went down.

The meal was a quiet, dismal affair. The preacher tried to pry a little conversation out of his neighbors about the party at the captain's house and the Christmas tree, but all his attempts "missed fire" as the miners said.

Allen left the table first and soon came back dressed for outdoors. When Jim passed him he said, "Goin' for a walk, Bob?"

"Iss, you, an' takin' the praycher with me," he whispered.

Together Jim and Jake went upstairs too. After so much time spent indoors, the outside was calling. In a few minutes they were facing the bracing cold and enjoying it.

"You've 'ad a good Christmas, boay," Jake said.

"A 'appy one," Jim replied.

Then, as was their custom, they indulged in a spell of silence. At last Jake broke it. "I was wonderin' if there hever was a gyarden that a snake dedn't get in un."

Jim did not answer.

"Christmas be like the streams that run a little way an' get lost in the sand. The Christmas stream make a hawful short run."

Jim did not follow him. "I feel sorry for Allen," he said.

"Better save yer feelin' for thicky praycher, to my mind," said Jake.

" 'E should knaw better," Jim said.

"I s'pose," Jake agreed, "I s'pose." But Jake was not to be deflected. He took his pipe from his mouth and quoted a part of the first Christmas carol.

"Us roll words like they under our tongue at Christmas time like's if they tasted good. Nex' day we spit mun out for another year."

Chapter Eleven

"MORRA PON" WAS THE CORNISHMAN'S parting wave to Christmas. The words had the same self-elucidation for him as the "Fourth." Cornishmen added the day to show their esteem of the Great Anniversary; but, of itself, it was an aid to recovery from heavy eating and copious drinking, and liberation from the numerous repressions that religion always assessed in its own honor. No day especially religious could be free and easy for them. Morra Pon afforded reprieve from the gloomy aftermath of their own excesses. The custom of taking the extra day way rooted in the slow method and small demand of older times in the Duchy. During the earlier years of Michigan mining, when Cornishmen captained the pits and supplied the skilled sinews of the trade, the custom was maintained. This year Christmas fell on Friday and thus the ancient custom lengthened the miner's holiday to a consideration. On Saturday some went to Calumet for enjoyments that the larger place might offer; some visited other locations within reach where lived some acquaintance from the old home. Pleasures were limited in variety and dwarfed in size for them in the old land, but the pioneer setting of the new reduced them still more. When Jim reported his letter to him, Jake suggested a journey to Central Mine to see the brothers as well as the town.

Jim agreed heartily. To both of them the place held more

than was suggested by the reunion. It epitomized America from the first day the name came to their ears. If America was the land of hope, here the fires of hope burned brightest. If it was the land of opportunity, here opportunity awaited in greater abundance than in any other place. The trappings that dreams accord to the unknown were draped about it or waved like pennants from its fancied spires, because it had extended rescue when they were threatened with despair. Jim and Jake wanted to see Central. Neither would let what he had seen on his way to Allouez, or what he had found there, mar his dream. Both waited for the comparison of the real with what they had fancied with the eagerness of children.

Saturday morning came with the vigor of a day becoming to a Keweenaw winter. The cutter they had engaged was at the door when they left the breakfast table. The driver stood while they got in and seated himself between them. A bearskin robe was tucked about their feet and legs, and they were off. The air stung their cheeks as if it were needled. The sky was clear save for drifting islands of whiteness that floated hither and yon like sheep without a shepherd. The sun was bright but without heat. The snow was as fine as powder and blew restlessly in swirls, or darted nervously like flicking tongues, across the road. In places it rounded into causeways across the track that previous sleds had made. At each mound the horses strained their harness, and the screech of the runners changed its pitch. On level and more open stretches the beasts trotted to the music of their bells in an appreciative, toilless sort of way. Trees overarched the road for miles. At their left, the vertebral cliffs of the peninsula stood perpendicularly to a height of five hundred feet, stood with bared breast to the winds that blew from the lake. Along its side, clinging with tentacled roots, scattered trees living on pauper's fare defied all weathers. Upon the top, forest again was visible, reaching with frozen limbs to the arctic sky.

Jake turned to Jim. "Do e like un, boay?"

" 'E's nice ridin', shore 'nough."

"I c'n see w'y young folks take to this way of travel."

Jake's face was as grave as a sexton's, but the driver chuckled.

Jim turned to look at Jake. "Thee would," he said.

Jake's whiskers responded to the ghost of a smile.

Occasionally Jake looked back, a well feigned fear in his eyes.

"W'at's the matter with e?" asked Jim.

"Afeard," said Jake.

Jim was suspicious of Jake's humor and said nothing. Jake looked back again. "This be the fust time for me in one of these things—an' for thee too. The awnly other I hever seed till I come 'ere was a picter. A woman sittin', hands awver 'er heyes, a man standin' drivin', beatin' the 'osses, the 'osses gallopin', eyes a-glazin', their nawses blowin' like exhaust pipes, an' be'ind mun—wolves!" Jake looked back again with well mimicked fright.

"A purty fancy," said Jim, smiling at his whimsical partner; "but the wolves bayn't likely."

"They be as likely as this thing was w'en I seed the picter."

"Be there wolves 'ere, driver?" asked Jim.

"Hunters see one once in a while," said the driver, "but they don't run in packs."

"I thought a wolf, just a single one, might hurry they 'osses a bit," said Jake, grinning.

The driver turned for a glimpse of his face, but Jake was looking back again in a mockery of fear.

"Dawn't pay no 'tention, driver," said Jim. " 'E's just 'omesick t' see his fambly."

With the passing of the miles small mining communities appeared and disappeared. They nestled in the angles of the cliff side and the road level, the inevitable shafting, black chimneys, and rock piles in the background against the cliff.

"They look lonesome an' frail too, as if they couldn' last long."

"Beginnin's be frail as well as ends, comrade," said Jim. "They'm awnly startin'."

"You'm right, my son," said Jake, glad that Jim was taking that view.

Again they were in the forest and under its spell. When they spoke it was in memory of their first impressions. Its apparent endlessness, its straight-bodied, clean-limbed growths drew their wonder and admiration. In places they could see the forest floor between the close-set boles and remarked how clean it was.

"Jim, do e s'pose towns an' villages will hever be close 'ere, like they be 'ome? an' farms fill the spaces atween? Did e think, comrade, us 'aven't seed a farm?"

"Could farms live through the winter 'ere, Jake?"

The questions were unanswered. Wonder was big in both of them. They were content to voice their amazement, their comparisons, to put their questions to the future and leave them.

"Be they mines awned, do e s'pose, by dif'runt comp'nies or by one?" Jim asked.

"Did e ever think that maybe a w'ite man never stood on the ground around us, an' that a plow never scratched the sod in the open places us see?"

"Jake! Allen said they villages be awnly twenty-five or thirty year old at most. Did e ever think of the place afore that? Awnly animals an' wind an' snow an' rain an' trees an' time—time passin' with nobody t' notice."

Thus they speculated in monosyllables and disconnectedly as the journey lengthened, approaching within finger reach of profound economics, of unwritten history. Naïvely they touched the garment of romance but did not recognize its texture.

"This is Central Mine," said the driver.

The village came into view with the suddenness of magic. A sharp turn in the road after the miles of snow, of cold, of trees, of isolation, and here again were habitations, columns of smoke, and people.

The cliff side had lost its hauteur and now fraternized with the plain. Its height had scarcely changed, but an hypotenuse had been constructed, mellowing the abruptness of the past miles into a long declivity that connected the highest point to the plain with accessibility. Around the village were the living walls of the forest. Not a tree had been allowed to stand within the village limits. A tree would be counted a faint ornament with such surroundings. And, besides, the rooted monarchs with the records of five hundred years folded like a scroll under their protecting bark were worth more as lumber and shingles, as shaft timber than as decorations. Stumps remained wherever they did not inconvenience the grocery wagon on its rounds or the construction of a house or barn or shed. All this was visible at a glance.

"Whoa!" exclaimed Jake. "Stop, driver! I want a look-see."

The driver pulled his steaming team to a standstill.

The village was almost entirely to the travelers' left, on the hillside. The dwellings were all small and were made smaller by the snow around them.

"Look like the snow be holdin' min w'ere they be set," said Jake. "W'at will 'appen w'en the snow melt or a bit of wind blow?" He chuckled at his own fancy. "Go t' bed up there an' wake up down 'ere."

Jim said nothing. Jake looked toward the mine which cut the village in two. "Well, comrade, a mine's a mine, even Central Mine. See they shaft houses an' burrows an' all else— A farmer's plow turn a green field black for a bit, but 'e turn green again in a fortnit an' then gold; but a mine— Your trade, my son, jus' lave a scab on a place."

Jim uttered a dubious grunt in answer to the little taunt, to which Jake gave no heed.

"See there!" he said. He pointed to houses with porches, glass doors, dormer windows, and picket fences, visible through the mine gear. "W'ere the nabobs live! Get hup, driver."

The driver started up the hill. "Where do you want to go?" he asked.

"Go to the comp'ny store," said Jim, assuming that there must be one.

"Just shanties," Jake muttered, "linhays!" He swept the place as he spoke, and his words seemed full of disappointment. "Put on the 'illside with plenty flat space below. Climb up an' skitter down."

"W'at's the matter with e?" Jim asked, surprised at Jake's faultfinding.

"Nothin', boay," said Jake, grinning at Jim's serious question. "You see, this place 'ave been a competitor with the rest of the world, an' I'm puttin' in a word for Allouez."

Jim saw his point and grinned back at him.

At the store porch Jake paid the driver and gave him instructions for their return.

While they were attending to the driver a voice, familiar and homelike, said, "See w'at 'ave come!" It was Joe with Tom and Bill at his heels. "Liv'ry 'osses dawn't make no choice of passengers, seem like." Handshakings and playful thrusts followed, and introductions to a few others who had come out of the store to see the cause of the slight commotion.

"Let's walk a bit to git our legs in use," said Jim. "Mine dawn't feel 's if they belonged t' me."

They strode off, taking the middle of the road for convenience. Jim and Jake shifted from one to the other of the Centralites, and at times they stopped in a cluster to enjoy more fully some tasty item of news. They went to the shaft houses, enginerooms and stamp mills, stood beside sleds loaded with masses of copper ready to be hauled to "The Harbor" warehouses on Monday.

"Now you knaw, comrade, w'y the mines back 'ome shut down," said Bill to Jim, "an' w'y they'll stay shut down."

"An' hev'ry mine you passed be coughin' up copper in pieces like that," added Joe.

They spoke as if Jim and Jake were not just as aware of the output from their Allouez experience. It was a simple evidence that their grief over the old home was not wholly assuaged.

Joe led them up the hill to the rim of the village. On a dormerlike spur stood the schoolhouse, set where the noise of the children at play would disturb less the rest of the men who worked at night and slept by day. They stood on the porch for a moment in silence breathing deeply after their climb.

"The sills of this 'ouse be 'igher than the roofs of most the town," said Joe.

"An', far's you c'n see, nothin' but woods," said Bill.

"A purty sight in summer an' fall, like's not," Tom added.

Jim peered into the school, counted the desks, and made out words on the blackboard. He looked at the desks again, prompted by the words. He smiled and called to Jake. Jake came and looked through the window beside him.

"Look, see," said Jim. "The desks be for the hinfants. They words be too, an' I c'n awnly make out a foo of min."

Jake patted him on the back. "They chuldern will grow up, my son. The words will get bigger. There be 'ope for you."

The others had gathered around, and they laughed together.

On the boarding-house stoop they took another view of the village. Jake's eyes twinkled, and his lips parted in a premonitory smile. He looked at Jim, whose thoughts he seemed better able to read than those of his brothers, nodded toward the spread of houses and said, "None of they 'ouses 'ave walls of jasper, an' the streets bayn't paved with gold."

" 'E edn' like w'at Cap'n 'Arry made me think 'e was like," said Jim.

"Dawn't blame Cap'n 'Arry too much, boay. Your fancy had summat t' do with un," said Joe. "Remember, thee was faced with a hempty belly then, an' a 'ongry man do see visions w'en 'e smell summat t' eat."

Bill opened the door and led the way into the dining room. "Us be the awnly boarders the missus 'ave just now," he said. " 'Er 'ave one hempty bed if you two dawn't mind sleepin' t'gether."

Each man took a chair from the table and sat down.

"I dawn't knaw nothin' about heaven," said Tom; "but this place be more like Camborne or Redruth. There be as many pasties made an' eat 'ere as there, as many saffern nubbies an' as much tetty cake. The Cousin Jack do sit on top of the heap. Hi dawn't knaw how they masses of copper would be cut if 'e wadn' a good man with a 'ammer."

" 'E 'ave 'e's awn way at the chapel too," said Bill. The awnly difference be the praycher dawn't line the 'ymns."

"Hi dedn' see no pubs 'ere," said Jake significantly.

"Right you are, my son," said Joe, "or 'e'd make 'is mark there too an' no mistake. 'E's a 'andy man at anything 'e take to."

The boarding missus came to the door, wiping her hands on her apron. Bill introduced the strangers, and arrangements were made for their stay.

Mrs. Bond was a large woman, tall and broad-shouldered. Her hands were large, her face had a look of perpetual challenge. Neither blond nor brunette, her eyes had a changing hue. Her mouth was large, firm, ready with rebellion on cause. She was big without being overweight. Her voice came from a long throat with a noticeable larynx and was almost manlike. After the few necessary words of the moment she left the room to attend to her work.

"Irish," said Bill. "A widda."

" 'Ard job for a widda," said Jake.

" 'E is," continued Bill. " 'Er man was killed in the shaft. Rope brawk, an' the cage went t' the bottom with ten men on un. W'at else could 'er do?"

"Able to take care of 'erself though. Throwed a man out once, they say. Took hold of un too," added Joe.

A woman's voice came to them from another room. They heard every syllable she spoke. The remark was pointless to them, but her presence and the clearness and unrelatedness of her comment surprised them. A man answered, and a conversation began.

" 'Oo's that?" asked Jake.

"Neighbor," replied Tom. "A double 'ouse."

Mrs. Bond stepped into the room as Tom explained, and her face darkened noticeably. She moved a chair and straightened a curtain. Jim was standing with his back to his companions, looking down the hill.

"Do the comp'ny awn they 'ouses?" he asked.

"The comp'ny awn everything 'ere, boay," said Tom.

"Look again, and think a minute." It was Mrs. Bond joining the conversation without invitation. Jim turned, surprised and embarrassed. He was speaking to the men. He had not heard her enter the room. She made no apology for her intrusion. She stood in the doorway now, filling it. The fight lines in her face deepened. Every wrinkle of her dress was belligerent.

"Think a minute," she repeated. "Would fifty people in their right minds build their houses alike and paint them alike? Surely some one out of the fifty would have some taste!"

Jim did not answer; nobody answered. The five of them were pictures of inconsequence. In their own homes over the sea, they would have spoken, and the women would have awaited and accepted their judgments. This woman held no such esteem for men. They did not need to answer. She was not asking their opinions. She would answer—and did.

"And the company wasn't in its right mind if it ever had one. Every house is too small if only two lived in it, and there are few families of two in these camps. A dozen pigs can live in one room, but two people can't. And some families keep boarders besides! A man is a brute or a fool who will keep boarders in a place like this! If the women weren't sheep—" She stopped on the precipice of disgust.

"Look at them!" she continued. "All the same shape, painted the same color, and set anyway—fronts facing backs, privies as public as the post office. A man's layout! The only convenience in them is a hole in the chimney for a stovepipe. Yes, these camps are all the products of the male mind." She looked from one to another of her five victims as if daring them to reply.

"You Cornish are an easy-going lot. You take what is handed to you, put your families into any place that will keep out wind and snow. You sleep in beds that can't cool between shifts, and say nothing, or—worse—do nothing. I wonder what kind of places you come from."

"Tedn' that bad, missus," said Bill. "Tedn' that bad."

She ignored him. "You live as though you planned to leave next week, or sooner; you just board or stay in company houses. Don't you want a home, a place to call your own? Don't you want a place your children will love and prize as long as they live? This mine has been running thirty years, and a lot of Cousin Jacks have raised families in these shacks. They have seen their children grow up in them and marry but keep on living as if they were sitting on needles and pins."

Her lips quivered a moment as if she were about to smile. "I have heard that an Englishman's house is his castle." She did smile. "I guess I have never seen an Englishman."

"That's cheatin', missus," said Jake, "an' you knaw it. I be a bach'lor, but I fancy a rented 'ouse can be made a 'ome."

She stared at Jake for a moment but did not answer him.

"And look at this thing," she said, including the premises in the sweep of her hand. "The company built this for a human dwelling—a home! It was all I could get. Two families as different as day and night compelled to live as one. Lucky for me, Mrs. Cruse and I can be sociable. We sit on the stairs and sew and talk—talk through the cracks and pass needle or thread or scissors to one another. Before she moved in, an Italian family lived there and kept boarders. You know what that meant! To be decent, all hands had to go to bed in the dark."

Joe verged upon some waggery, but a look at the militant woman restrained him.

"When can a family in any of these abominations have privacy? They can't whisper all the time."

"Hi never 'eard nobody complain afore," ventured Bill weakly.

"No, because all you Cousin Jacks think about is your work and your meals. You never think of your women and children."

Jim was thinking of Mrs. Uren and Pol. Bill was wishing he had not spoken.

"When you are through with your supper you go over to the 'stump' or the store and talk. After the dishes are washed, what does your wife do? Sit on the porch—if it is big enough to sit on and if it is summer—with a baby in her arms, and chat with a Dago or a Swede if they can talk English enough to talk back."

She left room for an answer but got none.

"I am not finding fault with the foreigners. They are as good as you or me. But we are too different to live under the same roof."

Mrs. Bond had changed her tone. Victory had come too easily. She was apparently sorry for those she had vanquished. Perhaps her reference to the woman and baby did it.

"W'at would us do, comin' 'ere if the comp'ny dedn' 'ave places for t' live in w'en us come?" asked Bill.

Mrs. Bond did not answer immediately—not that she was defeated. Battle had had too long a preemption of her face to show defeat if she felt it. She looked straight at Bill for a second and then included the rest.

"I don't know what you would do. I only know what your Cousin Jack brothers have done—and—what—my—father— did. He went to a new country and built a house with his own hands to have a home. He lived in a covered wagon while he did it."

"W'ere did yer father go?" asked Jake.

She swept the question aside. "The folks in these things breathe the spirit of them without knowing it. The mine threw them together to last till it had gutted the ground. You live in them with your bags packed for a hurried get- away. You own nothing and care for nothing. You never drive a nail to improve them; the house is not yours. You have no responsibility and no interest. The children may kick the plaster off or smash the windows. It's a company house; the company will mend it. You raise no garden, plant no flowers, maintain nothing—because you're not going to stay. The youngsters learn no respect, have no reverence. They and the women suffer most."

"But w'at would us do w'en us come?" persisted Bill.

"What you do when you come is one thing; what you do when you stay is another. As a stopping place this sort of thing will pass, but as a place to stay in it is an outrage. Aren't there any homes in England—in Cornwall?"

The men were mute. This was new. A woman hushing them, defying them, answering back! They felt like children. Their place of power had slipped away from them, was in the keep of a woman! A lesson he had been recently taught came to Jim: If 'e be true—if 'e be true, I must face un. And some of it seemed true. Mrs. Uren was a slave. Eighteen men crowded a house built for a half-dozen. Penglaze, Johnson, and others he knew proved the woman's point.

Jake was thinking of the frail growths as he called them that he had seen along the way to Central Mine. His own remark about them seemed fitting. "As you say, missus, they places dawn't look t' last long. They might shut down awver-night. Then w'at?"

Mrs. Bond paused at that. She spoke slowly in reply as if feeling her way over unfamiliar ground in the dark. She had spoken with a woman's resentment against the enemy of woman's sphere—the home. But now difficulties were appearing that were complex. She had no respect for mining as a job for any man. Her husband had come to the range on a different mission and had taken work in the mine to fill a gap. An accident took his life. She scanned the camp and wondered what any one would do if the mine did close. There was no railroad. The summers were short, and the soil poor. She had brought about a predicament for herself. But she was sure she was right. There must be a way out. Then she spoke again.

"One generation has been raised here already. You miners know what the prospect is for another to grow up here. This country is developing by leaps and bounds, and if there is copper here it will be needed more and more. If you must stay in the mine, then think of your home for your family's sake. Do you want to live expecting something to happen? You make me think of my father's sheep. They kept themselves poor, jumping fences. If mining doesn't offer the certainty you need, why not do something with more certainty to it? This is a big country."

Mrs. Bond broke into a smile.

"In spite of your whiskers, you are only boys—young enough, I should think, to learn some other work."

The woman gave up argument for reminiscence. She had dispelled her resentment toward her setting by her talk.

While her smile lingered she said: "I don't know why I let myself go. Maybe I was homesick and didn't know it. I think often how proud Father and Mother were of the place they built. From year to year they added to it. They built their hopes and desires into it. They became a part of it, and it was a part of them. We children loved it, and the ground it stood on. Do miners ever love a mine? I never heard one say."

"Be Father an' Mother livin'?" asked Jim.

"Father is. The house they loved burned in a prairie fire. Mother died soon after—we thought, of a broken heart."

Mrs. Bond's face softened with the memory, the belligerent lines of her usual expression showing only faintly through the diffusion of her affection. The softness lasted only a moment. A voice from the other side of the partition wrought the change. The hard lines came back. "The company house," she said. "I hate it." She turned and went into the kitchen.

Jake got up and went to the window and looked out into the twilight. "There be truth in w'at 'er say. If a man dawn't 'ave a 'ome, 'ow can a take root in a place?" He turned to Tom. "W'ere be thy concertina, boay?"

Tom fetched it from his room and said, "W'at will e 'ave?"

" ' 'Ome, Sweet 'Ome'—for the missus," said Jake.

With the last words came a deep silence that threatened to wreck the visit. It was a dangerous moment, and they all knew it. Youth saved the day.

"Jim, us 'ave some purty tunes in the chapel 'ere," said Tom. " 'Ark t' this one." And he sang an air alone.

"Never 'eard none like thicky back 'ome," he added.

The danger was past. They were themselves again, happy to be together, to enjoy their brogue unrestrained and such talk as would shuttle them back and forth between the old world and the new. And to sing. To sing after their long separation, sing to their hearts' content.

"Let's 'ave 'Diadem' again," said Joe. "Us 'aven' singed 'e since the last shift."

They sang it to the end. Joe's bass rolled and romped through it, Jake keeping him company with a softer voice and more seriousness. Joe's was a singer's enjoyment and not a worshiper's. He rejoiced in the power and smoothness of his voice for its own sake. He sang as a man eats who has a good appetite. The others enjoyed Joe's frolicsome abandon when once he was warmed up.

"Thicky 'ymn was made for bass singers, shore 'nough," said Jim, smiling.

"Hev'ry cheel try t' sing bass t' show 'e's grawin' up," said Bill.

Joe turned to Tom, the other tenor. "Well, my son, do you 'ave yoor say ready afore I speak?"

Tom shook his head laughingly. "I 'gree with William 'Enry."

Joe tried with poor success to look annihilatingly at his tormentors. "I be sorry for the three of e. I be sorry for a boay with a maid's voice. But there, be good boays, maybe 'e'll change w'en you be growed up." He laughed with the rest in their good humor and said, "Let's 'ave another."

"Monmouth" followed and "French" and others—substantial chapel hymns.

"Now let's 'ave a bit of real singin,'" said Bill. "Us 'ave been in chapel long enough. Let's go down t' Fools' Corer for a w'ile."

Immediately Tom's concertina fell from grace and frolicked with the blither things that enlivened the Cornish twilight after the day's work and supper, while the youths of the villages waited for their maidens.

As stopping places in her labor occurred, Mrs. Bond stood in the doorway to listen and watch, enjoying the odd accents, the boyish happiness, the taunts, the praise that passed around from time to time. Then she said, "Supper's ready."

"I be holla as a drum," said Joe.

"You sounded like it," flashed Bill.

"The hemptier a bass singer be, the better 'e sing," Jim added.

"But the fuller 'e be, the better 'e talk," retorted Joe. "You penny w'istles wait till I'm full."

Still laughing at Joe, they took their places at the table.

When bedtime came Bill and Jim climbed the stairs together. "Do e knaw anything about the boardin' missus?" Jim asked. "' 'Er kind edn' common," he added to apologize for his curiosity.

"Not much, my son. About all is that 'er have had a 'ard time of un. W'en 'er started a boardin' 'ouse, all the women in town talked about 'er an' made 'er life miserable. An' the men wadn far be'ind. W'en 'er went down the street they made all sorts of remarks about 'er; but she 'ave made good, an' now 'er 'ave the best 'ouse in town. 'Er won't take more'n six men at any price. There be a rumor that 'er 'ave a bit of money an' plan t' go back 'ome as soon as 'er 'ave anough."

Bill winked and said, "Gittin' t' like a bit of gossip, comrade?"

"' 'Er be a oncommon woman," Jim answered, ignoring Bill's little gibe. "Hi never 'eard a woman talk like she. 'Er bayn't English, that's plain."

Next morning they all went to chapel. Rumor of the singing heard the night before at Mrs. Bond's had preceded them, and the choir leader asked Joe if they would sing for the service.

"All you 'ave t' do, my son, be t' give the key, an' if you dawn't 'ave un us c'n do without."

Just before the sermon, the minister announced a special number, and the boys stood in their pew and sang. With the first line, every Cornish émigré present was seeing the walls of his little home chapel. Wives sat beside most of them, and children around them. People long unthought of and faces all but forgotten appeared in the mist. To the last word they stayed among the old scenes, tempted by the clearness of their fancy to reach for hands they could not touch; and then, with a handkerchief, they wiped the scene from their eyes and saw the singers sitting down.

After the service many came to meet the strangers and wished that they might stay to sing together again and again. One man lingered until most of the congregation had gone and then came to them; Joe introduced him as Cap'n Harris. He complimented them too and said he regretted that he could not hear them often.

"Us 'ave tried t' persuade mun t' hask for a job," said Bill, "t' be t'gether as us belong t' be."

"In the spring, w'en the shippin' 'ave opened," said the captain, "I'll make places for you."

"Thankee, Cap'n," they said.

At three o'clock, as Jim and Jake had ordered, the cutter returned for them.

For a long time they rode in silence. Both had much to think of. The visit had raised their spirits, had purged their minds of anxieties for a time. It was pleasant to retain the mood the old fellowship had created. Finally Jake spoke. "I be glad the boays dedn' wait long t' git jobs. Us all was lucky. An' I be glad Tom bayn't undergraound no more. In the machine shop 'e c'n learn a trade."

Jim thought long of the captain's offer. He and Jake had been offered a job without having to ask for it. Because they could sing! That was a new experience. He felt a sense of importance and a deepened sense of security.

"Allouez!" said Jake, as they came to the edge of the town. "As fair a city as Central, to my eye."

" 'E won't be aysy t' leave this place, comrade," said Jim.

Jake did not answer, but he was no stranger to Jim. Jim just waited his pleasure.

"Barrin' the Collins brothers, the folks in Central bayn't

'andsomer than they be 'ere. An' I shan't forgit the day us got a job."

"Aas," said Jim. " 'I was a stranger, an' ye took me in,' was true of we an' this place. A job in Central with the boays would be temptin', but I sh'll always be in debt t' Allouez.

Chapter Twelve

TUESDAY MORNING CAME, and the mine whistle blew at six o'clock. It split the silence with a frosty hoarseness and awakened every man in the house. The day men lingered a few minutes to indulge in the warmth of their beds while their minds cleared and they gathered courage. When the sound had died away and they settled back into their pillows and hooded their heads with the covers as if to stay there the rest of the day, small trickles of vapor again found freedom from the blanket's edge, spread in thin clouds over the pillows, rose a short distance, and disappeared. By comparison with the open space of the room, the bed was the bosom of luxury. A night man in Jim's room who wanted to sleep longer and knew what commotion was yet to come, called to the day men: "W'at's the matter with you fellas? 'Fraid of a little cold, be e?"

"Iss," said another, "go t' work, you slaves, an' let your betters sleep."

" 'Urry up, an' be quiet abaout it," added a third.

"All right, my sons, 'ere we go," said Jake, and his feet went straight up, carrying the bedclothes aloft as they went, leaving his bedfellow with only his underwear between himself and midwinter. The man in the next bed got out quietly and decorously, dressed and started for the stairs. As he passed the foot of the bed he had left, he snatched the cover and dropped it on the floor, leaving his partner bare. At the bedroom door, he and Jake stopped to laugh while the second victim hopped from bed to retrieve the clothes. Jim made no attempt to take part in the play and showed no appreciation of it. Jake wondered what was wrong.

While Jim dressed he remained silent, and the scrambling men, stepping gingerly on the cold floor, reaching for their bedding and muttering violent imprecations, brought no smile to his face. He was wordless at breakfast and on his way to the pit.

Down in the level, Jim's unwonted silence continued. Jake was puzzled. Somethin' be wrong, shore 'nough, he thought. Hi'll try t' pry un loose.

"I c'n think of a score of questions I minded t' ask the boays but forgot," he said while he held his candle for Jim to take a light.

Jim fired his wick and held his candle aslant so that the small flame could lick the grease and gather strength, but he said nothing.

"An' a score of things t' tell, but forgot," Jake added.

Still no answer.

"You might 'ave wraute yours down, you knaw," continued Jake, thinking to tease Jim back to himself.

"W'y dedn' you write yours down?" Jim retorted, every syllable edged with bitterness.

"Aas, w'y dedn' I? Fair anough, comrade. Tit for tat be a purty game," Jake answered, knowing that his ruse had failed.

As they entered their own drift, Jake stopped. He put his hand on the first set he and Jim had put up—their first visible production in America. "Us ought t' put a brass plate on thicky set with our names an' date on un an' a line, fitty an' to the point! W'a's tha say?"

"Do e think you'm that important? I knaw I bayn't."

Before the day was ended Jake's suspicion became conviction: his partner was homesick. And homesickness he considered a real disease, like some headaches he had heard about that doctors couldn't cure. He knew something about the ailment from experience. His trip to Central had not left him untouched. Before he and Jim reached home he had felt his world closing in on him, and had set himself against it. Once his father had left him alone in Cardiff for a week. Once was enough. He looked at Jim many times during the day, and each time thought, If I felt the way I did, I knaw 'e feel worse. 'E look like a cheel that 'ave been flogged.

Over and over Jake counted the possible causes: the Christmas doings, the trip to Central, the singing, the woman's crake—all had something to do with it. Three months had passed since he left home—long enough to make any boy homesick. Jake wondered how long it might last: the thought worried him. If he could get the boy to talk, to change his mind! But Jim defied every effort. When he spoke at all his words had the sound of a lash and stung as if the lash had knots in it.

Jake thought the week would never end. A chance to shock Jim out of his sullenness came, so Jake believed, when a clean drift end, neatly timbered, greeted them and drilling was their next job. He knew Jim's pride in his skill with a hammer, and, hurt or no hurt, Jim's nerves being as they were, Jake wouldn't trust his hands under the poll of Jim's mallet. Jake picked up the hammer and squared away for the first hole. Without question Jim selected a drill and the shift began. When Jake tired and set the hammer down, Jim picked it up.

"No, my son," said Jake quietly. "I'll use the mallet t'day, an' you'll twist."

"Hi c'n beat a drill as good as you," said Jim bluntly and bitterly, holding on to the hammer.

"Hi knaw you c'n, my son. There be foo better'n you if there be any, but not t'day. Hi dawn't want my wrists brawk."

Jim grunted, and his grunt creaked with resentment.

"Very well, boay. I'm goin' t' grass. My hands be wuth a day's pay, or a week's for that matter. Hi'll tell the hopposite shif' I was tooked sick—got fainty like from bad air."

"Be a liard, will e?" Jim asked, a Methodist's threat of hell in his voice.

Jake stopped, faced Jim and said, "Aas, my son, I sh'll lie, an' let God A'mighty make the most of un."

With a kind tolerant eye, Jake watched Jim. He saw that Jim ignored his books and his classes, avoided everybody, spoke only when compelled to and then as little as he could. The boy was acting as though he thought every man was his enemy. At times Jake was tempted to pay Jim in his own coin —"give un as good as 'e bring," to jolt him into his senses. He wanted to take him by the collar and tell him what a fool he was making of himself, but concluded that that was no way to treat a sick man, and forbore. So the week ended, Jim still touchy, tragic, and aloof.

Sunday morning came—the First—and Jim stayed in bed after the others had breakfasted and most of them had gone. Jake waited, thinking he should speak to Jim, but did not know what to say. When he came to Jim's side he noticed that Jim's body shook convulsively. His last shred of resistance had gone. He was weeping like a child. Jake looked on for a moment, his own lips almost beyond control. Feeling completely helpless, he tiptoed downstairs.

It was easy for Jake to put himself in Jim's place and picture the scene that Jim was seeing. It was Sunday morning, the day that would try the boy as no other day would or could do. Jake knew every feature of Jim's cottage home: its furniture, the pictures on the walls, the chimneypiece, stove, and hob. He saw Pol sitting there alone, her eyes focused on a scene that had form only in her imagination, a scene in a foreign land, the center of which was Jim. Footsteps outside would call her back. Men from down by the brook would be going up the road, walking slowly, talking with low voices, dressed in their Sabbath black—going to Class. Jim would be joining them if he were there. Jake fancied her bending over the deal table, sand-scrubbed and white, resting her head on her arms while her tears fell on the spotless board unregarded. Shore 'nough, Jake thought, that's w'at's done un.

And the scene Jake saw, Jim was seeing. It was so real to him that he put out his hand to soothe the sobbing girl, to caress the shoulders that rose and fell or trembled under his touch. He could hear her say, "I miss e so much." But she was four thousand miles away! That was why he wept even as she did.

When Jake stepped into the dining room he saw Allen in a chair looking dreamily out the window, his feet crossed over another chair. Knowing Allen's custom, he was surprised.

"W'a's the matter, Bob? Gun brawk, or aout of powder an' shot, be e?"

"Neither one, Jake. The hoist needed some repairs, an' they've been workin' on her since the last load last night. If the job be too long, you knaw w'at'll 'appen. The shaft will freeze, an' the cap'n will be a-needin' men."

Jake nodded his understanding of what was said but he did not fail to include the man who said it. "I've never seen 'is like," was a sentence Jake used often about Allen.

"W'ere's Jim?" Bob asked.

"Still abed. Today be a 'ard day for un—'e's 'ardes', I fancy."

" 'Omesickness is a cruel thing. I've seen boays in school sicken like they'd die—lose flesh, that is, get thin! A trip 'ome would cure them—if they could go. I never knawed one t' die."

"Might be, seems t' me like," said Jake, his eyes darkening as he spoke.

Allen shook his head. "For Jim, a change of mind's the thing."

Jake drew his pipe from his pocket as if to change the subject.

"Look see!" said Allen. "That be the cap'n comin' naow."

Both men watched the captain's approach until he reached the gate. A half-dozen steps, and his footfall sounded on the stoop. Allen went to the door to meet him.

" 'Aow many men 'ere? I need three."

"Three," said Bob.

"As soon as you can, my son," the captain said, and went back to the mine.

Jake started for the stairway, but Allen stopped him. "Let me go," he said, and Jake stepped aside.

Bob found Jim still lying on the bed but apparently calmed.

"Jim, my son," said Allen, "we be needed at the mine—right away, boay. The cap'n's in trouble."

Jim did not answer or turn his head when Allen spoke, and with the last word Allen left the room. Before he reached the bottom step he heard Jim moving about.

Jake and Bob changed and left before Jim came into the washroom. When he reached the shaft, the platform on which they were to work was attached to the floor of the cage and was swinging over the mouth of the pit. A third man, a timberman, was also aboard with Bob and Jake. Jim stepped on the platform without a word, took hold of a corner rope, and the captain signaled the engineman.

"Four hours will be long anough, my sons," the captain said. "Hi'll 'ave relief 'ere in four hours."

The cage dropped slowly from sight, and the work was on.

Through the week-end rest periods, when the temperature was low, the cages and skips were kept running in downcast shafts—those through which the mine inhaled—to keep ice from forming and making the shaft impassable. A too easy confidence in a mild day, and a quick change of temperature, meant that ice had to be cleared before hoisting could be resumed. Failure of the hoisting plant in a sub-zero spell made the job inevitable.

It was hard, dangerous work, and bitterly cold. The draft from the surface against which they fought, the spray of flying ice, the cold handles of their axes, the stiff oilcloth suits combined to make the men dread the job. Most of the work was single-handed as one hand was needed to hold to the ropes that ran from the corners of the pendent stage to the floor of the cage overhead. The men chopped until their bodies steamed beneath their heavy clothes the while their hands blued and stiffened with the cold. At intervals the cage was rung up to clear the water line and dropped back again to keep the timbers already cleared from clogging while they worked.

Talk between the workers was almost impossible. The game was too concentrated, the work too obvious, discussion was unnecessary. Candles sputtered and threatened to go out in the showers of ice that flew from the ax bits. Particles fell inside collars and sleeves to melt and add to the men's distress. The floor on which they stood became slippery and treacherous. But the work went on.

Four hours was long enough; indeed, it was longer than ten spent in stope or drift. The cold, the tension of their muscles, the sustained control of nerves left them wearier than hammer or shovel could make them. Fortunately, the ice was seldom allowed to get such a start, such was the vigilance maintained by the bosses; but it was inevitable at times that a Keweenaw winter should trick the confidence that men placed in their own judgment. This time the cold had had its own way for twelve hours.

The miners accepted their assignments as soldiers go into battle. Some of them damned the bosses, the mine, the winter,

the country and wished themselves out of it; but none refused
his turn when asked to go. Seriously they collected their tools
and placed them on the dangling floor and stepped aboard.
They did not talk as they went down, they did not jest as they
worked; but it was not fear that restrained them. Danger did
not keep them silent. The bitter cold changed everything—
their minds, their dispositions, their responses to life and
death. Talk had no sustenance in that temperature.

The four hours of the first team had almost ended when
the timberman dropped his ax. His lunge to retrieve it shot
the stage against the opposite side so suddenly that the others
dropped theirs and grabbed the ropes with both hands. Only
one candle was left alight. The timberman had slid toward
the edge of the platform where a space gaped wide enough
for a body to go through into the shaft. One foot caught on
the shafting beyond the space which his body bridged fear-
fully. Jim was nearest to him, and with one hand reached
for the man's arm and clung to his rope with the other.

"Jake, you 'old the stage steady till Jim an' me get the boay
back on," Allen ordered.

Jake threw one arm around a runner and held.

Allen braced one foot against a corner rope, and with his
free hand took hold of the prostrate man.

"Ready, Jim! Pull!"

They dragged the man to the sloping surface of the stage,
which Jake released slowly until its floor was flat again. Then
Jim and Bob steadied the trembling timberman to his feet.
The paleness of his fright showed plainly in the light of the
single candle, and the two rescuers continued to hold him
while he recovered. Finally Allen said, "Are e all right naow?"
and the man nodded, reached out his hand and grasped his
rope.

"Better light hup. 'E's time t' go."

Jake held his candle to share the flame and pulled the bell-
rope. Again silence. The four stood like statues, like men

straining to catch a sight or sound. But it was neither. They awaited the first tremor that descended the steel rope preceding actual movement. It came. Each was at his job again, keeping the platform clear as the ascent began.

As the cage neared the collar of the shaft voices reached them, and the first glimmer of light. Like a rapid dawn the gleam grew, and with it a voice came louder and clearer. In a few seconds it was fully day, and the retiring workers saw the captain standing with four men ready to go down.

"You've done brave, boays," he said. "Naow go 'ome an' rest till mornin'."

The new squad stepped upon the platform, and the captain repeated: "Be hawful careful, boays! 'E's a dang'rous job, but 'e 'ave t' be done."

The captain did not need to give instructions, and he knew it. The program was simple. He did not urge them to work. That was what they were there for. The men and families of their little town depended on them. And, of course, it never occurred to the captain to go with them to spur them on. He knew that no Cornishman worked for a boss. It was their binding code not to move a tool in the presence of one. So, when the men came he was at the shaft only to greet and cheer them, whether the hour was midnight or midmorning.

On the way to the house and in the washroom, Jim said nothing. Bob and Jake kept the few comments they made during the walk between themselves, for which Jim was glad. It did not dawn on him until long afterward that they, with mutual understanding, did so for his sake. Jim was aware of a strange exhilaration that possessed him. He felt it first when the daylight began to glimmer in the shaft. It was in full flow when he reached the surface. He was prepared to greet the world with warm friendliness, to see commonplace things as pleasing symbols; he saw in the late afternoon sunshine a glow he had not seen before he went down. An old scriptural phrase came to his mind, "beauty for ashes," and he said it over and over, marveling at its fitness to his change of spirit. He had had such moments before. He recalled instances in which homesickness or mine accidents had no part. Once an event did give the sensation justification, but there were other times when the exaltation seemed to be a matter of the spirit entirely. His Methodistic life provided a vehicle for his concept. " 'E do feel like bein' converted!" He went from the washroom into the dining room, where some other boarders had gathered, with his head up, the slate swept clean by the translation of his mood.

Greetings came from all sides.

" 'Aow did a go?"

"Was a froze bad?"

"Was a hawful cold?"

"Did anything 'appen?"

All the questions were answered directly except the last. To that Jake replied, "Us chopped ice."

Then came yarns of former years, episodes from other camps, accidents, and humorous incidents—humorous now, but frightening enough when they occurred. Time had taken the shock from tales that aforetime had pimpled their skins with unmentioned goose flesh. What had happened "ten year ago" outclassed anything that could have happened in more recent years.

"This one's bad enough t' suit me," Jake said, trying to dismiss the subject, "—bad anough without no accident."

" 'E is that," Jim added.

But Jake did not succeed. A youngster, still in his teens, had tried to edge in with a yarn a time or two but had given way each time to his elders. With the stop Jake had put to the discussion the boy saw his opportunity. His name was Sleep, Absalom Sleep, a stunted mite of a lad with a sharp face and easy laugh, a recent addition to the house who had stepped into Sims's shoes.

His story was similar to the occurrence of the day that the three partners had kept suppressed. The victim was a Swede. Sleep's tone soused the foreigner in inferiority. He was not a miner, he was awkward, scared to death to begin with—had no business being underground! Sleep saw humor in the sprawl of the man on the swaying stage, in the clutching hands and feet feeling for support. " 'Aow 'e did pray!" he said.

"Are e shore 'e wadn' a Cousin Jack, my son?" asked Spargo, ignoring Sleep's last remark.

"Cousin Jacks be miners," retorted Sleep with a patriot's scorn.

"I was never undergraound in my life till I comed 'ere," said Spargo, "an' I'm a Cousin Jack."

But Sleep refused to be squelched so easily.

"The Swede becomed a praycher hafter that," he said, and laughed in his own applause.

Jake looked at the boy in his enigmatic way, giving no hint to the group of appreciation or disapproval.

"That's anough, my son," he said quietly. "You've said anough. A man was struck blind once afore 'e was called t' praych. Nobody laughed at that, that I knaw by. 'E was some bit of a praycher, too, I've heard. Looks t' me like you'm laughin' in the wrong place."

Allen sat looking at an almanac Marx had given the missus, which she had hung under the clock. He had a dollar in his hand and was toying with it as if he had no interest in the talk that was going on around him. He flipped it into the air and caught it. He turned it round and round as aimlessly as another might twirl his thumbs.

"Hi'll bet this cart wheel not one of e knaw w'at day 'tis," he said.

All eyes turned to him with the look of men who confronted a riddle.

"Friday," said Penglaze.

"Right you be, my son, though that bayn't w'at I meant."
A wicked gleam came into Allen's eyes with the temptation
he could not resist.

"I dedn' knaw you was a bettin' man, William," he said.
" 'Ere's the dollar."

Penglaze's face went red to Allen's apparent enjoyment.
"I dedn' bet, an' I dawn't want your dollar."

Without shedding his smile Allen spoke again.

"Hi'll bet un once more. Not a man of e knaw w'at day
'tis besides Friday."

Silence again.

"Dawn't all spayk t' once," he taunted.

"Very well, all keep still w'ile Hi spayk," said Jake. "I like
the looks of thicky coin an' c'n see no 'arm in takin' un on
thy own terms, Bob, boay. 'E's New Year's Day."

"Brave," cried Bob, and handed Jake the dollar. "I've
been sittin' 'ere wonderin' if the cows moan at midnight of
New Year's Eve, like they do back 'ome."

A few of the men laughed at Allen's whimsical question,
but those who had laughed with Sleep still rankled from
Jake's rebuke.

"I've seen no cows 'ere," Jim remarked.

"There must be; us 'ave milk on the table," said Bob.

"Then 'twould be aysy t' find out," said Jack. "A cow
wouldn' objec' t' yoor comp'ny fur a night."

This time all hands laughed. A joke on Bob was doubly
amusing.

"S'pose the cow dedn' groan! That's w'at I'd be 'fraid of,"
Jake said.

Spargo's eye focused on Jake quizzically. "W'at's important
abaout a cow moanin' at midnight?" he asked.

"Iss, you," added Jenkins. "W'at's important abaout that?
Hi dawn't see."

"T' me, nothin'; but t' some, 'oo knaw? A lot of folks get
savage if you disturb their fancies."

"You be your brother's kayper, my son," Allen said, trying to tease Jake along.

"I refoose on two counts," said Jake. "Aysier on me; aysier on he."

Allen knew Jake was done with that, but was unwilling to let the talk revert to the ice-chopping if he could help it. He counted on Jake and Jack as his best bets to aid his purpose.

"Did e make any resolutions, Jake?"

Jake turned suspicious eyes on Bob and searched his face for a cue; but the rest were looking at Bob too, so he gave no sign of his purpose.

"No, my son, I dedn', did you?"

"No. I forgot till 'twas too late," Bob said seriously.

Spargo laughed in spite of Bob's solemn face. "Let's 'ave a resolution meetin'; ev'rybody tell 'is resolution!"

"By the time a man's my age 'e hought t' knaw w'at 'e want t' do an' feel no shame in doin' un," said Jake.

"Most of we can stand a bit of improvement, an' the First be a good time t' start off," countered Jack. "Mines an' banks an' stores figger that way."

"A man's resolutions be 'is awn business," said Penglaze, his voice brittle and conclusive.

A look at Allen's face, and Jake knew that something was brewing. He knew Allen's good intentions were as weak as water where Penglaze was concerned. While debate was still evident on Allen's face Jake spoke.

"Resolves be a man's awn business," he said, "but tellin' mun seem t' 'ave a place too. Edn' that w'y church folks testify?"

Allen grinned sheepishly and said, "Thanks, Jake."

"The last resolution I made, that I remember," said Jenkins, "was w'en I was a boay. I used t' go minchin' from school,—playin' truant the Yankees call it—be reported an' thrashed. Awver an' awver I resolved, t' no good. The last time I resolved I was 'leven year old. Three days after, Father tooked me aout of school. Hi 'aven' minched since."

"That's keepin' a resolve, shore 'nough," said Bob.

"Hi dawn't call that no resolve," muttered Penglaze.

"See 'aow you like mine, William," Spargo said. "W'en I was ten or 'leven or so, I dedn' wash my neck an' hears very good, an' Mother done un fur me with a flannel rag. 'Er rubbed my ears tender. A couple a years I resolved t' do a bit of washin' myself, t' spare Mother, of course; but I'd forgit. Then I falled in love with a mite of a maid w'at sit be'ind me in school. 'Er dedn' knaw I was in love with 'er, but I 'ad plans fur St. Valentine's Day t' let her knaw. One day 'er leaned awver 'er desk an' said, 'W'y dawn't e wash yer neck an' hears?' Hi did, an' I've kep' my resolve hever since."

Everybody laughed heartily at Jack's tale, and some wanted to know more about the maid and the romance.

"The romance died right there, suddent like," said Jack, "an' the maid be still a maid—a ol' maid. Serve 'er right."

" 'Er's better off, likely," said Allen, squaring accounts with Spargo.

By the next morning the cages were running again, and the New Year was on its way, in nothing different, that anyone could see, from the last.

In silence Jim and Jake splashed their way along the level to their own place, Jim leading the way. In the mouth of their own drift Jim stopped.

"Do e still want to put a plate on this set that us put up?" he asked. "If you do, I'll go 'alvers with e." Jim was looking straight at Jake as he spoke, and watched the slow spread of Jake's smile.

"Hi knawed you would, comrade. I knawed you would," Jake replied.

That night Jake said he did not want to stay in the house longer than he could help. He told Jim he doubted his popularity at the moment and assured him that the gang was no more popular with him. "Us bayn't bad," he said whimsically. "Us just git hoff on the wrong foot too aysy."

Without plan or apparent forethought they walked into the store. A dozen men were lounging around the stove, a huge boxlike thing that swallowed cordwood in full length. Penglaze and Jenkins from Uren's house were there. Not a greeting passed. The atmosphere was tense. Jenkins and a stranger to Jim and Jake were looking at each other as though to keep alive an argument while waiting for suitable words to come to mind. Jim wondered how Harry got mixed in a quarrel.

The stranger was in his middle thirties, of medium height, broad-shouldered and inclined to overweight. Jim noticed that he was heavy-jowled and wore a large mustache that drooped to the border of his jaw. He was about to speak again, his lips apart, his teeth showing in an angry snarl. One tooth was missing, which added to the ugliness of his rage. Jim glanced over the group again and recognized only one man in addition to Penglaze and Jenkins—Lobb. He was sitting behind the big stove, half hidden, his face turned away from the quarrelers, apparently indifferent to the argument.

"W'at did a want t' be nawsin' abaout for, spyin' on the men?" the stranger asked.

"The cap'n knawed 'twas a dang'rous job an' was hint'risted in 'is men," said Jenkins.

"Hint'risted in 'is men!" snarled the stranger, "A bloody slave driver! That's w'at 'e is."

"Do you knaw the cap'n, Prisk?" asked Harry.

"No, an' dawn't want to. I knaw 'e's kind. Hi'm for the men always." He looked around for approval but got none. "Hi never seen un till I asked un for a job."

"'Ark t' me, Jabe," said Jenkins. "The cap'n do knaw thee likely anough, like I do. Thy mouth cost thee thy job awver t' Calumet, an' still e took thee on. Dawn't e 'ave any thanks in thy guts?"

Prisk moved closer to Jenkins, his fists clenched and ready to brawl. Jenkins, tall and slender, seemed utterly inadequate to meet Prisk's fury, but he stood still, making no show of fight or retreat.

Jim wondered what Harry would do and prayed fervently that Prisk wouldn't strike.

"Step back, 'Arry!"

Lobb had left his hiding place and come up to Harry's side and spoke before Jim noticed him.

"This bayn't no argyment for a churchman. I'll take awver." He pushed Harry aside.

" 'Oo be you?" asked Prisk, standing his ground.

"My name be Lobb. Ever 'ear of me?"

Prisk's snarl came back. "I 'ave," he said. "From St. Just. A bloody deserter from the navy." His fist shot at Lobb's face, stopped midway in Lobb's left hand. Lobb's right, wide open, reached for Prisk's left cheek, each finger a talon sinking into the flesh. Lobb's powerful hand closed, blanching the man's face and pulling the thick lips to thin, gray streaks over his teeth. He drew Prisk toward himself and then shot him backward between the counter ends. As Lobb's hand came away each finger was tipped with blood. He drew a red handkerchief from his pocket and wiped his hand, walked to the stove, and threw it into the flames. As unconcerned as if what he had done was sanctioned by every law of heaven and earth, he turned to Jenkins and said, " 'E'll 'ave somethin' t' remember you an' me by as long as 'e live."

The manager of the store came running to the group. "What's the trouble here?" he asked, his eyes wide and face white.

"No trouble," said Lobb. "No trouble at all." And he walked out. Prisk was struggling to his feet, four gouged, bleeding rents in front of his ear.

Jim and Jake left the store in silence.

Outside, Jim said, "I be glad Jinkins be a Cornishman." He was thinking of Harry's defense of the captain and his fearless stand before Prisk.

"That other image be, too, my son," replied Jake.

"Oosh!" said Jim softly. "There mus' be a big fambly of Simses."

"Scattered all abroad," said Jake. "A foo like thicky idjit c'n give a lot of people a bad name."

" 'Ow 'bout a foo like Jinkins?"

"The rule dawn't seem t' work that way."

"Thy father used t' say, 'If a man dawn't 'ave nothin' t' think about, 'e'll think evil.' "

"Father wadn' always right, comrade. Us all 'ad about the same t' think about, there an' 'ere, but us bayn't all like that bloke an' Sims."

The two men walked in silence. They turned corners and rounded blocks with no attention to direction. From time to time the knocker line broke the silence to be followed by the first straining effort of the hoist to take its load, the short rapid puffs of the engine at full speed and the final slowing until the exhaust gasped spasmodically and stopped. A few seconds, and a car emerged from the shaft house, a blot against the sky, creeping along the burrow top. At its journey's end the trammers tripped the gate and freed its load. The sound of the rock rushing down the burrow's side came in a whisper to their ears.

The streets were unlighted. The windows of the houses they passed were closely curtained. The paths they followed were black in contrast to the unbroken snow between the walk and sled way in the middle of the road.

Occasionally some one was met and passed, the passers stepping into the snow in mutual courtesy. The good evenings or good nights were spoken with varying inflections and accents. Humorous attempts to "pass the time of day" in a foreign tongue passed with the day, or at least with the light. All the partners met were content to use only their best How-do's, now night had come. Jim and Jake had noticed the habit of using both greetings and curses in borrowed words, the Swede trying Italian, the Italian trying Swedish, the Englishman trying all of them. This bit of play had had its turn in the drift. Both of the partners had noticed the practice early. Men at the house swore in one language or another at small annoyances. "Seem like they be swearin'," Jim had said when he first heard it.

" 'E do, shore 'nough," Jake answered. "Aysy on their consciences w'en they dawn't knaw w'at they'm sayin', I s'pose. An', besides, Uren dawn't like swearin' in the 'ouse, 'tis said. They bayn't swearin' s'long's they dawn't knaw w'at they'm sayin'."

Each time Jake responded to a passer he did it with a western inflection and dropped back into his Devonese when he resumed talk with Jim. After a few such changes, Jim asked, "W'ich be the aysiest for thee?"

Jake answered Jim's question only with a chuckle of recognition. "Language bayn't my strong point, thee's knaw," Jake said slowly. "Hi dawn't knaw good from bad, but I see laughable bits now an' then because of un. There be some—most, in fact—'oo wouldn' change for a raise of pay, an' there be odd ones 'oo hurry t' be rid of all the old marks."

"Oosh," said Jim to betoken attention.

" 'E's a touchy subjec' with the boays, I've noticed. There's so many of min 'ere, they see no need t' change, an' they sneer an' scorch if a newcomer begin t' 'you bet' or 'Hi guess' too soon. ' 'E's a-pickin' of un up fast,' they say, like's if the new speech was a crime. The ol'-timers be 'lowed liberties, but they dawn't take mun—not often, that is."

Jim thought of the old-timers he knew. They spoke little better than the new arrivals.

"I've seed that," Jim said. "I feel as strange among the westerners as I do amongst Americans."

"An' I've seed that," said Jake playfully. "But you'm outnumbered. They'm as much at 'ome 'ere as they was in Cam-borne."

"You lived in St. 'Tossle' a long time. Tell me more about mun," said Jim.

"I dawn't knaw much, boay; awnly w'at I was told." Jake hesitated as if he preferred to let the subject drop. Then he continued: "Hi 'eard a lot of tales about their grandfers an' great-grandfers—of plunderin' an' fightin'. They would leave the field or their meals or church even t' rob a ship that run aground, or maybe light lights t' slock one on the rocks. An' they wadn' afeard t' kill sometimes. They do tell such tales."

"Do tell!" said Jim in surprise.

"Dawn't git vain, comrade," continued Jake. "I've 'eard Father say our parish wadn' a paradise w'en 'e was a boay." Jake waited for a retort from Jim but got none. "They lived 'ard lives, they did. Minin' be 'ard, fishin' be 'ard, an' farmin' be 'ard in Cornwall. An' that make men 'ard."

They were well beyond the farthest house of the village on the north road. A lone and very small house stood beside the road, a flimsy-looking thing to call a home. Around the shade of one window were narrow seams of yellow light.

"A farmer of a sort, I s'pose," said Jake.

"That shanty look like 'e wouldn' keep out the wind," Jim said.

"W'at 'e keep out edn' as important as w'at 'e keep in, com-rade. If us could see, I'd bet they boards be new an' the chim-bley pipe shiny." Jake grunted commendation to his own thought as if he was grateful for it.

"Spaykin' in parables, be e?"

"I dedn' knaw it if I was. But, Jim, to be plain, I was thinkin' of the 'ope that live in thicky wooden shanty, an' the want of un in the stone 'ouses back 'ome. Even if the bal do knock, I still say, in this country be 'ope; and w'ere there be 'ope be a good place t' live."

Both men seemed interested only in the small jets of vapor they emitted into the night air. Each kept to his path in silence until they reached the walk again.

"The trouble 'ere, my son, with us Cousin Jacks, be the same as 'e is back 'ome."

"W'at do e mean?"

"Hi was thinkin' of thicky idjit in the store an' Sims an' the boay at the 'ouse. Nothin' t' do but eat an' sleep an' work."

"I still dawn't see—" began Jim.

"A man can't live by bread alone. An' they boays prove the sayin' true. Tedn' anough, Jim. Tedn' anough." Jake's voice was more expressive than his words. He puffed at his pipe in silence for a short distance, and Jim thought he was done with the subject. Then he spoke again, and his voice lowered and softened. "I s'pose Lobb an' Prisk be t' blame for our plod t'night, but they bayn't all bad. Foo of min be bad all through. Most of min can be praised. They be true to their 'omes an' their wives. An' they try 'ard t' be good Methodies —a hard job, my son, a 'ard job."

"Thee's ought t' 'ave been a praycher, Jake."

"Because I've talked like a cheap-Jack t'night," said Jake, stopping and glaring at his partner. Slowly his lips softened into his enigmatic smile. "No, my son, you'm mistaken. I dawn't like hedges an' fences well anough. I prize bein' free too high."

That was the word, thought Jim. Being free. As long as he had known Jake, he had seemed to live and think by that rule. He went his way with quiet indifference to anything that did not interest him. Not that he did not notice it. He appeared to keep notes on the oddities and quirks he saw for future reference. Never did he criticize the enthusiasms of others or suffer discouragement when criticized. Jake had sat unmoved through revivals that had run like fire through the community back home. The brethren said he was cold, indifferent, needed a work of grace, but Jake was satisfied with the grace he had. Jim admired his strong resistance, his self-preservation under assault, his lonely independence; but he wondered even as he admired.

Chapter Thirteen

THE DAYS AND THE WEEKS were alike. Although the days were short, the weeks were long and without variety. The days differed only in name, and the weeks in figures on the calendar. Such was the monotony that to one from a town of another sort or from a farm it would have been appalling. But to the Cornish miner it had no conscious weight. He had come from a place where the bleak moors stood stark and brown long months through, to be relieved for a short season only by the yellow blooms of the furze and the purple of the heather. Not a house, perhaps, had been added to the stone tenements of his native village within his memory. The hedges that sided road and lane and girded his fields bore on their crests testimony to changelessness, in growths a century old. All over Cornwall were huge stone memorials of labors that had been spent before this era began and would remain for the next millennium to see. The Duchy was a changeless place.

And underground was forever underground. The damp blackness, the dry airlessness, the mute timbers supporting their burdens with their last strength, the heaped ore or rock awaiting their shovels, and the hard breast defying their drills were all the same. The variations to be found in the miners' search for ore were insignificant parts of their program.

Drifts might be larger, timbered or timberless to the need, the stopes might be overhand or underhand; but the breath of the pit, the blackness of it, the grime of it, the relentless danger, the heavy labor were forever the same. These men had breathed monotony with their first gasp, had looked upon it from infancy; they had inherited monotony from parents who for generations had searched the gravel and stone under their feet for pay dirt. Most of them were not aware of it, but they all suffered from it.

It was not yet light when the day men went down; it was dark when they came up. It was dark when the night men went down and they returned before dawn. These latter found breakfast waiting for them at the boarding house, and the beds still warm with the body heat of their recent occupants. Good sleepers awakened to lamplight and supper. These frequently saw no daylight from Monday to Sunday. The day men fared better. They could spend their evenings uptown, or, on occasion go to Calumet.

Seldom did the men at Uren's stay at home an evening through. The weather had to be more than usually savage to keep them housed. The small rooms brought them to too close quarters. Pipes and the small events of the mine were not equal to keeping them respectfully distant. Personal flaws became too visible. As they rebelled against bright lights underground because these revealed too much, they objected to being so close together because it enlarged faults and dislikes. Jim and Jake noticed how short-lived their discussions were. "And," said Jake, "they end sour."

Jim mentioned it to Allen. Bob nodded recognition but waited to shape his answer.

"What is there to discuss, my son?" he asked. "Would you like to hear them talk religion? They were all brought up the same. That leaves no room for argument." He smiled. "They all sin against their beliefs. They have no curiosity for more. They know nothing about politics—not a newspaper comes to the house. Not more than a half-dozen come to the town—weeklies that become fortnightlies when the weather is bad. All they have is the mine, the town, their hungers and memories. Sameness is like a disease in a place like this."

Jim looked at Allen, slightly bewildered. " 'E do mean the 'ouse, not the country," he said.

Occasionally the glow of precious metals caught their eyes, and fabulous yarns their ears. The West! The West was golden or silvered, alluring always, and to a few, seductive. Gold and silver were romantic and provided a lot of talk, but the tales about them were always tarnished by wildness. The Cornishmen shook their heads when booted and spurred gunmen raided saloon or bank or held up a stage and left corpses to mark their trail. The quiet of their snowbound, forest-walled villages was more to their taste. Penglaze said: "I 'ave seen a foo come to the 'Point' t' mine copper. They was none the richer for all their minin' silver or gold."

Hearsay brought word of fields being sketched on the prairies south and west of them, of sod houses and barns that hopeful builders called home. Farms could be had for only squatting on them or for a pittance per acre. Tales of the homesteaders' struggle against the adversities of nature, ailments of their crops and stock and themselves, tales of Indian raids that swept the prairies clean of the white man's toil sifted through the encircling bush to the men of the mines. But all this provided only garnishing to a pipeful of tobacco and was repeated to fill a tiresome hour.

"Some be took in by un," Northy said when the subject came up. "Tregellas from Welch's 'aouse skimped belly an' back t' buy a farm in Wisconsin, an' they Johns brothers too; but they was hinds back 'ome. They was never miners."

One man said: "I dawn't want un. The mine dawn't leave a smill on a man." A short silence followed, and then Jenkins said, "I wonder 'aow they'm gettin' hon—Tregellas an' the Johns boays, that is." But nobody answered.

One night a boarder came in from some place on Main Street. All eyes followed him expectantly and in silence while he found a place to sit. He knew news was expected from him and was glad he had something to tell. "A woods foreman was in town t'day lookin' for men, I 'ear."

"That's nothin'," said Northy. "That 'appen a dozen times a year."

"Oosh," came from others in agreement.

"Nobody pay attention t' they 'cept a foo Swedes or Irish," Northy added.

Jim was at the window looking into the night, the cold breath of the glass chilling his cheeks. "I be glad I bayn't in no lumber camp this weather," he said.

Talk about camp life began, began on a low note and with a touch of reluctance. "Six months in the woods be transportation, shore 'nough." "No wonder they brawl." "A lumberjack's crumbs make me want t' scratch just t' mention." "An' the dangers they run on ice an' water!" "W'at dangers they run in town be worse than ice an' water." The last speaker lowered his voice. "They be some awful."

"W'at be they, Griffin?"

Griffin looked around the silent group and toned his words with self-rebuke to make them acceptable. No man who wasn't shameless would tell such things as he had to tell. Allen and Jake looked straight at him disconcertingly. Some looked blankly into space; they must not be eager for what another was ashamed to tell.

"S'loons! Women! Women in s'loons for they special. I 'eard that 'cross the river from Michigan towns along the state line be 'aouses standin' 'lone in the woods like pest-'aouses. The s'loons fetch the painted maidens from they w'en the jacks come t' town. The good people shut doors and blinds t' keep aout the sights."

Spargo broke the heavy silence with a chuckle. All hands looked at him questioningly. It was no time to laugh.

"Hi couldn' 'elp un, Griff. They 'aouses in the woods, the blinds drawed, an' all that. I wondered 'oo patternized they maidens afore an' after the jacks come. 'Aow do the poor dears eat?"

Penglaze saw a duty in Spargo's behalf, showed it plainly, but was stumped. He returned to the lumbermen. "Fallin' trees be solemn sights," he said. "The dangers they men run be bad. 'E's a wonder sich things dawn't solemnize mun."

"Sailors, sojers, miners, an' lumberjacks bayn't famed for piousness, William," said Allen.

Before William could reply, Jake spoke. He knew Allen's weakness; it was William. Jake ignored Griffin's tidbit as completely as if it had not been told. "Northy, my son," he said, "you said 'e's nothin'—the woods bosses' man'unt, that is—'e 'appen a dozen times a year. T' my fancy 'e's a purtier sight w'en work be lookin' for men than men lookin' for work. W'a's tha say?"

Northy did not answer, but he was not displeased.

"I for one be sick of lumber-camp talk," Spargo put in, his face sober and his voice intent. "This be the third time for camp plods this winter. All in favor of no more jacks, lice, brawls, an' maidens, say Aye." He got enough response to satisfy him and a laugh for good measure.

Penglaze said Spargo was light, could not be serious, would see comicalness in a blind man's cup. Allen said Jack was sharp, and Jake said, " 'E's like a light in a dark place."

Northy suddenly pulled his watch from his pocket and said: "The stage be late t'night. I'm goin' awver."

"That's right," said Spargo. "That's right."

"W'at's right?" asked Jenkins.

"Goin' t' meet the stage," he said. " 'E deserve the notice. Thicky stage be the best friend us 'ave. 'E give us v'riety, keep us from rottin' daown. See 'aow important 'e is by all the folks 'oo go t' meet un. 'E dawn't look like much but 'e's somethin' from the aoutside. People glaze at un soon's 'e come in sight, like 'e's a myst'ry. Their faces say: 'W'at news be on un? 'Oo's ridin' in un? W'at's their business?' Thee's knaw, Jim, thicky skitterin' thing keep the place in touch with Hengland an' where the other furriners come from." Jack grinned at his own imaginings and expected Jim to laugh too; but Jim did not. What Jack rattled off as fun, Jim saw as fact.

"The stage," Jack went on, "be like the papers the chuldern get in Sunday school. There be tales that begin an' end in each, an' some that run along. The driver do get 'is news in Calumet. W'at 'e add to un afore he get 'ere, I dawn't knaw. You see, Jim, the stage be a great institootion, but 'e be better if 'e 'ave a good driver."

Jim laughed with Jack this time as the others did.

"The driver's talk be mos'ly big black lines atop the column—no small print below. 'Jesse James, a aoutlaw chap, robbed a bank in Iowa or a train in Missouri.' 'A fire, daown the line, a foo 'aouses saved by a change of wind.' 'Miners strike water in a shaft bottom on the Menominee range; mine filled up t' top; run awver.' Us swamp un with questions but 'e 'ave a timetable t' keep, so us be left in the dark."

One winter the stage brought a corpse found frozen beside the road. In the coach were a man, a woman, and two children. When the driver saw the body in the twilight, he stopped, called the man passenger and they put the body atop the coach. The driver surrendered his robe, rolled the body in it and they lifted it to place. The baggage rail would keep it from rolling off. When the stage came to a stop at the office, the frozen face of the corpse was wedged under the rail, turned toward the assembled crowd. Some one said, "Look there!" and all eyes turned accordingly, the driver's with the rest. It was the first time he had deigned to look at his extra passenger since loading him. To him, the body was only so much extra weight for his team. And then some one denounced him, said he had no respect for the dead or regard for the living because he had left the corpse uncovered. He stepped from the coach to the stoop and stamped his feet to restore blood flow to them and his legs, paid no attention to his accuser, but turned to the lifeless passenger.

"By damn," he said, "he ride free; he pay no fare! I geev heem my blanket, an' he lose heem! I was damn' fool, me! He froze already; I freeze for not'ing!" He shrugged his shoulders. "Soon he wear ze wood Mackinaw he no lose." He looked around, addressed the man who had criticized him: "You geev me lift—take heem down. He ride far 'nough!" The man shrank from the job, but the Frenchman took him by the arm and drew him to the coach. "You have what you call ze respec'," he said. "Grab holt." Others lent a hand, and the body was carried indoors. The Frenchman threw off the mail, borrowed a robe, and was gone. He rode off into the forest and the night as though nothing had happened.

Each time the yarn was told, some one said, "Hi seed un with my awn heyes! 'E's heyes was open an' w'ere I stood 'e looked like 'e was laughin'. I couldn' forgit un for weeks."

And some one asked, "Wadn' that driver some caution?" Which brought the tragic tale to an amusing end.

When the first line of the story was recited for Jim's and Jake's ears, one man said, "W'at, again?" and left the house; but the rest took it with the same stoicism as they took the holdovers from previous meals at breakfast.

"But 'e build out Jack's claim for the stage," Jim said.

"Mustn' forgit, my son," said Jake, "that most Jack claimed was in 'e's awn fancy."

One night Penglaze said: "I seed a boay board the daown stage t'night. 'E comed this mornin', lookin' for work. Couldn' git none. Goin' back daown t' the Hiron Ranges. Said 'is name was Nicolls. Come from Devoran."

The room was full of men, and Penglaze spoke, evidently just to add a quid to the talk. Immediately questions came from all corners.

"W'at did e say 'e's called?"

"Nicolls."

"W'ere did e say 'e comed from?"

"Devoran."

"That's w'ere Samp Nicolls come from—the pumpman! Wonder if they be relations!"

"Did a ask for Samp?"

Penglaze was getting uncomfortable. " 'E dedn' ask for nobody. 'E'd knaw Samp was 'ere if they was relations," Penglaze said irritably.

"If Samp dawn't write, 'e wouldn'," Jim answered, thinking of his brother who had been in the States five years and had never written.

"No hexcoose for that," said Penglaze curtly.

" 'Aow did a look?"

" 'Ongry, col', shabby an' tormented like," said Penglaze.

"I dawn't mean that. Hi mean 'is face an' heyes an' hair."

" 'Air was sandy like. 'E 'ad blue eyes an' a thin sharp face."

"That's a lot like Sampy all right."

Heads nodded all around.

"W'y dedn' a stop on the Ranges fust, I wonder."

"Copper would be more like 'ome to un, same as t' you an' me. The iron locations be mos'ly new too."

Up to this point Jake had kept silent, and Jim was wondering why. He knew Jake did not like Penglaze overmuch, and he knew Jake would have deep pity for the homeless, shivering boy.

"W'y dedn' e bring the boay 'ere for a mite t' eat? an' stay the night? A man w'at be lookin' for work edn' bad."

"The missus wouldn' like that—bringin' in a stranger."

"The missus! Stranger! Ugh! Say the hidee dedn' enter thee 'ead! The missus took we in!"

" 'Oo'd pay the bill?" Penglaze retorted, trying for escape.

"You would, be cose. An' if you couldn't, a foo of we would chip in."

"You bayn't rich, Collins," snapped Penglaze.

"No, William, I bayn't rich. You'm right," Jake said. "I bayn't." And his voice dwindled as though in hopeless defeat. He got to his feet and looked the crowd over with the smile Jim understood so well and the others understood better from day to day. Every face turned toward him. "If you boays 'ave some buttons t' sew on or a stockin' t' mend, I b'lieve 'e'd 'elp. Tedn' Sunday, an' the missus won't objec'."

Jim marveled that nobody snarled at Jake, and that they laughed instead.

"Now let's go, comrade," Jake said to him, and donning their coats, they went out.

"W'ere to now?" asked Jim when the door closed behind them.

"The Cliff Road be good anough. Anyw'ere t' be out of that," he answered.

On the road Jake continued: "Hi used t' wonder w'y women always carried a bit of sewin' 'r knittin', but I knaw now. If they dedn', they'd sclum one 'nother's heyes out. A passel of men ought t' 'ave w'ittlin' 'andy."

At the end of the board walk they stopped.

"There's a little shop down the road a mite, an' I be out of bacca. Let's go on," said Jake.

"'Oo keep the shop?" asked Jim.

"Hi dawn't knaw, comrade," Jake answered. "Us might be on the trail of a 'appenin'."

It was an odd place for a shop. Whoever kept it must have hoped that the passers toward town would be tempted to shorten their journey by patronizing him, and that those leaving town might have forgotten something. The shop presented two small windows to the road, one on each side of the door. In one window groceries were stacked, slabs of bacon wrapped in canvas with pictured labels stuck to the canvas, hams similarly clothed and decorated, and tobacco, both in open boxes and in packages. In the other were overalls, heavy underwear, and caps of various patterns adapted to winter use. Two smoking kerosene lamps lighted the exhibit dimly.

On the porch they stopped to kick the snow from their boots.

" 'E make me think of thy Aunt Maria at Kelly Bray," said Jake, "the little shop 'er 'ad. So hones' 'er was with 'er customer, 'er'd bite a raisin in two t' make weight, an' so hones' with 'erself, 'er'd spit t'other 'alf back in the barrel." Both laughed like two children at the memory. "Folks can be too hones', seem like, comrade," added Jake as he opened the door.

Five men sat around the stove. Two occupied the wood box, two sat on nail kegs and one sat on a chair. The owner of the store leaned against the counter. Four of the guests were in their forties; one of the keg sitters was within easy reach of thirty. As Jim and Jake approached, the young man was saying: "Hi'll be sailin' in two weeks for 'ome." With that the conversation stopped, interrupted by their approach.

The merchant was a short man, smoothly shaven save for a mustache; his features were round, and his dark eyes sparkled in an expectant welcoming manner. He came toward the two with a decided limp.

"W'at can I do for you?" he asked.

"Hi want a bit of bacca," said Jake, "F.O.B."

The tobacco was provided, change made, and the pair started for the door.

"Won't e come hup an' meet the men?" asked the shopkeeper. "You'm Cornishmen an' strangers, I b'lieve. My name is Burt, John Burt."

"He's Jacob Collins, an' I be Jim Holman."

John Burt shook hands with both.

Jim and Jake had seen all of the men either about the mine or on the street.

Burt introduced them in American fashion, adding the names of the places they had come from: "Thomas Doney from St. Ives; Edward Treloar from St. Just; Isaac Williams from Helston; Jack Dunstone from St. Dominick; Stanton from St. Cleer. I come from Newlyn."

"A saintly lot," said the Helston man. "You'd think Cornwall was a chip off the 'Oly Land, an' all the Cousin Jacks was pious."

All laughed but Stanton, but the laugh was short. Dunstone's announcement had received no comment.

"Dunstun say 'e's goin' back 'ome in a fortnit," said Williams.

"Iss, you," Dunstone said, looking at Jake and Jim. "I be sick of this eternal winter."

" 'E's 'ard, I agree," said Doney. "The winters do grind a man daown, but 'e's 'arder back there." And then, with a touch of apology, "To my mind, that is," he added. "A man can stand cold an' 'ard work an' low pay better'n 'e can stand warm weather, frien's, no work an' a hempty belly."

The young man had evidently spent his reasons in his one denunciation of the winter, so he got up and left the store.

"Hi be sorry for un," Treloar said when the door closed. "The pore boay be 'omesick, I b'lieve. That's w'at's the matter with 'e."

"An' 'e live in a big boardin' 'aouse—eighteen men," said Williams. "Nothin' 'arder than that on a man's sperrit."

" 'Aouse builded fur five or six! They must pile up awver Sunday like cordwood," said Doney. "There ought t' be a law agin such doin's."

"Hi knawed a Collins awver St. Tossle way," said Williams, looking at Jake. " 'Ave relations there, do e?"

"My people come from there," replied Jake.

"I've been t' St. Cleer," said Jim. "I 'ave a uncle there." He spoke to Stanton.

Stanton nodded but did not look up or speak.

"Not much t' say for St. Cleer, boays," laughed Doney.

"Hi 'ave 'eard of nine maidens that was turned t' moor-stones up there," said Treloar. " 'Aow 'baout un, Stanton?"

"I've seen the stones," said Stanton. "Seven stones, they be. The maidens danced on Sunday. Punished so."

"Did e knaw any of the maidens, Jimmy?" asked Jake.

The men all laughed except Stanton, and he did not answer.

"Did e hever see Lady 'Oward drive 'er coach of bones aout of Tavistock, Collins? That's close t' you. A chap from there tol' me that plod once," said Doney.

"No," Jake said. "I never seed 'er."

" 'E's a purty tale," said Doney. "Th' ol' maid was some savage. 'Er 'ad four men an' killed mun all. Their bones was made into a carriage with a 'ead on each corner. 'Er 'ad t' drive t' Okehampton ev'ry night as a punishment. But that wadn' all. 'Er 'ad t' pick one blade of grass there an' carry un back t' Tavistock. W'en all the grass in Okehampton was give aout, 'er could lie in 'er grave an' rest."

Doney waited a few seconds for his yarn to sink in and added: "Iss, shore 'nough! A plenty 'ave seen 'er. Bad as 'er was, she 'ad a good point or two. She always ask folks 'er meet on the road t' ride with 'er."

"Hi dawn't b'lieve I'd want t' meet 'er of a dark night," said Jake, turning a solemn face toward the story-teller.

Jim looked at him in surprise, traced with wonder. The merest flicker of an eyelid told him Jake was merely taking part in the tournament of yarns.

"Daown w'ere I come from," said John Burt, "seein' an' hearin' piskies be common anough. An' they wadn' always seen by folks on parish pay. Doctors an' lawyers an' praychers seen mun. An' not awnly cowards. Sailors an' sojers comin' 'ome t' visit met mun an' was led aout of their way by mun. I be hones' t' say, Hi dawn't knaw w'at t' make aout of un."

A silence followed, in recognition of Burt's seriousness. Then he went on.

"I remember a tale from awver Hayle way—abaout ten mile from my place. Aout on the hopen moor is a chapel called Lelant. You mus' knaw the place, Doney, an' maybe the tale." Doney nodded. "A doctor was comin' home across the moor of a night—late—from a call on a sick body. Sudden like, 'e 'eard the Lelant chapel bell ring—toll, that is—faint like, an' he wondered. It was midnight an' after. 'E thought 'is hears was deceivin' un, but the bell ringed again an' again. Then 'e seen the chapel an', shore 'nough, a glimmer of light come from all the windas. Bein' as 'ow 'e was a doctor, 'e wadn' afeard of ghosts, so he determined t' take a look-see. 'E got off 'is hoss an' crep' up t' the winda, pulled hisself up so's t' see, an' the chapel was full of dim light, like candlelight, but no candles to be seen. Then he see the haisle was full of little people goin' hup t' the haltar. 'E looked that way an' there, afore the haltar, was a little body laid aout with a craown on 'er head! In his excitement, the doctor slipped an' made a clatter. 'E climbed up again but the chapel was dark an' the bell stopped tollin'." Burt hesitated a moment and added, "The doctor was a Christian man too."

"Hi'm glad you said that, John Burt, or I'd want t' knaw if 'e tippled a bit. Doctors do sometimes, thee's knaw," said Williams.

" 'E's a fancy tale," said Doney, "an' I've heard un many's the time."

"Did e knaw the doctor?" asked Williams.

" 'E was gone afore my time," replied Doney.

Tales of piskies followed, of ghosts, of voices in haunted places, appearances of the devil, witches, mermaids in weird procession. For each tale told, some one vouched with due assurance. Nor did the occasional laugh rid the listeners of the conviction that the teller believed his tale.

"An' then there be they stones, like Seven Stones! They'm scattered all awver Cornwall, I've 'eard say," John Burt went on. "They be stood araoun' in circles, in patterns, like somebody put mun there on purpose." He paused and looked over his company like a man looking for help. "Do you boays knaw 'oo the Droods be? I've 'eard said, they put hup the moorstones."

No one answered.

"Well," said Jake, "you boays 'ave 'ad anough of we, an' us must be goin'." And turning toward the door he said "Thankee" to Burt's "Come again."

"I be glad you wanted a bit of bacca," said Jim as soon as they were outside again.

"There be lots of gains in smawkin', my son."

To Jake's respects to the weed, his partner made no answer. Instead, he said, "Do you b'lieve trade like that?"

"You remember old Granny Johns seed Dick Crago after 'e cut 'is thrawt," replied Jake.

"An' Pol's brother George was pisky-led on 'is way 'ome from the doctor's w'en 'is father died," observed Jim.

"Couldn' say 'e went t' see 'e's maid, because Lizzie Jane dedn' live that way," argued Jake.

"An' George dedn' tipple."

"No. 'E was pious then."

They walked in silence.

"Jake!"

"Aas, my son."

"Us dedn' 'ave ghosts underground back 'ome, an' plenty of men was killed t' 'ave sperrits on ev'ry level, in ev'ry stope, climbin' ladders in all the shafts."

"Strange that! Hi never minded that afore. An' no signs!"

"Not t' 'mount t' nothin'. A man wouldn' w'istle in the bal or hand a light through a ladder."

"An' some wouldn' work the last shift."

"But the devil never got down the mine, nor witches nother."

"S'prisin' too that Bet Bunt dedn' go down; 'er went ev'ry place helse," said Jake laughingly. "Hint'restin' subjec', my son."

"Hi keep wonderin' all the time w'y they dawn't 'ave ghost tales 'ere."

" 'Ow did e like Jan Burt? I liked un."

"It sounded a bit like 'ome t' 'ear Stanton's St. Cleer talk. 'E's the fust I've 'eard."

The next night Jim went to school. He resented the break in his schooling caused by the holidays but was ashamed of the time lost because of his melancholy. He understood the increase in the master's work up to the holidays and his preparations for his classrooms after the holidays. He had seen Mr. Frost take on Walters' job at the organ and knew he prepared much of the Christmas program. All this he resented but excused. It postponed the day when he could read what his wife wrote to him, and when he could, without help, write to her. But his homesickness which had the same result, he branded as disloyalty; and he was humiliated at the thought of it. Like a man offering a petition he said, "Forgive me, Pol. Forgive me, maid."

After his lesson Jim lingered. He had something to ask, but it was difficult for him. He sensed that what was puzzling him might be a simple matter to a man of education. It was a confession of ignorance comparable to his inability to read and write. And, too, the questions he had in mind concerned his own country, about which he ought to be better informed than the teacher who was an American. Still, he remembered that the teacher of the parish school at home knew more of America than the men who had been there.

"Mr. Frost, I want to ask a question, but I fear 'e will sound foolish."

"What is it, Jim?"

"W'y dawn't we 'ave ghosts an' witches an' sperrits in this country? Cornwall is full of min. An' piskies an' mermaids."

Frost was puzzled. The question was asked seriously, and he must answer it so; but he had not thought of it. He had always charged such things to ignorance, superstition. It was impossible that a modern man could believe them. He had read the myths of other peoples but had not felt the need of explaining how they came to be. The absence of myth, of superstition was the result of education. To speak plainly, shortly, would be hurtful. He compromised, but honestly.

"Jim," he said, "I have not thought enough of that to give you a satisfactory answer. Let me think it over, and we will talk about it the next time you come. Is there anything else?"

"Yes, sir. W'at be Droods?"

"I don't know, Jim. I never heard of them. I know what Druids are. Perhaps Droods are relatives of the piskies you Cornishmen talk about."

"One question more, Mr. Frost—if I dawn't wear e out. 'Ow do us 'ave so many places in Cornwall called saint something or hother, like Saint Jus', Saint Ives, an' the like?"

"Again, I don't know, Jim. I'll find out if possible and tell you."

What would be the source of his information, Jim did not give a thought. For his own edification only did Allen come to his mind. "P'r'aps 'e'll knaw," he murmured.

The following Sunday, Jim was alone in the front room thinking of these problems when Allen came in. As was his custom, he had ranged the woods since early morning, enjoying the unsullied companionship of the wind, the snow, the uninhabited distances, the whisperings that come out of primitive vastnesses. He had regaled himself with the air that had swept the lake and was as clean as the snow about him. He would have denied that his habit had anything of worship in it, but he always returned from his tramps renewed, ready for the new week with increased zest. He smiled at Jim as he came in.

"I hear the pupil has been puzzling the master with his questions," he said.

Jim's heart warmed to the man in spite of a slight fear that Allen might be laughing at him. For a moment he censured the schoolmaster for disclosing his questions, but then he suddenly thought that Frost would naturally turn to Allen for his information.

"Hi thought 'e'd knaw," said Jim simply.

"A man can't know everything, my son, even if he is a schoolmaster." Again Allen smiled as if to reestablish the younger man's confidence in his teacher. "All of us take life as we find it and don't ask many questions about it. You lived in Cornwall twenty years with pisky tales all around you, and you waited until this week to ask questions about it. Isn't that right?"

"That's so," said Jim.

"How did it happen, Jim?"

Jim told of his visit to Burt's shop.

"You asked no more questions about the Seven Stones set in a circle than you did of the hill they were on. Did you think God set the stones as you did that He made the hill?"

"Hi dedn' think about un at all," was the honest answer.

"Exactly! Curiosity was born to you that night in John Burt's store. Curiosity is a precious thing, Jim. Your job now, boay, be t' keep it alive."

Allen's eyes showed his earnestness as did his slip into Cornish. His lips curved into a faint smile as he began to speak again.

"The schoolmaster doesn't know much about Cornwall," he said. "Few folks do. The Cousin Jacks themselves don't know much of anything about it. He could get nothing from them. You see, my son, he has a lot of things to read and learn for his job, and Cornwall was never of interest to him before." Allen smiled. "He will have a bit of curiosity from now on too."

"Did a ask you, Bob?"

"He did."

"Did you knaw?"

"I know a little, Jim, boy. A little. Nobody really knows much about Cornwall."

"Tell me w'at you told 'e. Tell me w'ere piskies come from."

"Not where they came from, Jim, but how folks invented them and then believed in them. You see, the master knows there is no such a thing, but he wanted to see his way clear to tell you without hurt. He thought you might believe in them."

In simple terms Allen told Jim the possible origins of myths and fairy tales. He drew illustrations from many lands and then came back to Cornwall. The men began to come in for tea. After they had eaten, he and Jim put on their coats and caps and went out.

Under the cold clear sky they walked for a time without talk, listening to the snow complaining under their feet. To Jim, much that Allen had told him savored of what the preachers called demonism. Allen said it was the fancying of the race in its childhood. "You like to hear a child talk to its toys," he said, "make them laugh or speak or go to sleep. The human race was young once, my son."

That was new to Jim. For him, man had begun full-grown and world-wise in Eden. He knew nothing of the long history of mankind, but Allen was patient and led his pupil by easy paths and simple stories.

"Seem like there be a lot for me t' read, some day," said Jim. "W'at did e say about folks comin' back from the dead?"

"Old wives' fables, Jim."

Jim remained silent, unsatisfied.

"Did you ever hear of a good man coming back?"

Jim hesitated. "I dawn't b'lieve I did."

"The bad don't seem to rest well, Jim."

" 'E look like it."

"Religion has made the veil between the two worlds very thin, my son. The Bible tells of angels appearing, the dead rising, and the like. In our experience it is a short step from this world into the next. It is easy to think that the step back is just as short. But it isn't, boy. The dead coming back is a fancy of the folks still here."

"W'y dawn't the people 'ere 'ave ghos' tales?"

"Ghost tales and myths live only among people who have a long past. America is new. Such yarns won't transplant. Remember the maid who said, 'Thy people shall be my people, and thy God my God'?"

"Aas."

"She knew she couldn't transplant her gods. Ghosts, goblins, and piskies can't survive where people are intelligent, Jim. Another generation, and such plods will fade out, be laughed at back home, or used only in illustration and mentioned only in history."

"Tell me a little about Droods, Bob. That is, if thee edn' tired of talkin'."

Bob laughed. "Jim, you remind me of my mother. When I was a nipper I'd come home hungry and eat no end. Mother would say, 'Bob, thee't like a clock case.' You remember the old clocks, as tall as a man and hollow from face to floor."

The two laughed heartily, and Bob said: "Not tonight, lad. We've had enough. Let's leave that to the master."

Chapter Fourteen

THE REVIVAL—it was so named in advance—had been announced several times from the pulpit as a certainty of the near future, and the divine blessing had been asked for it in prayers. It was anticipated as the high spot of the chapel endeavor for the year. If successful, it would be its own best defense; if a failure, the less said about it the better. To the boarders of the town and the loungers in public places it was something out of the ordinary, looked forward to as was a circus or the Fourth or Christmas, one of the few noteworthy events of the year. Consciously or unconsciously, time was the major problem of the locations: what to do with it, how to squander it, how to "kill it." The Revival gave a solution to the problem as long as it lasted. It had in it many elements of chance which would enliven talk and inspire attendance. Old-timers who had proved their professions to be deciduous plants would be subjects of bets as to how long they would resist. Others were sampled as possibilities for the coming Pentecost, and the wager was whether they would or would not succumb. Most of the Cornish would attend. No one regarded attendance as a certain evidence of religious interest. One went to hear and see what in ordinary services would be unusual or even unseemly. By so doing, some very unlikely guests were often netted and added to the roll of the saved.

Already the Revival was the subject of widespread conversation. Jim and Jake heard talk about it in the mine, at the store, and at the boarding house. Jake remarked that it was doing what few subjects were able to do: it held the men in their places after they had eaten, until the missus had to shoo them away. The meeting was generally spoken of with respect but not always without humor. Comments about some who were certain, from past experience, to take part in the meeting were sometimes heavy-handed, and names were mentioned without restraint; but more frequently laughable items were told and followed with guffaws.

"Just like back 'ome," Jim said.

"Oosh," was Jake's only reply.

At Uren's, talk of the meeting began in fun. The boarders laughed at oddities of phrase or manner used in prayer or testimony by some of the old-timers when they got warmed up. One insisted on starting a hymn who had no sense of tune or pitch. He was rescued sometimes by some one who caught the words and could add the tune, but he oftener lost himself in mid-air. "An'," Northy said, " 'e'll do un awver an' awver."

When the laugh had died down, Spargo said: "You've 'ad your laugh. Naow confess that hev'ry man you tipped a grin at be a good man."

" 'Ear, 'ear," said Jenkins, but no one contradicted Spargo.

A moment of awkward silence followed Jenkins' approval of Spargo's dare when a question was tossed into the open for any one to answer. "Do e think the meetin' will be as excitin' 'ere as 'e belong t' be back 'ome?"

Jake winked at Jim and answered. "You 'ave the same blood in the pulpit an' pew, my son. Cousin Jacks dawn't change awvernight. Remember the leopard an' 'e's spots."

"You'm a Cousin Jack, the same as we," said the man truculently. "W'a's tha mean?"

"Iss, you. I'm a Cousin Jack with no excooses, the same yesterday, t'day an' forhever," said Jake, and grinned innocently at the questioner's squallishness.

"Preparations be afoot naow, I 'ear," Northy said.

"'Aow?" asked several together.

"The praycher be visitin' 'omes, readin' Scripter an' off'rin' prayer," said Northy.

"'Tis so," said Mrs. Uren. "'E's comin' 'ere t'morra an' want all of e t' bide in after supper. I 'ope you will." She spoke at first like a conscious-burdened disciple forcing herself to an unpleasant duty. Her last sentence was lighter, having in it the lilt of victory over her reproachable reluctance— her own mite thrown into the coffer.

"It take a brave man t' do that," said Spargo seriously.

"'Aow's that? 'E's aysier than minin'," said another.

"Hi'd ruther mine," insisted Jack.

"If you 'ad the call," said the missus, "'e'd be aysy."

"A call wouldn' blind me t' the 'ard spots of the job," said Jack. "Goin' w'ere you bayn't wanted an' doin' w'at embarrass ev'rybody be like givin' sulphur an' m'lasses t' the kids."

"Jack Spargo, you hought t' be 'shamed of yourself," the missus retorted. "You saound like you 'ave fallen from grace."

"The pulpit 'ave been a way aout of chiselin' copper an' drillin' iron ore for a lot of they," said Allen, throwing another chip on the fire.

"W'at do e mean?" asked several together.

"I'll bet there be a half-dozen men in this 'aouse 'oo prayched back 'ome—or tried to. If they'd been good, they wouldn' be in the pit t'day, would they?"

"Be they t' blame for that?" asked one, thinking Allen was critical.

"No, my son, not if they dawn't like minin'. Praych or plow if you dawn't like t' mine."

"W'at abaout the call?" persisted the missus.

"A manner of speakin', I fancy," said Allen. "Some folks

feel deeper than others, develop a fellin' for w'at they do; others just plod along. I never 'eard of calls that I knaw by back 'ome. The parish passon was gived a church for a livin'. Some of they was good 'unters, liked t' fish, chased butterflies, wraute poetry that wadn' religious, an' prayched t' live. You all knaw that," he added generously.

"You saoun' like a onb'liever, Bob Allen," chid the missus.

"Dawn't be hasty, Missus," answered Bob gently. "You knaw 'aouw the boays got on the plan."

"Shore 'er do; us all do," Jake put in to divide the effect of Allen's remark. "The boay was tried. If 'e was frail, couldn' say 'is piece, 'e was dropped. Awver 'ere, seem like, praychers be called. If they make good they 'ave un; if they be poor an' stammery they say they 'ave un. That make a union man of un."

"Well, well!" gasped Mrs. Uren. "Hi declare, I dawn't knaw w'at my 'aouse be comin' to!"

" 'E shore 'nough need a revival t' my mind," said Penglaze, looking from Allen to Jake.

"I'd ruther mine," Spargo insisted.

"Fair anough, comrade," said Northy. "Us all knaw you dawn't 'ave no call."

The men laughed at Spargo, and he laughed with them. Popular as he was, they enjoyed a joke on him because the joke usually came from him. Jack was a churchman, but his humor kept him from high esteem as a religious man. When the laugh died down Jack said, "A laugh be as good as a meal."

"I dawn't see you miss no meals," retorted Northy, trying to prolong the merriment.

"No, a laugh with a meal be like cream on a tart."

Some of the men began to push back from the table. As if speaking for those close to him only, Allen said, "I've seen times when a laugh was better'n a prayer." But Penglaze heard him.

"That's anough," he said, his voice filling the room. "That's blasphemy."

"Shore 'nough," added the missus. "Leave the table at once."

The men arose and withdrew to the middle room. Some continued upstairs for coats and caps and came stamping down again to seek new company to pick up the happenings of the day. Some stood around in indecision, hands in pockets in search of pipes and tobacco. Some went to the windows for a look at the winter-wrapped scene while they made up their minds what to do. One by one they sat down, Jim, Jake, Bob, Penglaze, Northy, Jenkins, and a few more. The room would have seemed crowded if they had ever been used to larger quarters.

"So you dawn't prize a laugh, William," said Bob as he straddled his chair.

"Devilment's afoot," muttered Jake.

Penglaze turned his whiskered face toward Bob as though measuring his man before answering. But Bob knew Penglaze measured nobody. "Duty" was the big word in Penglaze's code. "A man's duty be t' speak for 'is faith," was his favored injunction before the Class, and, whatever Penglaze enjoined, he practiced.

"Not w'ere religion be concerned," he said. "Us be told the Lord weeped, but no place say 'E ever laughed."

" 'Oo fixed a man's face an' heyes so's 'e can laugh?" asked Northy.

"But the Book dawn't say—"

"Shore 'nough, William, you'm right. The Book dawn't." Bob seemed suddenly to lose interest in the issue. His sparring fists had dropped to his sides in concession of the fight. Jake and Jim wondered why his surrender, wondered where he had intended to lead Penglaze and to what end. They knew nothing pleased Allen like an argument with William. They were disappointed. Allen surrendered the bout with a smile on his face.

Jenkins had looked on and listened in silence. With Allen's withdrawal, he spoke.

"I think I hunderstan' naow w'at you meant by praychin' bein' a way aout of the mines. Hi'd like t' 'ear more abaout the call you spawk of, Bob. That is if 'e c'n be done withaout bad feelin's."

"Hi never 'ad one, 'Arry, boay," said Bob. "All I'd say would be jus' theory—nothin' more."

"Saoundin' brass an' tinklin' cymbal," said Penglaze.

"Thankee, William," said Bob. "You'm the kindes' man I knaw if I may be 'lowed t' lie t' thy face."

Jim and Jake were troubled, as was Jenkins too. Jim had sat silent through the table talk wondering, part of the time, what set William and Bob at swords' points. Different sensations assailed him as words had come from this one and that. He kept still because, he told himself, he was too young and inexperienced to talk about subjects like these. He did wish that Harry's question had been aired a little. During his chapel experience he had never heard of a call. As he puzzled, from somewhere came a voice saying, "Follow me," and he saw a hand beckoning men away from their jobs to do something else. He thought of their names. And there was Saul, too! Straight calls! He was interested. And then a happening in the old country took shape in his mind. He had no thought what it would prove; it seemed to fit, that was all. Before he was aware of it he was speaking.

"W'en I was a boay, a man come to a close-by Wesleyan chapel—Moors, us called un—an' 'ad a revival. He was young, in 'e's fust thirties; no more. I c'n see un yet. 'E 'ad a full, square beard, like Jake's, with a shade of red in un. 'E wored dark glasses. Everybody said 'e was 'andsome, but 'e was as blind as a adder. 'E read the Scripter with 'is fingers. I never seed the book 'e had, but the sayin' was, 'e could feel the letters. W'en 'e spawk, 'is voice sounded like a harmonium note—a bass note." Jim suddenly became self-conscious and stopped, turned to Jake, his face red with confusion and said, "You tell un, Jake."

"No, boay. You'm doin' brave," said Jake.

"Spayk on! Spayk on!" said others.

Jim looked from face to face, and some said "Oosh" to the request; others nodded.

"The revival 'e 'ad shook the parish from core t' brim. Men an' women was changed, shore 'nough. People talked of 'e's secret. Some said it was 'e's voice. 'E's talk was like low moosic, an' w'en 'e raised 'is voice 'e sounded like a note in a hanthem. Some said 'twas because 'e was blind—pity was stirred t' begin with. Some said 'twas 'e's looks—that 'e looked like the picter of Christ, but for 'e's glasses. W'en 'e talked 'e stood still, kept 'is 'ands t'gether in front of un. 'E looked out into that 'ouse like I looked out awver the sea at night, w'en crossin'. 'E's words warmed the very air. It was a strange thing. People sat so still an' quiet, 'e must 'ave wondered if the 'ouse was hempty. W'en 'e said, 'Come,' folks comed like chuldern to their mother."

Again Jim stopped and turned to Jake for help. He had not thought, when he began, the story would take so long. His first thought had not included the things he was saying. He was bewildered at his own speech. But Jake only said, "Go on with e."

"He was borned just across our parish line an' lived in a thatched cottage. 'E was borned blind. I've seen the place, an' I'd 'eard of the blind boay 'oo lived there. Jake, too. 'E was seldom spawk of. It come out that w'en 'e was fifteen 'e said, 'Ma, I want t' praych.' 'Er was troubled: 'e 'ad no schoolin'. Then 'e asked the chapel for a place on the plan. 'E was told 'e couldn' read, an' 'e mus' read t' praych—a deceit because we 'ad praychers 'oo couldn' read. 'E dedn' knaw w'en 'e was converted, if hever after the fashion. The story went through our parish an' his too, but nobody could 'elp in a case like that.

"One day, so 'tis said, a lady with a cob an' trap come to 'e's mother's 'ouse; an' a bit later the boay was gone. There was rumors, but they died down. Nobody knawed nothin'. The boay was forgot. Next come the Moors chapel meetin'. 'E was the idol of two parishes. He was invited 'ere an' there for tay or dinner or supper an' t' stay the night, but after hev'ry service 'e was drove across the parish line to the cottage an' 'e's mother. W'en the meetin' was finished it was like somebody'd said 'Hush!' an' for weeks ev'rybody waited t' spayk."

Jim sat back in his chair, wondering why he had told the story, how it applied to the conversation that had preceded it, if it did at all. He had followed an impulse he could not explain. He wondered if the tale sounded pointless, foolish. The men still looked at him intently. He felt painfully conspicuous. He wished he had not spoken, that some one would break the silence. He looked at Spargo and Jenkins. Their faces were lighted and kindly. They seemed to be waiting for more, but he had no more to say. He looked at Penglaze but saw only a mask. Jake was looking at something far away. Jim did not know what it was, but he did know Jake was with him, always with him. Then he looked at Allen. He did not want to seem foolish to Allen, to have talked and said nothing to Allen's judgment. Allen, like the rest—all but Jake—was looking at him, too; but his look was different; it was not expectant. Jim thought he could make out surprise in his eyes, that he was pleased. Allen's lips parted, and a faint smile spread over his face. Spacing his words, he said, " ' 'E that hath ears t' hear, let him 'ear.' Jim, my son, your tale 'ave answered the question better'n a world of hargyment. I'm glad you told un."

To Jim's surprise and Allen's too, Penglaze said, "Amen."

Then he turned to Bob and said, "If you liked that plod, Robert, you'm not far from the kingdom."

To Jim's delight and Jake's too, Allen said, "Thank you, William."

When the two partners went upstairs, Jim said he was glad Penglaze and Allen had come closer to friendliness. Jake faced him as his custom was when he wanted to make a point. "Did e notice thicky 'Robert'? That show 'tis awnly a truce. W'en William bury a 'atchet, as the Yankees say, 'e leave the 'ilt stickin' out of the ground."

On Sunday the meeting was said to begin with the morning worship, although the service differed only slightly from its predecessors. The pastor devoted most of the sermon period to exhortation. He pleaded with the members of the congregation for cooperation. There must be unity of purpose, conviction of the need of such a stirring as only a revival could give, and faith to believe that God was willing and waiting to do more than they could "ask or think." He urged promptness in testimony and prayer when a request for either was made. Responsibility for the success of the endeavor was quite equally spread over pulpit and pew. He was sure the pulpit would not fail.

"We do want more in the choir too," he said. "I 'ave 'eard good voices in the congregation that ought t' be in the choir. Tonight we shall put more chairs up 'ere, an' we want they full." He argued that the choir must do the will of the preacher—"for the time bein,' that is." The brother who was coming was expert in directing the music of a revival. Wouldn't all the singers forget their differences and consecrate their voices to the saving of souls?

The first week would be devoted to preparation; the church must be prepared to receive what the Lord had in store for them. He hoped every member would put other things aside and be in his place every night. The pastor showed no sign of misgiving that any one would fail to attend because he was to preach during the week. "Next Lord's Day, Brother Noble will be 'ere, a man mighty before the Lord, an' will continue as long as the Sperrit do show 'E's favor."

During the first week, Jim and Jake were night shift and could not attend the services, but the boarding house was full of talk about them. What those who had been to church said was quoted and elaborated by those who had not. The preaching was poor, dull, fireless. The members did not want to pray when called upon, and the testimonies prodded out of them were flat and lifeless. The choir had taken offense at the preacher's request that they forget their differences. The loyal few who sang for him were depressed by the empty chairs around them. Hope for a revival was pinned to the stranger.

Tozer did his best, but the general judgment was, " 'E will never make a revival."

Saturday night, the boarders lingered over emptied plates and cups. The talk had no enthusiasm. It was sourly critical, produced mostly by those who wanted a show, an entertainment. Those who had a genuine interest in the welfare of the church and the outcome of the "effort" were defenseless. If hope is to flower it must have a trellis to climb. A promising beginning would, at least, give all a new strain of conversation, perhaps start a few good arguments. There was the gloominess of reprisal in all that was said, perhaps because the undertaking was so nearly Cornish. Loyalty called for something better. Pride smarted under what looked like failure.

"That boay would be dropped from the plan back 'ome, and no mistake," said Northy. " 'E wouldn' git as far as 'andlin' a meetin' alone."

" 'E's doin' the best 'e can," said Penglaze.

"A poor best never look as bad as in a pulpit," retorted Northy.

Tozer's sermons were dire, dutiful things. They lacked sparkle, lilt, exaltation. They dealt with the uncertainty of life, mine accidents, baleful quotations from the Scriptures, stories of retribution, descriptions of fervid conversions in England, much of the golden streets and more of heavy, fiery punishment. Revival was unfelt at the end of the first week; the last day was as fervorless as the first.

Sunday morning, at breakfast, Spargo said, "I'll bet Tozer's glad 'e's through."

" 'E bayn't the only one," said Northy.

"From all accounts, 'e's like a right-'anded man tryin' t' beat a drill left hand afore."

"More like a man w'at never seen a 'ammer in 'e's life."

"Dawn't be too 'ard, my son," said Spargo soothingly, trying to close the discussion.

"I bayn't as 'ard on 'e as he is on the cause, t' my mind, an' no matter w'at I be, I 'ave respec' for the cause."

No one came to the preacher's defense. Even Penglaze was silent. And yet no one seemed to think the preacher had missed the point of his gospel, that in his words was no precious ointment, no inspiration, no light for dark places or heart's ease for trying times. What he said, they were used to; the way he said it was what damned his effort. He lacked something; they called it "the gift."

After his first service it was agreed that Mr. Noble had it. The men who attended were unanimous. To begin with, he could sing, and he made song of topmost importance. He tossed a small jest at singers in general—after he had sung. He smiled at his own humor, smiled with the rest at himself, something poor Tozer could not do. Tozer's singing almost disfranchised him as a Cornishman. His big voice could carry only the airs of hymns at bass level. "Let us sing," he would say with utmost solemnity and lead off an octave too low. "We'll sing unto the Lord a new song," said Noble, "—today! We'll make old songs new by the way we sing them." He walked over to the singers' corner of the platform, put his hand on an empty chair. "This chair can't sing!" he said, as if imparting information. "Who'll give this chair a voice—a soprano, a tenor, a bass voice?" A moment of nudging and whispering in the audience, and shortly every chair was filled. Ignoring the audience, he spoke to the choir, swelled their importance. Vividly he portrayed the scene at Galilee— waves, boats, men and nets, and a man on the shore calling. "They answered as you have done today, answered, each according to his gift. You will sing for Him."

Then he assumed their direction; between stanzas, he instructed and demonstrated. He selected hymns familiar from youth to most of his congregation. Before he was done, a poignant homesickness swelled the hearts and filled the eyes of nearly all before him. An accent that the remainder of his life would not erase showed where he had learned the songs they sang.

And then he preached. His theme was "Our Heavenly Home." His text: "He looked for a city which hath foundations, whose builder and maker is God." He detailed two homes at the end—one, any of his hearers might have known —a thatched cottage with birds nesting in the thatch, a garden with Father the gardener, the season's blooms with Mother the florist, the orchard and fruit to the taste of childhood, honeysuckle draping the enclosing hedges, filling the air with an ecstasy of perfume. The other! Here fancy flew from spire to spire. "Eye hath not seen, nor ear heard!" Like Whitefield, his great predecessor, he knew how to put tears into his voice. This home they might miss! He sobbed with the heartbroken who could not enter the gates of that city, and shuddered as they sank into darkness. "You miners are acquainted with darkness. But you have a match if the candle blows out. You say always, 'Daylight is waiting overhead!' But these! No match, no candle, no daylight save as it lives like a flame in memory! Today you may enter. Harps, viols, voices for your home-coming." The citizens of London might have seen what he depicted, but his hearers had looked at such only in dreams.

At Uren's dinner table it was agreed that the revival was sure.

" 'E's a gifted man," said Jenkins.

" 'E is that," replied several together.

"An' he's a Cornishman," added another, a compliment they were all reluctant to give Tozer.

" 'E 'ave been a good scholar under a good teacher, I'd say," another approved.

"Us'll be thinkin' we be back 'ome afore 'e's through."

"The 'aouse will be craowded t'night, shore 'nough," Spargo prophesied.

"Oosh," came in a chorus.

" 'E'll likely throw the meetin' open t'night," Spargo continued, still visioning the future.

But Spargo was mistaken. However uncertain life might be, the preacher would gamble with it. Hell might yawn, but sinners must wait the preacher's convenience. He had a plan of campaign to follow.

In midweek, Noble discarded the old tunes and substituted what he called revival songs. He had ordered books especially adapted to such services. These songs were sung rollickingly, softly, pleadingly, or hummed.

" 'E'll 'ave e w'istlin' the gospel next," Jake told Jim.

Noble instituted afternoon meetings for the benefit of the night-shift men. Some one objected that the men needed sleep. His retort was, "Could ye not watch one little hour?"

The first week was devoted to kindling the membership— to doing what Tozer had been unable to do. They were coached in prayer and testimony, urged to be bold for the Lord, to seek a second blessing, to regain their lost estate. Each night seemed auspicious to the men at Uren's.

" 'E's losin' time," Northy insisted. "W'y do a put off the call?"

"The praycher do knaw 'e's business," Penglaze told him.

Noble's second Sunday morning service was dignified, quiet, studious. It seemed like a rest period. But the waters were troubled, none the less. All the men sensed a pending surge. They were not being let off. That night he talked of Naaman, the Syrian leper. A single spot was fatal! All human righteousness was as filthy rags! He sent Naaman off, reluctant, hopeless—a man grasping at a straw. With Naaman out of sight, the preacher portrayed the waiting, praying wife. She counted the days to Jordan and back, then stood in the doorway to watch for his return. Noble saw wives in the doorways of Allouez and the doorways of Cornish cottages waiting for their Naamans to come home.

"Will you disappoint her?" he asked. "Tell her no, tonight."

He waited for the answer with a certainty that it would come. And it came! Men moved out of their pews, and women came with them to strengthen their resolve. A sign to the choir, and the organ breathed a chord that the choir took up and followed until men and women could find no place to kneel at the preacher's feet. The revival had come!

At the boarding house, after that meeting, some of the men showed unmistakable signs that the services were affecting them. Witticisms were noticeably absent. Criticism had a new quality. One man asked, "W'y do a think women be always pious?" But the question was heard in silence. One of them said afterward, "They was solemnized." The boy Jake had rebuked was deeply disturbed. "Hi wanted t' go for'ard," he said, "but was afeard. 'E 'adn' asked for sinners yet."

"That's w'at I say," said Spargo, agreeing with the implication of the boy's remark. "S'pose somebody be killed in the pit, or die afore the invitation be gived! 'Oo's responsible?"

"Us must pray that dawn't 'appen," said Penglaze.

The middle of Noble's second week came. Three sermons had been pointed at the unredeemed. When the third was finished the organ began without announcement, "Who'll be the Next?" a song of the village chapels throughout Cornwall. The minister stood silent while the instrument wooed the audience with unspoken words. The first stanza finished, he said, simply, "Who?" The choir took up the refrain softly, pleadingly as instructed. At its end he again said, "Who?" Suddenly a man's voice sounded from the audience. "Hi will," he shouted, and went to the altar. Again the minister said, "Who?" and his voice vibrated with the appeal of generous welcome to all. "Who?" It seemed so easy to induce them. The rustle in the congregation almost stopped the singing, and, more, the choir itself grew smaller. From every pew some one was groping for the aisle. The altar rail became crowded from end to end. Tears, promises, confessions came from the converts as they arose from their knees. One man stretched out his hands while he still knelt. "I knaw naow," he said, " 'oosoever mean me. 'E mean you too! Anybody." A widow pleaded with her daughter: "Come es on, Annie! Come es with thy mother t' see Father!" Mr. Noble said it was Pentecost over again.

At the beginning of the third week the minister suggested prayers for friends. People were urged to name the person or persons they wished to see saved. The names mentioned were mostly of strangers to Jim. He thought the suggestion was indicative of generous interest, of a Christian spirit. For some of the persons who arose and made requests he had a deep respect. They were good men, pious men, solicitous for their friends. But when Penglaze stood up a foreboding filled him. A fear numbed him as he waited. Said Penglaze, "Hi want t' ask prayers for Jake Collins, a backslider, an' Bob Allen, a agnostic." Jim's heart went cold. He wanted to stand up and contradict the statements, to say that both were lies. He wanted to leave the place but sat helpless and silent. He hated the incriminating words, he struggled with a hate of the man who spoke them. But this was a revival. "Souls" was the magic word which sanctioned all the extremes of it. Penglaze was in earnest if his earnestness was misguided. Penglaze did not know Jake. Jake had never made a profession. Not one of the people present understood Allen. How could Penglaze openly accuse, condemn, without knowing? True enough, Jim himself did not know where to classify Allen in the category of the church, but both Allen and Jake represented the best he had ever known of kind, friendly living. Jim knew it was a miserable misunderstanding. Filthy rags! Interest in souls! The meeting lost its glow for him, became a Babel of sound. Babel! Misunderstanding.

The week totaled a hundred conversions, and Noble said his work was done. Fervor was at white heat, but he had to go. Some remonstrated, argued, censured, but he must go. Other fields were "white unto harvest." He must go.

And he left. His itinerary must be kept.

He left a fire of his own kindling for some one else to tend. He said it tore his heart to leave. The fire would cease to flame. After the flame, embers would glow for a time, darken, and then die. The converts would sing the songs he had sobbed for a few weeks; they would remember the tales he had told, relive the emotions of the high moments of his endeavor. But then what? They would find the food he had given insufficient, lacking in nourishment for the strength they needed. Resolves—all too many of them—made in such a surge of excitement, would be like writings on sand or, worse, on water. The void his departure left, poor Tozer could not fill. Tozer's best advice was that they "be strong in the Lord." If he had misgivings, his heavy features did not show them.

The gossip of the village took stock of the situation and cast up its accounts. Blunt comparisons of Tozer and Noble were made wherever people met and were free to talk. Noble did not escape assay, and the process became more and more cruel as the meeting receded. He was a showman. He didn't teach; only excited. He left while his credit was good. The folks he had coaxed to a frenzy deserved a week of his time for serious counsel. Perhaps the collection wouldn't have been as large after such a week as it had been the night he called Pentecost.

They prophesied—and not always with derision—the period of regeneration for the converts they knew. Bets were paid in words that had been made about those the meeting would not touch. Some quiet inconspicuous soul escaped analysis.

In the mine, Jim and Jake took several turns at it. Jim had been an eyewitness of the meeting; Jake had only a hearsay of it. He said: "I dedn' need that. They'm all the same."

Jim did not reply to many of Jake's comments, and he let that one pass.

When the meeting had ended, Jim was glad it was over. He was not sure he was not sorry it had happened. To Jake, he said, "W'at now?"

"Aas, w'at now?" answered Jake. "What 'appened after the last? An' the one afore that?"

"W'ere?" asked Jim.

"Anyw'ere," said Jake.

Jim did not answer.

"The better the revival's said t' be, the worse 'e is, seem like. The more the 'citement, the frailer the converts. They'm like chuldern borned afore time."

Jim grunted recognition of the idea.

"You an' me both 'ave seed good come out of a revival, comrade, but the harm they do be more'n the good."

"Oosh," said Jim reluctantly, more in respect than in agreement.

"A man w'at make a show of 'e's self in a revival an' then fail must do somethin' to 'isself you can't see n'r measure."

Both men remained silent until the next rest spell. Both had stayed with the subject through the work period, and Jim was sure Jake would resume it in spite of his playful, "Time t' blow a bit."

"Dost tha remember the time the Peters 'ouse burned, back 'ome?"

"Aas."

" 'Tis said the mother went in the blazin' buildin' t' get a cheel. 'Er wrapped the babe in some beddin' an' brought un out, 'erself in flames. The cheel was saved, but 'er died of burns."

"So I 'eard."

"If the Cousin Jacks us knaw ever be saved, that's the way 'e must be done—wrapped up in a blanket an' carried through the fire."

Again Jim grunted, but said no word.

"The Methodee salvation dawn't save, my son. 'E leave too much of the job to the sinner."

Jake was in dead earnest. His feelings were touched by the futility he tried to illustrate. After a short period he smiled and spoke again.

"Let's forgit un, my son. Maybe that's the way 'e will happen, even if Cousin John dawn't knaw it. Just wrapped in somethin' an' carried through the fire."

Chapter Fifteen

JIM TRIED TO FACE THE ISSUES that the past weeks, the recently past days had brought him, without being troubled about them. He tried, as he said, to hold them in his hand and look at them. That idea, he conceded, he got from Allen. Although he called it a brave notion, he found it a hard one to put into practice. Jake had the knack of it, had come by it naturally. Few things outside his immediate loyalties moved Jake. It was this that made others think he was indifferent. He was not indifferent; he was different, that was all. No one but Jim knew how he had grieved about Tom, when the boy went to his brothers in another camp. Jake stayed with Jim for a reason Jim understood with an appreciation akin to pain. Both Jake and Allen had a way of sorting, choosing, sifting, that set them apart. Jake said, "My rubble pile do grow fast, a lot faster than the ore. But a bit of hore be worth a mountain of rubble." Allen was of the same mind. He said, "Mind the truth, boay; never mind the rest." There was no name on Jim's tongue for this process of looking at things, at ideas and keeping one's mind free from resentment, passion, or other emotions, but Jim coveted it. " 'E is 'ard t' do —'ard for me, that is," he said. He realized, too, that he could not select "the ore from the rubble," with any certainty because all he knew of what he deemed the source of the truth, he knew by hearsay only. As always, when confronted with a predicament, he wanted to talk to Allen about it.

Frequently enough Allen had surprised Jim by seeming to know what he was pondering. Numerous times Allen had seemed to read his mind. Jim smiled as he thought of it. " 'E must be a wizard," he said. So, he was not surprised when, one evening, Allen came into the room where he was sitting and said, "If you need a light, my son, maybe I could find a match."

"Thanks, Bob. I knaw," said Jim eagerly.

At Allen's suggestion they left the house for the open air. For a time they walked in silence. Jim liked the wordless stretches he and Allen often walked together. And Allen was assured by Jim's confidence. He wanted the younger man to sense his sympathy. It was assuring that Jim felt free to be still.

As they walked, the memory came to Jim of that first racking loneliness, when he left the house and climbed to the hill-top where he met Allen. The subjects that had absorbed him then came back to him. That seemed like a long time ago— like years, he thought. Others, just as perturbing, followed in rapid succession. Fancy gave them face and form as they moved through the gloom. As each came and went and came to go again in the rapid recall and dismissal of his thought, he wondered if all of life's problems were to be guessed at only, were without answer, their solutions varying according to the minds that mulled them. Finally Allen broke the silence.

"Jim, my son!"

"Aas, Bob."

"A lot of things have happened since we met on this hill."

"Aas."

"Out of the lot, what has seemed most important to you?"

Jim's answer came easily and quickly: "W'en I fust made out the word in the book."

Allen had not been thinking of the weight Jim's uppermost desire would have on his choice; the answer he received, therefore, was not what he expected. So he remained silent for a while.

"What did the meeting do for you, Jim?"

Jim was slow in saying. To tell just what it had done for him seemed like disloyalty. He maintained a family sense in his church relation. To speak to an outsider of dissensions that might occur in church, of its faults and misadventures, seemed a sort of treachery. Still, to think of Allen in such terms halted him too. This man exemplified to him something no other had ever done unless it was Jake. The two were akin in so many ways. Bob was waiting, but Jim remained silent.

"I heard prayers were asked for Jake," Bob said.

"Aas."

With a word Allen had shoved him against the very thing he would have avoided. He was sure Allen must know prayers had been asked for him too. He wondered what Allen would say. Allen could swear—Jim had heard him. Allen would fight. That Jim had seen. Would he go to Penglaze if that fact should slip and perchance Allen had not heard of it? If so, what would happen? Jim hoped—

"Did you hear Penglaze ask prayers for Jake?"

"Aas."

Jim's answer was half voiced. He felt the sharp sting of rebuke from his esteemed friend. And yet how could a man defend another at a time and in a place like that? Bob could hardly expect that. Perhaps Allen had already spoken to Penglaze! If so, what had he said? The words between the two would be cruel, and Allen would have the advantage. But Penglaze, slow-witted, blunt, short-tempered, could say nasty things, and he would.

"I wondered, Jim, how you felt when you heard it."

Jim told of the meeting, the requests and his suspicions

when Penglaze arose. He mentioned his resentment, his impulse to defend Jake. As he had felt, he spoke, cutting close to the truth. "Penglaze dawn't knaw Jake," he said. "A man ought t' knaw afore 'e spayk like that. Hit spoiled the meetin' for me."

"Yes, my son. But the meeting is past and gone now. Did it spoil anything else?"

Jim did not know what Allen meant, and said so. Allen knew he would have to come closer to his point if he were to give Jim the help he had hoped to do. He waited to formulate his approach. The while, the snow crunched under their feet, and sleigh bells tinkled in the distance. Once the knocker line jangled, and the hoist answered with coughing, gasping breaths.

"I dawn't think, Jim, that learnin' letters be the biggest thing that 'ave 'appened t' you. I b'lieve you will find I be right, some day."

(Allen dropped into Cornish when he became earnest or talked to himself. He often wondered if it would be so to the end of his days. "They words an' phrases seem t' carry my feelin's better," he said.)

"When Walters died, you questioned the preacher and you questioned the Book."

"Aas."

"You questioned a lot of things, smaller things, and now the church has lost something. Am I right?"

"Aas."

"Questions are dangerous, Jim."

" 'Ow c'n a man help 'isself?"

"Some seem to make a success of it. They are led through life. They learn words and phrases to steer by as they learn to behave at the table. Life is a set of manners for them."

Momentarily Jim hoped Allen had forgotten Penglaze.

"The things you questioned and the reading you plan to do are details, my son, the details of life."

"If they be details, w'at be the big things?"

Allen gave minutes to his answer before he gave it voice. He knew well enough the moorings some minds required to be kept from wreck—how many said, "Damme, it's no use," and turned themselves adrift. He wondered if he had the right estimate of this boy. He wondered, too, how he came to have such a profound interest in Jim. Did he dare say what he had in mind? Safety for most people lay in the size of the pool they sailed, their seas of life. Their little guidebooks and charts suited the size of their craft. This boy seemed headed for wider horizons and more trying journeys. When he spoke, at last, his voice was subdued, serious, his words slow and Cornish.

"You be the bigges' thing in the worl', Jim, so long as you be hones' with yourself. Hones' men dawn't ask questions an' then be 'feard of the hanswers. 'Tis the hanswer you want. Hi 'ave 'eard of folks afeard t' ask questions for fear of hoffendin' God. They must live in 'ell. Hit seem like a hinsult t' God t' be afeard of un. You wouldn' want your cheel t' be afeard of you."

Your cheel! The words stirred every nerve in Jim's body. He was to have a cheel! Pol said so. For a moment the present slipped away, and again he heard her words that last evening at home. In that moment he traveled the months to the time when the babe would be in her arms. Allen was forgotten, and his questions, for many oblivious steps. Jim returned as he had gone, suddenly. He answered. But Allen did not surmise how far Jim had traveled since he had spoken.

As though speaking to himself, Allen said, "Few seem to know what He meant when He said, 'Our Father.' "

There was something in Allen's voice that spoke to new depths, new and fuller understanding in Jim. Jim wished others in the boarding house might have heard it. But would they have grasped it? Allen's tone soothed an anxiety that had gnawed at his peace since the night he had rebelled against the preaching at Walters' funeral. Doubt, he called it; and doubt was proscribed by the code he had learned. He wondered what Allen would say about it.

"Bob, Hi find it 'ard t' keep from doubtin' sometimes."

"Why try, my son? Doubt is natural to a man. Your stomach takes some food and refuses others; your mind does that, too. What you would not eat a year ago, you eat and like now. Again, so with your mind. We've got to take honest minds to religion as well as to mining—honest minds. Understand?"

"Hi b'lieve so, Bob."

"But that's anough, my son," said Bob, sliding again into Cornish. "I was afeard you might be hupset, driftin' like, because of the praycher an' Penglaze. Mustn' let that hupset e, boay. Religion be as close to a man as the marra of 'e's bones or the color of 'e's blood. Christianity be the finest face religion ever wore. Penglaze an' the praycher, hones' though they be, be poor, splotched mirrors reflectin' a fine picter, that's all."

The two men were back in the village again. They passed the humble cottages on the outskirts in silence. There was nothing about them to distract their thoughts or provoke a comment. Each little house represented a fragment of some foreign peasantry. The bosses and tradespeople lived on the other side of town. On their left the school loomed, a large, boxlike shadow. At sight of it Allen asked, "How are the studies doing, Jim?"

"A bit slow, Bob. Hev'rything 'ave t' wait on readin' an' writin', an' both of they 'ave t' wait on talkin'."

"How's that?"

"There bayn't no letters fur the sounds of a Devonshire man's words, an' so, no way of spellin' mun. Hi must learn new ways of sayin' things."

Bob saw the difficulty. The teacher might advise in correct expression, but where was the pupil to practice it? For

Jim to drop the old-land idioms too soon meant jeers and mockery.

"Jim!"

"Aas, Bob."

"You asked me to talk to you as I do to the master. Suppose you talk to me as the master wants you to talk!"

Jim shook his head. "Hi b'lieve 'e's aysier t' write one way an' talk another—for a w'ile, at least."

Allen understood the timidity that restrained the boy, and let the matter drop. He knew that gradually changes would work themselves into his speech. The influence of his reading, the use of better language by the more Americanized of the population, and that of the handful of Americans in the town would have a progressive effect. But it would be slow. Jim would spend most of his time with foreigners in the mine who would be of no help, and with his kinsmen in the boarding house who would help him less. And besides, the welcome that the Copper Country extended to the brawn of its population included no criticism of their efforts in speech. Bosses, store people, saloon men willingly adjusted their minds and ears to the Babel of accent, the oddities of lip and tongue, and left the speakers to their own devices.

Suddenly Allen's picture turned, and he smiled to himself. "The Cousin Jacks' forms and inflections are taking root in their adopted soil!" He had laughed at a Cornishism used unwittingly only a few evenings ago by the schoolmaster. They be contagious, he thought. The flavor of Cornwall will last on the peninsula a long w'ile hafter the Cornishman be extinc'.

It was late when they reached Uren's. The house was dark except for a candle left burning in the kitchen. Jim swept the snow from his boots and handed the broom to Allen.

"Hi tried my 'and at a letter last night," he said, lowering his voice.

"Did you post it?"

"Hi dedn'. Hi was afeard of the henvelope."

"I'll fix one for you, Jim."

"Thank e, Bob, but I want t' say more."

Allen pinched the candle wick, and they went to bed by the light of the snow on the ground and roofs.

Two nights later Jim was sitting on his bed with his overcoat thrown around his shoulders. On his knee was a small square of board he had found and assigned to this very purpose. On the board were sheets of lined paper he had partially filled. His letters were in the large uncertain style of a beginner, done with a pencil.

He had reached the limit of his learning and sat daunted by the things he wanted to say. One moment he was thrilled at the sight of his own words on the paper, and the next he despaired as he fancied what he had yet to do. "Still," he said, "three months ago I couldn' tell my awn name on the tailboard of a cart."

His face brightened to the ideas that trooped through his mind. Hev'ry day do bring pages of things t' write! The talks of the men, the tales they told, the retorts of the touchy and suspicious! And Spargo's wit, that turned trouble aside and even made the men laugh at themselves. That would be worth telling. Penglaze couldn't be missed. He would make Pol think of old Blatchford back there. How often he and Pol had laughed at him and pitied him too. Jake's calm, steadying comment, his unwavering friendship would light the whole scene. John Burt's store and the plods he heard there would make a letter alone. They 'ams an' bacon with clo'es on. He smiled broadly at the thought of it. And Stanton! What an oddity he was! He would be misplaced, no matter where he was. The weather, too, the snow, now sodden and gray, now refreshed and brightened by a new fall to become dull and gray again in a few hours. It would all be new to Pol.

Writing was like painting a picture. It caught events and

people on the run and held them fast, fixed them as paint fixed a stream, a tree, a cloud, that a day or a season changed. Mother, he recalled, put flowers between the pages of her Bible—the Bible she couldn't read—and sniffed them after the gardens were dead. Jim smiled at his own fancy. He wondered if Mother did it as "tribbit" to the Book she could not honor otherwise. No, it was to preserve the flowers, their color, their fragrance beyond their day. The Book lingered in his mind—a thick, black, hard-covered volume, a ribbon tooled on its back in a circle with a bow at the bottom. In the circle were the words, "Holy Bible." It was fat and springy because of Mother's whim for flowers, and its leaves were stained from their moisture.

Jim looked at his scrawls again with eyes that saw magic. "Writin'!" he said. "An' I've 'eard some say they hated a pen, despised writin', couldn' drive theirselves t' write!" And then he wondered if he would have felt as he did if he had learned to write in his childhood. He pondered. Perhaps, what had made parting from Pol so hard, had given him his greatest anxiety since reaching Allouez was, after all, the best thing that could have happened to him. How was a man to tell?

Jim was still deep in his reverie when Allen said, "Fitchered, my son? At the hend of your rope?"

"Aas, you, fitchered."

Allen stood over him, smiling. "The sperrit be willin', but the pencil be weak."

"Hi wonder if 'e'll always be that way!"

" 'E's oftener the other way, Hi b'lieve, my son. W'en my pencil do stop, I'm forked. Can I 'elp e?"

Allen took the pencil, a fresh sheet of paper and said, "Strike."

"Tell the maid," Jim began. And Bob wrote until Jim said: "That's all. Thanks, Bob."

Bob took an envelope, and Jim repeated the address which nearly covered its surface.

"That's a lot of address t' find a village no bigger'n a mole'ill."

"W'y izza, you?"

"There may be a 'alf-dozen places of the same name in the Duchy, an' all this be t' make it aysy for the postman."

Allen watched Jim as he moistened the seal, thinking of the effect reading and writing would have on the boy's life.

"Well, Jim, I feel the same's if the cap'n was abaout t' give me the sack. My job be abaout awver."

Jim did not answer. Something in Bob's look stopped the thanks on his lips. Hi've seen un there afore, but never as plain as this time.

Allen turned to the stair and went down. A Cornish village, a Cornish cottage, a Cornish girl were before his eyes. The girl held a letter in her hand. I 'ave seen parents glow awver the first writin's of a child, he thought, but this woman— If she be 'alf like 'e, 'er will spen' the day thicky note come in a dream. Iss, she will read w'at I wraute but they other scribbles will be like copperplate t' she.

Jim stayed in the room puzzled by that look. Hi wonder could a be? he asked himself. 'E never mentioned nothin'. 'E keep 'is awn counsel awful close. 'E's a man, ev'ry inch of un. Hi wonder. Writin' such letters must be 'ard on un.

Jim knew there were many Cornishmen in the village who could not write. Some could read "easy print" as they called it, but never tried to make a letter. He recalled the old woman at the chapel saying, "Lawzee, Jan can't write!" and then going away wiping the tears from her eyes. "Same as bein' buried alive, for she," he muttered. Carefully he tried to open the envelope without tearing it. He took the pages out and sought an open space. Allen had filled them completely. He took another sheet, tore it in half and wrote,

"Pol, tell my mother and father how I be, and say I'll write."
Again he closed the letter and held it until the flap was secure.
"Thank God," he said, "that that thought come to me." He
found comfort in the assurance that Pol would have told
them although he had never asked her before.

Allen found the middle room empty when he went down.
He looked out the window absently. He recognized most of
the men who went this way and that, to the stores, to the mine
or walked only for lack of a better purpose. " 'E take a bit of
courage for boays like they t' leave 'ome for Australia or
Africa or America, as they do," he said to himself. Again the
Cornish village came back. "An' they women bidin' there.
They bid their men good-bye—men 'oo can't write to mun—
t' go t' tryin' climates, strange work, new ways of life. They
bayn't all as steadfast as this one. Hi mind Jan Trevarrow.
'E's wife, awnly a bride, clung to un an' pleaded that 'e ask
some one t' write. 'Awnly a word an' I'll knaw the rest,' 'er
said. But Jan never wraute. The pore maid jus' faded an'
went in a decline. But Jan was a exception, I dare say. Foo
Cornishmen be of 'is stripe."

Next day as the miners stood about the shaft waiting for
the whistle to blow, Jake heard Jenkins tell the captain he
would not be out Friday. "Hi'll be goin' down to Hancock,"
Jenkins said. Underground, Jake told Jim what he had
heard.

"Well, comrade, w'at of it? A lot of men go to 'Ancock an'
Calumet, an' dawn't tell th' cap'n."

"That be worth mentionin' then, edna? Jenkins be that
dif'runt."

"Thee's got somethin' else in thee head. W'at izza?"

"Hi 'eard Jenkins was buyin' a bit of furniture an' 'ad a
'ouse rented. W'at do that mean?"

Jim did not answer. His own dreams and desires were close
to the surface. Jenkins was about to achieve what looked a
long way off to him.

At the supper table Friday night Jim noticed that Jenkins was absent. Spargo mentioned the empty place.

"You won't see 'e 'ere no more. 'E do 'ave a 'aouse of 'is awn," said Mrs. Uren.

" 'Ave 'is missus come?" asked Northy.

"She 'ave come. She come tonight by th' stage with three little ones, an' I do 'ear, a brother," continued the boarding missus.

"Good for 'er, 'er brother could come too. Two little ones be a care for a woman t' take across the ocean," said Northy.

"As if a man do 'elp a woman much at any time," said Mrs. Uren daringly.

"Not so 'ard, missus, not so 'ard," said Spargo.

"An' a thousand miles by land," said Northy. "That be the 'ardest part of travel. Can't make no mistakes on a boat. Once you get on, you stay. 'E's aysy to take th' wrong train in New York or Chicago."

"We found un a hawful long way from Chicago 'ere, longer than from New York t' Chicago, dedn' us, comrade?" said Jake.

"Aas," Jim said. "The train was hawful slow; no place t' wash or sleep, an' no time t' eat."

"Hi pity a woman travelin' with children," said Northy.

"But 'er 'ad a brother, dedn' e say, missus?" asked Jake.

"Iss. But little 'elp 'e was. More care than a cheel, I should say. 'E is blind as a bat."

"Blind!" There was a unison of voices.

"Iss, you. Blind. Both heyes shot aout by a missed hole. Been blind for years." Mrs. Uren was informative only, her tone showing no interest in the episode beyond telling it.

" 'Oo told e that? Shorely Jenkins wouldn' bring a blind man awver from the ol' country," said Penglaze.

"Mrs. Doney," retorted Mrs. Uren, nettled at having her information questioned. "Mrs. Doney got supper ready for mun w'en they got 'ere."

"Maybe 'e do 'ave a bit of money to keep un," suggested Northy, trying to smooth the surface Penglaze's bluntness had disturbed.

"Cousin Jacks 'oo do work in th' mines dawn't often 'ave money," snapped Mrs. Uren.

"Do e mean Jenkins do keep un, paid 'is way awver?" asked Penglaze.

"You better ask Jenkins. Maybe 'e will tell e," retorted the woman.

"There be poor'aouses in Hengland," said Penglaze. "There bayn't no call for a man t' keep 'is wife's brother."

"P'r'aps there be, Penglaze," said Jake. "P'r'aps there be." There was something that sounded ominous to Jim in Jake's voice. He thrilled with expectation. He knew that Jake chose his occasions and met them well armed.

"Hi dawn't see it," returned Penglaze, his words more growled than spoken.

"P'r'aps you need specs, my son," Jake countered.

"W'at do e mean?" asked Penglaze.

"Hi knawed a man back 'ome 'oo 'ad no ear for moosic," explained Jake. "'E used t' say a passel of ducks a-quackin' sounded no diff'runt to 'e than a choir. An' 'e was a good man too. Hi never 'eard 'e say there was no sich thing as moosic or a man was a fool t' sing. P'r'aps thy heyes be like 'is ears."

Jake's retort stung like a bunch of nettles. Everybody there knew of Penglaze's request in the revival, and all had wondered how Jake would balance accounts. Some said he didn't care, that he was a happy-go-lucky old bach; and a few charged him with fear. Some one said, "Bravo, Collins!"

"Good for you, my son," said another.

But Jake was done only as far as publicity was concerned. Penglaze was completely done.

Mrs. Uren, standing at the stove, was ill at ease. She did not like Penglaze any more than the rest, but she was afraid of arguments at the table. She knew the truculence of the breed she fed, and averted open trouble as best she could. A boarding house had a name to make or maintain. She wanted hers to be good.

"If you 'ave done eatin'," she said, "you can leave the table. Hi want t' go aout tonight an' must 'urry th' dishes through."

The men pushed back the forms and stepped over them. All went into the sitting room but Jake and Penglaze, who sat at the end of the table. Jake waited for him. When he came up Jake spoke.

"Penglaze, thee dedn' ask prayers for Jinkins, but thee hought t' ask Jinkins t' pray for thee."

" 'Oo be you t' talk t' me like that?" asked Penglaze.

"You knaw my name. Take my advice, my son."

There was no quarrel in Jake's tone, or fear, only the emphasis a man feels when a right has been infringed. Self-respect was finding expression, self-defense was being made. It had a double objective. It might do some good. Jake knew what had instigated Penglaze's public request. He knew the man's pride in his own righteousness. His kind was common enough among Cornishmen. The letter of the law was the whole law to him. Perhaps something of this sort would waken him. Jake knew his chance would come if he waited, and waiting for Jake was easy. He was never in a hurry. And so it had come. Penglaze did not answer; Jake said no more.

As was customary the men scattered to their rooms for coats and hats, and the house was soon empty and quiet.

Before a week had passed the news of Mrs. Jenkins' arrival had been discussed in every Cornish home and loafing place in the village. Most of the men sided with Penglaze. It was unnecessary, foolish, or, in simple Cornish, "plain maze." A half-dozen in the company store had had their say about it and gratified themselves with their own opinions.

"Iss, you, maze is right," said one.

"Soft with 'is missus, I spect—petticoat government. I do

like to see a man rule 'is awn 'aouse. A man do pay the bills,''
added another.

"A blin' man do eat an' wear as much as a seein' man. Some
load t' come off one man's pay,'' said another. "W'at do you
say, Uncle Billy?''

Uncle Billy had been a silent listener to most of the talk.
He was leaning against the counter, near the poor box from
which he had filled his short black clay pipe. He too was short
and black—black of eyes, beard, and hair—a stocky, muscular
man in his late fifties. Uncle Billy had been a "wrassler" in
the old country and "back wes','' it was said, a powerful man
with the jackets. His temper was known to be short and to be
avoided or soothed at the first gleam through his unbarbered
beard. No one in Allouez had ever seen him either wrestle or
fight. The tales told about him lingered around him, nur-
tured and strengthened by his surly demeanor. The question
asked of him was a sop thrown to Cerberus.

"Iss, Bill, w'at do you say?''

"In th' fust place, 'e is none of your bloody business; and,
in the second place, you be all goin' hoff 'alf-cocked.''

Uncle Billy looked his auditors over as though to catch the
first show of resentment and pounce upon it, but he saw none.
He was secure in his reserve, in his ambush of beard, the
shadow of his slouching hat, the fabled heroics that persisted
about him.

"Hi do come from the same place as 'Arry Jinkins. Hi
knawed 'is father an' worked with un afore 'e was killed. Hi
knawed Bill 'Unt afore 'e lost 'e's heyes. Hi knaw th' whole
tale from A to zed. Th' plod I can tell about 'Arry an' 'Unt
do make you look like a passel of old women.'' Uncle Billy
looked his listeners over again, and again was sure of his
ground. No one seemed to wish an argument. A "good man
with the jackets" was still a good man to keep in a good
temper. One man, anxious to fraternize with the old athlete,
said: "Good boay, Bill! Let's 'ave un.''

" 'Arry's father was poor as th' rest of us an' took th' boay undergraound w'en 'e was eight year old t' carry drills an' water an' twist a bit an' add a halfpenny or two to the pay. One Saturday night they dedn' come up, an' the cap'n dedn' miss mun. W'en they dedn' come 'ome th' missus—the ol' man's missus, that was—was maze with fright. 'Er run to th' neighbors an' told 'er tale. Th' boay Hunt went to th' mine halone an' went daown. 'E found the boay in the drift cryin' in the dark. 'Is light was blawed aout by th' blast. The ol' man was killed in 'is place. 'Unt took th' cheel on 'is back an' carried un two hundred fathoms hup t' grass. In the mornin' the old man was took up. Years after, th' cheel married Hunt's sister."

" 'Aow did 'Unt lose 'is heyes?"

"Hark to me, my son. Hi dedn' come awver 'ere t' crake all night. Ask 'Unt. Hi wanted to shaw e your bloody 'pinions was all haddle."

Uncle Billy filled his pipe again, snapped his fingers to his dog, and left the store without a nod or a word of parting. A silence followed his graceless going, and an evident relief settled upon his audience.

"Hi dedn' knaw 'e an' Jinkins was close," said one.

"They bayn't," said another. "Ol' Bill bayn't close t' nobody. 'E couldn' be."

Chapter Sixteen

Jɪᴍ ᴄᴏɴᴛɪɴᴜᴇᴅ ᴛʜᴇ ʜᴀʙɪᴛ he had formed at home of attending the Class Meeting, held each Sunday before the morning service. The Class was for men only, for such as took their professions seriously. Usually fewer than a dozen sat in the small alcove of the church at such meetings, silent, solemn men who appeared to have met for some weighty unhappy consideration. It was not a secret meeting, and yet, by most of the membership of the little chapel, it was unconsidered, ignored. Those who did not attend would say they were not good enough, were too worldly for the spiritual standards of the Class. It was for the pious only.

As the worshipers came into the meeting they either knelt at a chair or sat, bending forward in silent supplication. The end of the prayer was marked with an audible amen or a moaning sigh. They then waited in silence until the leader asked for a hymn, which they sang without books or the support of an instrument. Any one might start it when it was asked for. Penglaze lined the verse of the hymn he wanted. His favorite was:

> A charge to keep I have,
> A God to glorify,
> A never-dying soul to save,
> And fit it for the sky.

This was the battle hymn of their struggle. It gave the emotional pitch and expressed their endeavor better than they could do it themselves. Ministers said this body denoted by its size the spiritual strength of the church. No women attended, nor had the women a counterpart of it for their spiritual relaxation or exercise. As a result the singing lacked the lilt and completeness of a mixed congregation. Both singing and praying seldom had a note of triumph in them.

The leader read a scrap of Scripture or recited a bit from memory, speaking for a few minutes to its suggestion. The remarks were always grave, slightly admonitive, faintly hortatory. And then they testified or prayed at the prompting of the leader, uttering difficult, heroic phrases that bound them to their adopted purpose with thongs that cut both flesh and spirit. Most of them spoke slowly, laboriously, conscious of the heavy impositions they placed upon themselves. Occasionally one refused to add his voice to either song or prayer or testimony. Such a one was Stanton, who came and went from week to week in unfailing loyalty. Always a little wait occurred in the serial of testimonies in deference to him; always he kept his thought unspoken. Of course he was discussed. Why did he go if he wouldn't take part? Why should a man make himself so conspicuous? Why persist in being odd? Didn't he know the Class was meant for testimony and prayer? Once Stanton was reproached for his silence. He retorted, "Talk be the smalles' part of religion, to my mind!"

A story was told of him at which many smiled after sufficient time had elapsed to permit it. The wife of the only man he ever attached himself to became ill and died. During her illness, Stanton visited his friend daily. " 'Ow be e t'day, maister?" he asked. The reply vouched the hope or fear of the household. Stanton said not another word. After a stay of fifteen or twenty minutes, he arose and left. The day the woman died he called but asked no question. He drew a chair close to his friend and sat beside him in silence, with his hat on his knee. Without a word he got up, replaced his chair and hat, and left.

Once at least a laugh at the oddity of this tale died at birth when a St. Ives man said, "Th' tide dawn't make a noise, my son, a-comin' in."

Hunt added a new quality to the Class. The first Sunday of his American life found him there. He came guided by his brother-in-law. All eyes turned as the pair entered, to see the newcomer. Hunt was plainly but neatly dressed in black and wore dark glasses to hide his empty orbits. His face was covered with a network of blue lines made by the healing of unwashed wounds, the result of a blast. He walked with military erectness, his face slightly uplifted as though listening for difficult elusive sounds.

" 'E do seem like 'e 'ear heverything," one man remarked.

"Iss, you, an' be still 'arkin' for more," came a reply.

"Hi knawed a blind man back 'ome 'oo could tell w'en 'e passed a 'ouse by the sound 'is feet made on the ground," added a third.

And when he sat he maintained the same straightness of body as when he walked, the same alert attentiveness. Not once did he relax into the arch of his chair.

For three Sundays he came, sitting silently through the services. At the first meeting Jenkins introduced him, and after that Hunt called each man by name as soon as he heard his voice. His memory seemed unfailing. His celerity in coupling names with voices was discussed by all the men who met him.

Two pairs of miners underground discussed him.

" 'Is 'earin' and mindin' of names dawn't s'prise me! Hi always 'eard that blind folks get good hears and deef folks get good heyes. But I wonder w'at 'e will do in meetin'?"

"W'at do e mean? 'E will talk like th' rest, Hi s'pose."

"W'at do a blind man 'ave t' thank God for, is w'at I mean. Th' others will, for this or that an' a lot of things 'e can't."

Put on the track of the other's thought, the questioner added: "An' bein' blind, 'e's dependent too, a load on somebody helse. 'E mus' feel some bad habaout that."

" 'E's young, too, with years afore un. Hi should think 'e'd go maze thinkin' abaout un."

"Hi b'lieve Hi'd wish th' bloody 'ole 'ad finished me aoutright."

The pair came to the ladderway leading up to their stope. "So long," they said, and the question dropped unsettled. So the blind man, unknown to himself, was impressing the community.

Sunday came and went repeatedly, Hunt remaining constant in attendance and in silence. The Class felt his presence deeply, was affected by it noticeably, and puzzled over the problem of the blind man's unspoken thoughts, his unexpressed emotions. In their testimonies and prayers the men avoided phrases, references, narratives that they thought might impinge on the sensitive spirit of one so afflicted. It left them curtailed, restricted, and often speechless. Much of their former freedom was gone. The Class was suffering; occasionally an absence occurred.

One morning Penglaze read of a seaside meeting in which the teacher, sitting in a boat, spoke to an audience lounging or standing on the strand. The descriptive elements of the tale fell on accustomed ears. The audience bided the ceremony inertly, waiting for the comment, however futile, because, poor as it might be, it was more vital than the stumbling attempt to decipher the printed page. Penglaze ended his reading with the familiar lines, "But blessed are your eyes for they see and your ears for they hear." He felt no shock of inappropriateness. He did not observe the startled looks of some of his hearers. For minutes he spoke of the enjoyments of seeing and hearing. Penglaze ended by saying, " 'E must be awful t' be deaf or blind," and then called for remarks or testimony but got none. A second time he asked for a response, to be rewarded only with a stammering prayer. Penglaze arose from his knees to end the service. As he turned toward his little coterie of hearers he was surprised to see Hunt standing, waiting to speak. Every face was turned toward the tall, dark figure. His dark clothes, dark glasses, dark face, and black hair made him look like an effigy of gloom.

His voice saved the moment and the meeting—perhaps the Class. It had a deep baritone richness that suggested many possibilities. Years of blindness and the experience of being always on the border of social groups had led him to speak slowly. He spoke with a West Cornish cadence that he made no pretense to hide.

"Brothers," was his first word, "Hi want you to be that to me and let me be one of you. Hi b'lieve I knaw 'aow you feel just naow—'aow you 'ave been feelin'. That be natural. But I want e to be free. You 'ave heyes to see. Go on seein', an' tell me w'at you see. You mustn' make yourselves blind because I be. You 'urt yourselves. Dawn't forget there be some stars in a blind man's night." He hesitated for a moment as though debating his next words. And then, as though to assure them of his last phrase, he said: "Iss, there be! Stars!" Up to this point he had seemed to be addressing persons beyond the farthest wall of the church, but suddenly he turned as if seized with a longing for intimacy, for friendliness. He faced the men who, until then, were behind him, and went on. Jenkins alone was not looking at the speaker. His face was white and tense, his eyes fixed unseeingly on the floor.

"There be gains, rewards in blindness," Hunt went on, "compensations. You can't knaw: you 'ave heyes. But there be. Dedn' He say, 'Hi've meat to eat ye knaw not of'? So with me. Go on seein', see all you can, and share with me. Talk abaout seein'; talk abaout th' things you see. Dawn't ban beauty from your testimony accaount of me. Bring the aoutdoor glories of God into this place an' talk with gladness of 'eart. Hi'll be glad with e." Again he stopped. He had lost the focus of the faces before him which he found when he turned, and was looking oddly at a chair covered with coats in a corner of the alcove. His lips curved in a smile which lighted one-half of his face oddly. "Come awver t' 'Arry's 'aouse t' see me. Hi do get lonely sometimes. Hi want t' knaw e—all of e."

Penglaze did not know what to say, and after a brief silence the men arose, moved out of their places toward the door, and so closed the meeting.

Jim and Spargo walked back to the house together. They were almost there before either spoke. "Hi be glad 'e spawk, Jack."

"If 'e 'adn' spawk soon 'e would 'a' finished the Class."

"I be fraid 'e would."

That afternoon Jim and Jake were leaving the house—as Jake said, "To blow hourselves out a bit"—when Spargo joined them.

"Three be a craowd," he said laughing.

"Not too big in this case, comrade," Jake replied in welcome. "Come on for th' good of thy soul."

Since Jenkins' family had come, Spargo was very much alone. Jim and Jake understood and were glad to have his company. The three followed the main street to the outskirts of the town and then took the middle of the road, walking abreast.

The meeting of the morning, Penglaze's Scripture, the feeling of dejection and regret, the effect of Hunt's presence on previous meetings, and finally Hunt's talk were retold. As he had attended none of the meetings, Jake was a silent listener. Finally he spoke, spoke to himself, to the trees that arched the road, to the gathering twilight. His voice was low and vibrant.

"Stars in a blind man's night! I wonder w'at they be!"

"Hi dawn't knaw," said Spargo, "but after 'earin' un talk, Hi b'lieve 'e do see more'n a lot of we 'oo 'ave heyes."

" 'Pears like us might learn somethin' if us could get Hunt t' plod a bit," said Jake.

Jim knew that was Jake's "full stop" to talk about Hunt for the time being, and he glanced at Spargo to see if he got Jake's hint.

For a distance they walked without talk, looking down the road or into the snow-carpeted woods. The snow was no longer a light, fluffy coverlet, a plaything of the winds, drifting from place to place and beautifying what obstructed it. Rather it was a sodden, worn-out, poverty-ridden thing that had made a slow descent from fairy palaces to slums.

"The back of winter be about brawk," said Jim.

"Oosh," Jack agreed.

Jake said nothing.

Jack put no high value on silence. A few yards and he said: "I've 'eard spaych be silver but silence be gold. T' me silence be a waste of time if a man 'ave good comp'ny."

Jake looked at Spargo with a sparkle of appreciation in his eyes, but his lips did not move. Jim chuckled audibly.

"I 'ear Lobb an' Prisk 'ave left taown," Jack went on after he had cleared the way for more talk; "gone daown t' the iron camps—t' be minin' cap'ns, I s'pose."

"Did they leave by the same stage?" Jake asked.

Jim and Jack grinned, remembering the fight and the finger marks on Prisk's face.

" 'Ow be cap'ns choosed?" asked Jim.

"I wonder sometimes abaout that," said Jack. "T' 'ear the boays at the 'aouse, Cousin Jacks be always choosed because they knaw minin' an' c'n manage men."

"Thicky rule be too broad, my son," said Jake. "No race of men c'n be bundled t'gether an' ticketed that there way."

Jack was in his native element. "I be 'fraid you bayn't all Cornish, Jake," he said.

"Look at our cap'n," Jake said, "a fine man. An' then compare un with Cap'n Trezize awver 'cross the Portage— 'e think 'e's Phara an' 'is men be the chuldern of Isrul."

"An' I fancy they bayn't all miners. I knaw a cobbler awver Atlantic way 'oo was took by a relative daown on the Menominee t' be a minin' cap'n. Iss, you, 'e was a Cousin Jack. 'Is relative took un to the shaft talkin' abaout the work. 'Do I 'ave t' go daown there, comrade?' asked the shoemaker, pointing into the pit. 'Shore, if you be a cap'n,' the relative answered. The cobbler shook 'e's 'ead. 'Shoemakin' be awnly a 'alf a loaf,' 'e said, 'but I c'n do without tother 'alf.' An' 'e turned away. There's prob'bly more wearin' duck coats 'oo bayn't miners," concluded Jack.

"That be a purty tale," said Jim.

"An' 'e's true," argued Jack, "but I fancy most of mun be good miners."

"An' good men," said Jim.

"Most," agreed Jack, "but some be hawful praoud of their jobs. There's a himage in these 'ere parts 'oo comed 'ere early w'en the top boss was called a hagent. 'Tis told that a Cornish boay come to un, meek-like, an' said, 'Cap'n, playse, sir, could e give me a job?' " Spargo stopped, drew himself up, and glared at the imaginary and innocent suppliant and said, " 'Cap'n, did e say? Cap'n, my son! I do make they!' "

Jim and Jake laughed heartily at Jack's act. Both enjoyed his imitations. Jim said he had a gift. Jake said, "Jack, boay, I want e t' grant me a favor."

"Shore 'nough," said Jack promptly.

"W'en I be gone, dawn't tell no plods about me. You do mun too lifelike." Jake was as serious as a curate.

Jim grinned, but Jack looked woebegone. "You 'ave made me promise away a lot of fun, Jake Collins," he said.

"If you c'n be seryus, Jack, I'd like t' ask e summat," said Jim.

"Spayk on," said Jack, "if 'e edn' another favor."

"I 'eard the boays talkin' about the names of the camps: Calumet, Hecla, Osceola, Delaware, an' others. The boays said they'm Indian. W'at do they mean?"

"I dawn't knaw," said Jack. "I bayn't a Hindian."

"Dost tha knaw Allouez? 'Ow izza *way* an' end in zed?"

"Best go down t' Baraga w'ere there be Indians an' ask, Jim. I couldn' tell e."

"This be far anough," Jake said, and they turned around.

Before they had gone a hundred yards they noticed two men approaching whom the past two months had made familiar to Allouez. Arm in arm they came, one of them erect and attent, lifting his feet in a telltale manner as he stepped. The distance between them shortened rapidly. Jenkins introduced Collins to Hunt, who had already recognized Spargo and Holman by their good afternoons.

"Are e settled yet an' feel at 'ome, 'Arry?" Spargo asked.

"Iss, you, we be settled well anough, but 'e do take time t' feel at 'ome with new furniture, new kiddles an' pans, an' the missus strange t' hev'rything an' hev'rybody."

"Hi c'n see that, comrade, although I 'adn' thought of un afore," replied Jack. "Hi s'pose, by that measure, 'e was 'ard t' say good-bye t' kiddles an' pans too."

Harry smiled. "She did bring a foo fancy bits of cloam with 'er that 'er couldn' part with. 'Er 'ad mun wrapped like they was craown jewels."

"She will say 'er prayers t' they," laughed Jack.

"Hi be 'feard they won't 'elp 'er t' forget. She faound un 'ard t' leave home—'E be 'arder for maidens than 'e be for we; but she will get used t' things, Hi spect."

"Shore 'er will," assured Jack.

"You mus' come awver an' see us, Jack, an' you boays too," said Harry. "Hi want the missus t' knaw you, an' you t' knaw she."

It was too cold to stand long, and Jim noticed that Hunt

still wore elastic sides with only the added protection of rubbers.

As soon as the two groups had parted Jack said, "Hi b'lieve Hi'll marry a Yankee if one will 'ave me. A 'omesick woman mus' be some caution, you. W'at do e say, Jake?"

"I be thinkin' of the Indians as best for you an' me, boay. They bayn't partic'lar, which be a item, an' wouldn' git 'omesick t' boot."

"That 'ave been done afore now," said Spargo. "There's a St. Ives man awver on the shore 'oo 'ave a Indian wife. 'E was a poacher back 'ome an' 'ave been in the clink a foo times. 'E do 'unt an' trap an' fish for meat an' live in a shanty that would 'umble a pig. They say 'e wanted a 'ousekeeper an' 'er wanted a home, an' they both got took in."

What Jack began as a joke ended on a low note.

"Do they 'ave chuldern?" Jim asked.

"Iss, you, too many," answered Jack; "an' they would discourage any man. 'Aow a father could look at mun an' not want t' draown 'isself fur shame, I dawn't knaw."

"There be a rumor about that 'Arry plan to keep a boarder or two," said Jake.

"I 'adn' 'eard," said Jack. "Shore 'nough, 'is beds won't work doublers. 'Arry used t' hate that."

"There be too many at our place," said Jake. "No place t' call yer own, to sit with yer own thoughts or 'ave a two-sided chat."

The next night Spargo visited the Jenkins household and sought out Jim and Jake on his return. Again they sought privacy outdoors.

"Do you boays think you'd like t' change?" he asked. " 'Arry said 'e'd take four—no more."

Neither answered. Jim, as usual, waited for Jake, and in addition was thinking of separation from Allen. True enough, they would be only a half-dozen blocks apart, but he hesitated. He would miss the little encouragements and helps Allen volunteered so often.

Jack could not imagine why they hesitated. He said: "The board will be the same; hit be the same all awver taown."

"Hi wadn' thinkin' of that, you," said Jake. "I was won-d'rin' would a look like 'Arry was slockin' we away an' give 'e a bad name."

"The looks of the thing won't 'urt 'Arry," Jack said assur-ingly. "Hev'ry man here belong t' do w'at 'e like abaout changin' boardin' places."

"W'en will Jenkins be ready?" asked Jim.

"First of the month."

"That be two weeks—a fair warnin' to our boardin' boss."

"Hi never 'eard nobody spayk of that afore," said Jack in surprise.

"Worse they, then," said Jake. "Hit's awnly fitty. Did 'Arry 'ave nobody in mind?"

" 'E dedn' say, my son," answered Jack.

The first of the month came, and on that day the boys moved their belongings in three bulging carpetbags. Jake said, "Now us 'ave a bit of room us c'n git a Yankee trunk apiece."

April came with a warmer breath which started the *drip, drip, drip* of spring as well as growth of icy stalactites from every roof. They formed during the chilling afternoon to fall with frequent crashings during the morning. Snow and ice that had accumulated on the houses was loosened and slid off with a startling swish sounding, often, as though it were taking the shingles with it. Small pools formed in ruts to be covered during the night with glasslike panes of ice. Boots became more popular than German socks, which soaked too quickly in the slush. Horses hobbled painfully as their shoes filled with compressed masses of snow. The roads were like stony lanes when the rounded masses loosened from the horses' feet and froze again.

Colds, sore throats, and more serious chest ailments were soon numerous and formed a large part of the general conversation. Men brought their untouched lunches back to the house complaining that they could not swallow. "Missus, will e make a bit of soup or a basin of broth for me? Hi'm starved." But few ever stayed at home from work because of colds or sore throat. On all sides the men spoke of the weather with the vocabulary that had been worn out in the early winter months, resurrecting the weakened denunciations and ending always with the avowal that it was no place for a white man. But their arguments and denunciation lacked strength and pungence, perhaps because spring was in the air.

The days were beautiful if one could forget the discomfort underfoot. And the nights were beautiful too. Sunset and dark were close together. Soon after the sun had disappeared, stars began to peer like fearful eyes at the world the sun had left. Gradually the first comers grew bolder while the still more timid peeped over their shoulders. These soon took courage to vie with the first to shine. So, on into the evening they came increasingly to pulsate with frigid light. But more remarkable to the Cornishmen were the icy flames that palisaded the northern sky, quivering like living fire, cold colorful rays that rose above the forest to reach almost overhead. These men had seen the boreal light at home but not in such weird, frightening extravagance as in Keweenaw. Their voices fell to half-tones as they stood and marveled.

"I wonder what they be!" said one in a voice that expected no reply.

" 'E do look like the judgment," said another.

"Do e s'pose they be real fire?"

"God do shore 'ave ways of showin' man 'is place."

On a night of such a sky, Spargo came in from town. His step was hurried. He opened the door with a single thrust. His eyes were wide with wonder or fright or a mixture of the two. He found Harry and his wife still sitting at the table with Hunt and Jake and Jim, just as he had left them an hour before, still talking. He urged all to the door to see the ice-fires. " 'E do look like somethin' be goin' t' 'appen," he said, his voice lessening no whit the impression that fright was mixed with his awe.

All but Hunt arose and went to the porch, the men coatless and Mrs. Jenkins with a shawl snatched from a nail beside the kitchen door, thrown about her shoulders. They stood for minutes in silence looking at the sky, the men with their hands deep in their trouser pockets and arms pressed tight to their sides in defense against the chill. "They do look like they would break loose an' fall, they stars," said Spargo, his voice slightly strained. "An' did 'e ever see they lights so plain?"

"They make me afeared, they lights," said the woman. "My mother used t' say, 'God mustn' come too close.' "

The men went into the front room, to which Hunt had also come, leaving the kitchen to Mrs. Jenkins. She went directly there to finish her work. Before starting she went to the window, raised the shade, and looked out again for a minute. The shaft house and the smoking stack back of the boiler house partially hid her view of the sky but themselves stood clearly lined against the flashing heavens. For a moment she felt sorry for them as if they might be sensible of impending catastrophe. "Hi 'ope they be standin' in the mornin'," she whispered, and let the shade fall to place.

The boarders were loath to comment on the stellar and boreal display. It was too stupendous, too mighty, too fraught with unknown potentialities. Also they had not become free enough with the blind man to discuss sights and scenes before him. What had been done already, impressed them as a blunder. They waited for Jenkins to speak, but he remained silent.

Hunt sat as he did in church, his body erect, his face

slightly uplifted as though he were looking over the near things to something beyond the wall, beyond the street, the mine, the town and, when he spoke, were addressing persons near the horizon. The men felt like eavesdroppers to his remarks.

"Fifteen year ago t'night, 'tis, that I seen the sky last," he said. "Fifteen year ago."

No one spoke. If Hunt chose to tell a story, they would listen, but they did not feel privileged to comment. As though knowing that a tale he knew was about to be told, Harry slipped from the room to be company for his wife.

"Hi can see the night shift standin' at the shaft waitin' for the cap'n afore goin' daown. At last he come an' stepped on a candle box, his white duck coat makin' un plain in the dark." Hunt stopped to look the scene over again, to refresh his memory.

"Hi b'lieve I could mark exactly 'aow the men stood. Hi knawed ev'ry one of mun. They all wored bowlers made 'ard with rozum, with tobs of clay stuck to mun an' candles stuck in the tobs. Almos' all had a bunch of candles hooked into his shirt and danglin' on 'is chist. Hi dawn't remember any night like I do that one. Some 'ad drills in a sling looped around their shoulders, the drills 'angin' on their backs. You knaw 'aow—t' make climbin' aysy."

The men nodded in reply and quickly corrected themselves with an "Oosh," of approval.

"Cap'n Goldsworthy was sendin' stemmers 'ere an' there an' givin' a word to this pair an' that w'en, of a sudden, a man—it was Bill Trevry—fairly shaouted, 'Men, look, see, the sky!' 'E stopped the cap'n in 'e's words, but the cap'n tooked no hoffense; he looked with the rest." Again Hunt stopped and raised his face slightly for a better glimpse of the sky of fifteen years ago.

"They stars was all nervous an' widdery. They opened an'

shut like heyes an' yet shined steady too. Us felt like the sky was goin' t' change, the stars fall, or somethin' dreadful 'appen.

"The north sky was full of fire. It leaped an' blazed an' changed color with hev'ry flash. Wheal Tom is aout on the moors, you knaw, an' us could see all abaout—not a tree t' hide un. We 'ad all seen the Lights afore, but most likely in the village or on the road with hedges an' bushes t' hide mun. But that night they 'ad nothing for a screen. The flames reached awver our heads. The men was more solemn than if they was in chapel. An' there was some there w'at was never seen in chapel.

" 'Hit's from the throne of God,' said Trevry.

"For a long time—that is, 'e seemed a long time—the men stood silent, w'en Ol' Bennetts—Jeremiah Bennetts, the Class leader—said, 'Iss, 'e's from the throne of God. No man can see 'Is face an' live.'

"A amen or two saounded through the group, coming from the pious ones. Then we went daown, an' was glad t' go an' leave that sight be'ind.

"Most of the way daown, the men talked as they climbed.

" 'Do e think the Judgment will come like that?'

" 'The 'eavens will be rolled back like a scroll.'

" 'You 'ave t' 'ave fire t' make a scroll, dawn't e?'

"Bennetts was climbin' be'ind me, and 'e said, 'The great an' terrible day of the Lord.'

"A lot of fiery an' smawky Scripters come aout on that climb. Hi be shore that if the shaft timbers an' shaft had come together, they men wouldn' a been surprised. Right below me was Bill Buzza. 'E wadn' pious. The Wesaleens could never reach un. 'E poached an' gamed on any day. 'E 'ad a voice like a bull of Bashan. Suddenly 'e spawk, an' a dozen men both ways could 'a 'eard un. 'Hi 'ope my old dummon dawn't see un, or she will stifle 'erself in the bedclo'es.'

"Buzza broke the spell. Nothin' more was said of the fires

and of course, the men got fooer an' fooer on the ladders as they got to their plats an' went to their places.

"Me an' my comrade was drillin', finishin' a cut, until three in the mornin'. From three t' seven was a long time t' waste, so we charged up.

"We was usin' black powder. Fooses hadn' come in; reeds took the place of fooses—you all knaw."

Nods and audible "Ooshes" responded.

"Some parties was still usin' feathers an' tares t' break graoun'; but they be 'ard, like drillin' the 'oles twice awver. Powder do make minin' aysier if 'e be dang'rous.

"Us fired—four 'oles—got to a safe place, an' waited.

"Hi remember us both caounted aout laoud: 'One—two—three . . .'

"An' then us waited minutes. They was long ones too. Both together, as though we was timed, us said, 'Missed!'

"You knaw 'aouw you say un. That word 'ave a hawful 'ist'ry in Cornwall. Blind men, men with no harms or legs, men brawk an' useless.

"Aour candles blawed aout, but we waited on in the dark; then us lighted up an' went back t' the plat t' bide till the smawk cleared aout.

"Us dedn't talk much, an' us dedn' go back till five.

"My comrade was a boay. Hi made 'e stand back w'ile I worked. You better b'lieve I was careful. W'en I got close t' the 'ole, I used my fingers t' clean the maouth of un. Hi dawn't knaw w'at made un go off. Maybe the settlin' rock made a spark. I dawn't knaw."

Hunt stopped. He had told his experience without emotion, told it simply, in the phrase of the mines. His hearers could picture each step of the tale. They waited for him to go on, but he appeared to be lost, to have forgotten that he had been talking—lost in his black memories.

Finally Jake said, "Your comrade, William—was 'e 'urted?"

Only Hunt's lips moved as he spoke again. "Nayther of

us was hurt much—'cept my heyes. There was too much load on the 'ole, I s'pose, an' awnly the small dirt hit us. Hi was knocked back on the sollar an' stunned a bit. The fine dirt cut my face all abroad an' my heyes. My comrade was cut a little on 'is face. 'E do carry a mark or two, Hi'm told. 'E's in the kitchen with Mary Ellen."

Jake and Spargo lighted their pipes. They thought Hunt was done, but he spoke again.

" 'E be aysy t' blame a man for goin' back to a missed 'ole —aysy t' call un a fool. But you be miners an' knaw. A Cornish miner do gamble for 'is bread an' meat, an' the stake be 'is life or limbs or heyes. If 'e hever stop, somebody must stop un."

" 'Oo will do un, maister?" asked Jim.

"The bal authorities," said Hunt. "Sack, if 'e go back too soon. 'Ave a rule of a day or two days afore a miner dare go into a place w'ere a 'ole 'ave missed. Better a poor pay, a pinched belly even, than death an' widdas an' horphans like be scattered all habroad in Cornwall—or blind men an' cripples."

The men nodded and said yes in Cornish fashion but did not accept the idea readily. Each felt the Cousin Jack's disdain for all interference with his liberty in the mine. They conceived the dangers and safety of mining, excluding caves and floods, to be proof of a miner's skill and not a matter for outside interference. Their nods merely meant that they were listening.

Jim harked back again to Allen's comments on Walters' death and the resentful phrases that followed.

Hunt seemed to surmise the thought of their minds and said, " 'E will, my sons, 'e will, 'e'll come."

Argument with a blind man did not appeal to them had they an argument to give. They waited in silence, surmising that Hunt would continue. Surely there were things to be said. What about the intervening years?

"Fifteen year ago—an' the nights alike!" Hunt was speaking to himself. "Hi hope they be alike awnly in the sky. Men bayn't made t' live in the dark, but—thank God—they be made so that they can."

Again he stopped. The scene of that night still filled his mind.

"W'en I was gettin' well, ev'ry man in the bal come t' see me. Some kept comin' as long as they lived in the parish, until Hi come away. Stars an' faces! They faces look purty much like stars naow."

Hunt was silent again. Jim watched him, but his face was expressionless. Suddenly Hunt held his hands before his sightless eyes as if looking at them. "There mus' be somethin' I can learn um," he said. "Somethin'."

Hunt dropped his hands, and his tale was told. The curtain of silence still hid many interesting items, but it stayed down.

Jake drew his lever from his pocket and turned to Jim. "There will be a gittin'-up time in the mornin', comrade." He arose and went to the door, Jim and Jack following. They looked at the stars and the lights again. "Hi 'ope they be alike awnly in the sky," Jake said. The others agreed, and the door was closed. Hunt still sat as they had left him.

"Good night, maister," they said, and went upstairs to bed.

Chapter Seventeen

SEVENTY MEN STOOD AROUND the shaft waiting for the hooter to blow. The air had a slight edge to it, but the sky was clear; and they all knew that in an hour every building and trestle would begin to drip. When the shift was done and they came back to the surface, there would be less snow, more water, and bigger patches of bare ground. The whistle blew, and they grouped more closely around the shaft.

A man standing near Jim and Jake turned toward them and said, "Here's where we say good-bye to spring." He smiled as he spoke, but the partners got his meaning. Something in the man was resenting the need that took him underground—away from the day that was dawning.

Jake and Jim smiled in return and nodded.

Down below, Jake said: "Thicky chap be wrong. There bayn't no spring down 'ere, shore 'nough, in the way he meant. The timber dawn't leaf, an' the piles of dirt sprout nothin'; but my bones an' brain be agin the place this time of the year. I 'ave t' get a sweat up afore I c'n forgit the sunshine on top. I can't say good-bye t' spring that sharp."

"Same 'ere, comrade," said Jim. "The purtier the day, the less I want t' go down, an' the slower I be t' get started."

" 'E must be torture for the chap 'oo like t' fish an' 'unt." Jake shook his head as if condemning something. "A day-shift man do get a scrap of the mornin' an' a bit of hevenin'. The night-shift man often miss both." He stopped and stared at Jim. "Us be endin' our fust winter an' beginnin' our fust spring. Keep yer heyes open, comrade. You'm on the doorstep of the year." Jake grinned sheepishly at his own whimsy, and Jim smiled too.

Both knew that, for them and most of the others, warm weather meant more freedom of action, fewer clothes, more open air. The boys would stand on the corner, sit on the store porch, and gossip of "places," drilling, firing, lodes, a new shaft that was rumored, and an addition to the stamp mill. There was always the chance, too, of a raise in pay with the opening of the lake. Beyond that, spring meant only that the trees would tip with green and then the leaves would come out. Creeping things and things with wings would appear. Fancy roamed further in spring airs than it did in deep winter.

"Back 'ome, this time, us'd be turnin' up a bit of gyarden," Jake continued, "t' grow a foo tetties an' flatpoll cabbages. But 'ere, back yards be full of woodpiles an' covered with sawdust an' chips. Most of the men of the place be boarders. The furriners"—Jake laughed at the word—"the blokes w'at dawn't speak Henglish try t' raise a little in this stingy groot, I'm told, but Cousin John say, 'A day's work hunderground be anough for any man.' "

"I've 'eard un said," Jim replied. "That be a Cornishman all awver."

"You knaw, boay," Jake went on, "I think, sometimes 'e'd be good for all of we t' plant an' tend somethin', an' watch un grow. That be more natural, seem t' me like, than delvin' in the pit."

Jim did not answer that. He was thinking of what the few melting days had done for him. He had found it harder to take up his books, to stay indoors when the other men went out to enjoy the touch of the spring air. He thought that he was dulling, that his mind was less willing to submit to his purpose. He wanted to push his books aside, but he knew too that that was a test of his strength of will, of his loyalty to Pol. If spring meant new vistas and dreams to the other men, these books meant new vistas and dreams to him. Still, it required all his effort to resist the temptation to leave them and ramble with Jake or Allen, with leisurely talk.

"W'at izza that pull so 'ard?" he asked. "W'y can't a man work as well in good weather as in bad?"

Jake laughed at Jim's seriousness. "Books, comrade," he said, "be as onnatural as workin' in the bal." He looked at Jim as if to make sure that he might say what came next. "You 'ave jus' added one more enemy t' fight."

After his supper, one evening, Jim sat alone in the front room trying to make some figures intelligible upon a fragment of paper. He found the arrangement of figures for multiplication, division, and subtraction interesting and useful. They represented puzzles to him that led to solutions worth while. For years he had forced himself to do the necessary calculating of mining, as he said, "in my 'ead." To set footages, tonnages, and costs astride the symbols of arithmetic and see the answers he wanted emerge below the line was as fascinating as a game. First he did his sum mentally, and then, with the assistance of the rules his teacher had taught him. If the latter way ended in agreement with his own results he chuckled in triumph. He looked at the ranks of figures in deep appreciation. "The man 'oo invented they, was some smart," he said. The pleasure of doing sums subtracted somewhat from the disquiet of their revelation when they showed that he would have a small pay at the end of the month.

While he worked, Mrs. Jenkins came into the room, pulled a rocking chair nearer the window, and began to sew. Jim put the paper and pencil into his pocket: he was timid about letting any one see him trying to write. Per'aps 'er c'n write, an' I dew look clumsy t' she, he thought.

He watched her arranging her work, her chair moving gently to and fro. She looked frail to him, too frail to run a boarding house; but Harry would never let her keep more than three or four. Her hair was drawn back smoothly from her forehead to a knot at the back, like Pol's. It was oiled too, and shiny, like Pol's. And, like Pol, she never allowed herself to be idle. "There be halways somethin' for a woman t' do about a 'ouse."

Jim was most impressed with the idea that she looked lonesome. He did not count himself as company for her; nor did she look upon him as such, evidently. She had not spoken. Harry was underground; Hunt and Jake were "downtown." Something like pity was taking form in his mind when she said: "Us dawn't belong t' 'ave rockers in the old country, Mr. Holman. They be comfortable, 'aowever, an' I like mun."

"No, missus. They be aysier than a form or a settle."

Jim noted that she did not smile when she spoke. Rather, her face was drawn, sad, pale. She had a pleasing voice, and her western cadence impressed him.

" 'E's queer, people livin' so close together do talk so different." Mrs. Jenkins dropped her hands and work into her lap and said: "Do we 'ave primroses 'ere an' buttercups 'ere, do e s'pose, Mr. Holman? Snowdrops ought t' be comin' naow."

"Hi dawn't knaw, missus. I never 'eard nobody say," answered Jim.

"If there be no Lent lilies nor wallflowers, I shall be more lonely than I be now," she said. She stopped and looked out the window. "W'en I look aout Hi miss the hedges, too, an' the fields." Her voice trailed away as though following her mind across the distance that separated her from the things she was missing. Jim waited, thinking and questioning what answer he might give.

"Ev'ry country do 'ave 'e's growths," he said. "Us that be drove from 'ome must learn t' like w'at they be."

"Hi did love the trees back 'ome; but 'ere there be so many, so much woods, I get frightened."

"The mines be eatin' um fast, missus, an' all the 'ouses be made of wood," consoled Jim. "An' the iron mines do use more than we. A man said there be 'underds of miles out West w'ere there bayn't no trees, just farmin' land. W'en that be settled, they will eat up the trees."

Mrs. Jenkins did not answer that. The view was too long to ease the problem of her present. She seemed to be absorbed in the whirring wheels atop the headframes visible from where she sat and in the smoke curling and thinning into the evening sky from the mine stack.

"Bayn't e 'appy 'ere, missus?" asked Jim.

Tears came into her eyes, and for a moment she did not speak.

"Hi be 'appy t' be with 'Arry," she said, "but I do miss 'ome."

Jim was silent. He did not know what to say. That a woman should be happy with her man had been the whole of his philosophy. The idea came to him with a shock, that a woman might want more than that.

"Back 'ome, my sister an' mother lived awver past the plantation, a 'alf-mile away. Close by me was maidens Hi went t' school with, I could go t' see. Hi knawed ev'rybody an' their ways. If I wanted t' walk down the lane alone, I weren't afeared. 'Ere the town be wrapped up in woods like a bundle. There be wild beasts in mun, too! W'ere could a body walk 'ere?"

Again Jim was without an answer. A question was rising in his mind that was of greater importance to him than hers.

To his silence, she said: "An' the people be diff'runt. Hi c'n feel it. Hi dawn't feel aysy with mun."

Jim thought he had an answer to this that might be helpful, but refrained from giving it, thinking it was not his privilege to advise her. While he pondered the matter the children came in, in distress, the older one crying loudly. Mrs. Jenkins went to him hurriedly and tried to coax from him the cause of his trouble. At last she quieted him sufficiently to get from him his tale, but not until the younger one had said breathlessly: " 'E 'ad a fight, 'e did. 'E 'ad a fight."

"They laughed at me, at my talk—called me 'Old Country'; an' at 'er too," he said.

Mrs. Jenkins found that the anguish was not so much from injury as from humiliation, and perhaps was meant to lessen the chance of a scolding from her. Her idea of a difference between the people here and at home was substantiated even by the children, Jim thought. She took them to the kitchen to wash them in readiness for bed.

Their chatter came through the partition and stopped only when the mother said, "Kneel down now, an' say your prayers." Together they recited the Lord's Prayer, after which, at her prompting, they added, "God bless Gramma, Uncle Will, and Da." A silence, then "And Ma," was added. Jim's curiosity was aroused by the order of the prayer. He dismissed the suggestion that came to his mind, saying, " 'Tis just a cheel's way of doin' un."

Just as the mother bade the children good night, Jake and Hunt came in. As Harry was night shift, Jake had substituted for him. As soon as Hunt was in his chair Jake said " 'E be still early, comrade. Do e want t' do a turn?"

Jim found his hat and coat and followed Jake out.

"Us will 'ave t' stick t' the boards, Jim, boay. The roads be runnin' like leats."

Jim smiled at Jake's Devonshire. Since Jim had been studying, Jake seemed to enjoy his native jargon the more. At every opportunity he avoided an American form and emphasized a Devonian substitute. Once when Jim laughed at his phrase, Jake said, "Hi be afeard thee wust furgit."

"No danger of that, you," countered Jim. " 'E's too 'ard t' change. I speak from hexperience."

"All in the method, my son," said Jake. "All in the method. I bayn't no prophet, Jim, but I give un two generations t' die out."

"Good riddance to un," answered Jim.

"Hi wouldn' say that, you," said Jake slowly. "I wouldn' say that. 'E's too bad books an' writin' be one way an' spaych be another, but 'e seem t' me like a lost spaych of any sort be a pity."

"W'y?" asked Jim.

"Hi dawn't knaw as I c'n tell e, comrade. Hi dawn't knaw exactly, but 'e feel that way to me."

"W'at will make un die?" queried Jim.

"That's aysier, my son. There be a barm a-workin' in Cornwall that will change un: edication an' travel. Did e hever 'ear a chap 'oo 'ave been abroad come back talkin' the same?"

"No."

"An' in this country—" Jake hesitated and spoke like one thinking out a new scheme of things. "If you bring Pol 'ere an' you 'ave a cheel, 'e won't spayk like you do."

That seemed easy and likely, too, to Jim; but his first question was more interesting to him. "Jake do always sterry up things 'ard t' settle." But Jake smoked on in evident peace of mind. He turned neither right nor left to notice passers or the windows. Jim looked at him in friendly understanding and admiration. 'E 'pear t' think a answer will come in time like fruit to a tree, Jim thought. But he was impatient for his answers. He prodded Jake again.

"Hi wish thee'd hexplain w'y a lost spaych be a pity."

"I be thinkin' of a plod Ol' Parent, my father, told, about Jan Dydge an' Bat Dingle. Both was seventy-five to eighty year old. Now Jan was a bad man in 'e's youth. 'E was a sailor then. W'en 'e come 'ome 'e disgraced his folks by his swearin' an' fightin' an' drink. Neighbors brought un home from the pub w'en the bobby dedn' take un to the clink. 'E got religion; got un like Saul of Tarsus. It tooked a blaze t' stop un, but the light never left un. It burned quiet an' steady an' warm in un all through 'e's life. Bat Dingle was diff'runt. 'E was a quiet man—always was. 'E dedn' curse an' 'e dedn' drink. 'E worked an' was hones', but religion dedn' int'rest un the least bit. Not he. W'en the air was thick with revival Old Bat passed the chapel door an' dedn' turn 'e's 'ead. One day Jan Dydge was weedin' 'is gyarden. 'E stopped at the end of a row to rest a bit, leanin' on 'is hoe, thicky fashion." Jake stopped and showed with cupped hands upon an imagined hoe how the old man rested. "Old Bat was comin' hup the road just outside w'en they spied one tother. Bat comed awver t' plod a bit an' rest—two tired old men, pantin' an' sweatin' an' trembly like. Bat braced 'e's stick agin the hedge an' leaned on un while 'e catched 'e's breath. Jan said somethin' about rest ahead that 'e'd come by soon—no weeds, no weariness, no ache in 'e's bones, 'is old heyes shinin' like they always done. Hi dawn't knaw w'at else 'e said, but thicky light must 'a' blazed again that blinded Saul. Or maybe 'twas Jan's eyes. Bat's stick falled to the ground, an' 'e said, soft an' quavery like, 'I zee't Jan Dydge! I zee't!' "

Jake chuckled quietly to himself for telling such a yarn and said: "Put that plod in fancy language, my son, an' 'e will sicken an' die. Try un!"

Jim was deeply moved by the tale as well as satisfied that Jake had made his point. Then he said, "Be that all?"

"No, you. There be a little more. Parent said, 'Old Bat was never absent, as long as 'e lived, after that from the chapel.' He said, ' 'Twould bring tears to your heyes just t' see th' ol' man sittin' an' list'nin' to ev'rything that was said, drinkin' of un in, thirsty, like a man 'oo'd jus' crossed a desert.' "

"That's w'at I meant," said Jim.

"I knaw, boay. But dawn't miss the point. W'en I think of the tales, the jokes, the odd sayin's in that lingo that I knaw, Hi can't see un go with no regrets. They be like jewels wrapped in rags, maybe, but they'm jewels none the less."

As he had done many times before, Jim marveled at the aptness of Jake's easy figures of speech. "Picters," Jim called them. In the silence that followed, he repeated Jake's phrase: "Jools wrapped in rags! Jools wrapped in rags!" And then he felt that the talk about dialect had led him away from a farther-reaching, more important subject—the questions and disquietude Mrs. Jenkins had disclosed to him. Jim found that almost every experience, every talk, every idea that came to him, bore somehow on Pol, on his future, on their home—their home in America. A body would think it was settled that I'm goin' t' stay 'ere. In his heart he was far more certain that his future would be spent here than that he would go back to England. Pol loved primroses and buttercups! He remembered "her tree" down by the spring in the garden! Would she be afraid of the forest? Yes, Mrs. Jenkins' talk was more important, more vital than Jake's dialect.

And so, in the mine the next day, he told Jake of Mrs. Jenkins' unhappiness, of her longing for the coming of an English spring, for the fields and hedges and her friends.

Jake said nothing.

"Hi was thinkin'—" began Jim.

"Hi knaw w'at thee't thinkin'. Thee't thinkin' about Pol. 'E dawn't pay t' think too much, my son, hunless you think fitty things. Hi mayn, you bayn't thinkin'; you'm worryin'. Wait till thee'st turned un awver in thy brain for a month. Then thee cus call un thinkin'."

"W'at do e mean by 'fitty things'?" asked Jim.

Jake held a bit of candle in his hand and toyed with the softened grease around the blazing wick. His pastime seemed to be absorbing him entirely. When the tallow he had squeezed high about the wick melted and ran, he watched as though it were a new phenomenon to him. He smiled at his childish endeavors and said, "Did e ever see thy father, Jim?"

Jim did not answer. He knew Jake's question called for no answer.

"Let me shaw un to e, boay," said Jake. "Hi'll paint 'e's picter for e. He tippled a little, smawked, swored sometimes, and 'e seed ghosts. He never paid 'tribbit' to 'is betters an' seed nobody wuss than 'e's self. Religion never touched un; 'e seemed t' look at un the same as 'e looked at tipplin', an' 'arked to un like 'e would to a ghost tale. 'E'd give h'up a day's pay t' 'elp a neighbor. Everybody liked un, but 'e's wife abused un."

Jake threw the bit of candle away, struck a light for his pipe, and with it fired a new one.

"Now, thy mother. Moosic never comed from 'er mouth, nor praise. 'Er was religious but sour. As a cheel, you was afeard of 'er. She smiled w'en 'er said, 'I told e so.' 'Er could find fault, but 'er advice was never good. Thy father learned no 'ardness from she, an' she learned no kindness from 'e."

Allen's words came to Jim's mind: "No man is born with a clean slate." And he added to himself: Father or mother or both do start a cheel off, shore 'nough. Of the two portraits Jake painted, Jim knew the one he resembled. He knew his tendency to weigh others in the scales of the dogma he had learned. And he knew what it did for him as he tried to be true to it. "Let your communication be, yea, yea; nay, nay," was no figure of speech to him. It made him wordless where the speechfulness of others produced a laugh. With difficulty he tried to suppress his censure of the chatterers; but his censure was not without wonder. He was afraid of compromise because compromise meant indictment. He said, "My blood an' brain an' my raisin' be agin my bein' free."

Jake knew his question would call out no answer. He was

sure Jim would understand the portrayal of his father and mother. When again they threw their coats over their shoulders for another rest, Jake reached for his candle and began his molding all over again.

"There be some good in the worl', Jim: 'nough for a man t' 'ave some faith in. 'E wouldn' all die if you did—an' me." At his supplement, Jake grinned. "Yer father was a man of faith, comrade, faith in tomorra, in folks, in hev'rything. Had too much, p'raps, but 'e dedn' worry. You 'ave faith—a little—an' worry. Too much of mother an' not anough of father."

Jim said nothing although Jake's silence was expectant. Jim could think of nothing he called "fitty."

"There be things in the worl' t' laugh at, too, Jim, or folks wouldn' be made t' laugh. Dogs dawn't laugh that I knaw by. They can't!"

"No."

"Livin' with no laughin' be like Mrs. Uren's grub—no flavor. Lor'! I'll never forget they meals."

"They was some sad affairs, comrade," said Jim. "But w'at be e aimin' at?"

"Givin' thee a gladder outlook," answered Jake. "There must be, an' is, some bright side to havin' Pol out 'ere. There mus' be some way t' be 'appy livin' in America. Aas, an' livin' with thee."

Jake looked at Jim with a smile that Jim failed to return.

"'E's askin' a lot of a maid, comrade," said Jim, "to leave 'er mother, 'er relations, a climate like Cornwall, for one like this."

"Jim, a old bach bayn't nobody to hadvise, maybe. But standin' t' one side an' lookin' on, a man can see a foo things."

"Aas."

"Let's forget the climate. There be wood an' stoves, clo'es an' money t' buy min. In the nex' place, Pol edn' no baby, an' 'er edn' no invalid. 'Er c'n trade American flowers for Cornish ones, an' frien's made out of strangers be better than relatives 'oo take e for granted."

Jim's eyes were unflinching and expressionless, and Jake could discern no effects of his words. Maybe they'm just bouncin' back like a ball throwed agin a wall, he thought. His next words came in a lower, a softer tone.

"You done a brave thing, my son, w'en you gived 'er up an' come away. You was forced, I knaw, but 'e was brave. W'y not let 'er 'ave 'er bit of bravery too? There be foo things a dummon won't do for 'er home. Dawn't forgit, boay, ' 'ome' be a big word in any tongue. 'Omes 'ave t' go on, no matter w'at they cost."

Caught by the idea, Jim broke his silence involuntarily. "Oosh," he said.

Jake smiled in recognition of Jim's assent. "There be another item, Jim. 'E be dang'rous t' leave a maid there too long. Dost tha remember Mary Jane Hally?"

"Aas, the strumpet. 'Er lost 'er weddin' ring playin' Drop the 'Andkerchief at a picnic."

"That's w'at the village said," answered Jake, "but I wouldn' say un. The village forgot, an' thee's forgot, that 'e was a Sunday-school picnic, 'eld in broad daylight in a medder. Remember 'er was a young woman, 'avin' a little fun with 'er neighbors. Losin' a ring dawn't mean nothin'. Tom could buy 'er another."

"Aysy 'nough for thee t' talk," broke in Jim, "but w'en Tom sent for 'er, 'er wouldn' come."

" 'Xac'ly! An' there's the point! Tommy 'ad been 'ere—out Wes'—five year, an' never wraute. 'E couldn' write—never tried t' learn. Asked nobody t' write for un. Jest sent a little dab of money each month. Love dawn't live on that, my son. 'Er 'ad lost a ring that comed t' mean nothin'. W'y should 'er come to a man like 'e?"

"Wadn' it 'er duty?" queried Jim.

Jake did not answer the question immediately. He was not through with Tom.

"Seem t' me like, if I loved a woman an' 'er wouldn' come t' me, Hi'd go to she an' find out the trouble. 'Er be worth that, seem t' me like. Edn' that so?"

Jake waited for a retort but got none.

"Thicky duty thing be a narrer creed, my son. An' belikes he be all one-sided. A lot of women 'ave come for duty, I s'pose. Come with 'earts that be cold to a man whose 'eart edn' warm, come bringin' chuldern 'oo be strangers to their father. They 'ad better stayed 'ome."

Jake stared at his candle as though its next flicker would disclose what he ought to say.

"Cornish women be a brave lot, comrade, an' show a lot of sense sometimes. Sometimes they show more braveness than sense. But you dawn't hear of many bein' honfaithful."

"No," said Jim.

In their next spell of labor, with common consent they turned to their coats after shoveling fewer cars than usual. It was not the first time they had turned to rest after a shorter turn with their shovels. "Is the air gettin' bad in 'ere, or bayn't us as good as w'en us landed?" Jim asked.

"Us be in considerable furder than w'en us began," said Jake. "I fancy the air edn' so good as 'e was."

Both looked back into the gloom and speculated on the distance they had come since their first shift. Then Jake spoke again. "Partner," he said, "if thee bayn't tired of my clack, I want t' tell e I was called to the cap'n's dry last night."

"The cap'n's dry?" said Jim.

"Aas. 'E sent for me."

Jim did not speak. He thought of only one thing as a reason for such a call—they were to be let out.

" 'E wanted me t' be a shift boss," said Jake to Jim's relief.

"You might say w'at you done," said Jim impatiently.

"Hi dedn' take the job, comrade, for two good reasons."

"They be?" said Jim questioningly.

"Another man was considered, a married man 'oo 'ave a 'ome 'ere. I be a rollin' stone. So I said: 'Let 'e 'ave un. As I be, I be free.'"

"That be one reason," said Jim.

"Thee cus cipher fitty," laughed Jake. "Thy schoolin' edn' all for nothin'. But that reason be anough."

Jim said nothing, but he thought, 'E's the selfishest man in the world an' the most unselfishest.

Chapter Eighteen

THE TWO PARTNERS, drifting at so much a foot, had had no big pays. They had difficulty keeping in the forties and seldom approached fifty closely. They had talked the matter over frequently but found conclusions difficult.

"A foo weeks ago us was beggers out of hand, an' glad t' work for anything," Jake said. "Best wait aw'ile."

Jim conceded the point but, after a little summing, inevitably came to the same result. Something for Pol, his board bill, and a dollar or two put away for the unforeseen or, what was increasingly important to him, the possible passage of the maid across the sea, left him with nearly nothing. For reasons easily seen, impatience stung one while the other could remain untroubled.

Something else, harder to define, sharpened the teeth of the perplexity. Jim tried to express it. "W'en a man put 'is strength an' sweat into a job, 'e 'ave a right t' somethin' more. A man can't respect 'isself in our fix."

The margin Jim desired meant shingles and boards and nails, doors and windows for the air castles he built from day to day. His reasoning resolved itself into a primitive demand that burned deeply into a man when it was denied.

Jake was not entirely surprised when Jim spoke to the night captain about it.

"If you dawn't like un, my son, you knaw w'at you can do," was the answer he got.

After the captain had gone out of the drift, Jim said: "I made a mistake, spaykin' to he. Should 'ave waited till we was day shif'."

To this Jake agreed.

After that the night captain was not encouraged to linger when he came into their place. Sometimes no words passed between them except a neutral good evening. After a look around—at the timber and "brist"—the boss walked out in suggestive silence.

" 'E mus' be a purty thing t' feel safe on a job," said Jim after such a visit.

"Hi wonder if 'e do!" replied Jake. "There bayn't many jobs that be safe, my son."

"Seem like a workin'man—" began Jim, but Jake headed him off.

"Dawn't take un too much to 'eart, boay," consoled Jake. "Thee might be a boss next, an' no tellin' w'at would 'appen t' thee then." His eyes sparkled humorously.

Jim ignored the jest. "Hi dawn't b'lieve I—" he began.

"Hi'm shore you would give a man a civil answer," said Jake, cutting him off again. "Cousin Jacks be good miners, but w'en they'm made cap'ns they change—seem t' change for the worse. They like t' show authority."

"The day cap'n be a 'ception to the rule, lucky for we," said Jim.

"Fair anough, boay, fair anough," said Jake. "I'll take back w'at I said. They words took in too much."

"W'a's tha mean?" asked Jim.

"W'en you've been 'ere a bit, you will 'ave friends 'oo be Swedes an' Eyetalians an' Finns. If somebody ask e do e like Swedes an' Eyetalians an' Finns, w'at will e say?"

Jim looked at Jake blankly for a moment, as if he had

spoken in a foreign tongue. Suddenly his eyes brightened, and he said, "Oosh! I see."

" 'Owsomever," continued Jake, "the night man told the truth. If us dawn't like un 'ere, us c'n move on."

"That be a 'ard sayin', comrade," said Jim. " 'E leave a man feelin' purty low."

"Not so low 'ere as 'e would back there, my son," said Jake.

When the day captain came around next he said, "The night man told me you was complainin'."

"Not complainin', cap'n," said Jim, "just askin'. An' besides, I done un. My partner dedn' say nothin'."

"Hi be sorry you spawk t' he. Things be a bit uncertain, an' I can't raise e. Your pay be abaout the same as the rest of the mine. Hi wish us could pay e all better."

Neither man answered the captain, but both felt better for his considerateness.

"Hi dawn't want 'e t' leave," continued the boss, "but if you can better yourselves, that be hev'ry man's privilege. There'll be no 'ard feelin's."

The big man smiled when he said his last words, perhaps thinking of the night man's attitude.

"Us dawn't want t' leave, cap'n," said Jake. "Us thought, no askin', no receivin'. That's all."

"Better times be comin', boays," said the captain, and continued his rounds.

"That's better," said Jim. " 'E dawn't leave a man feelin' like a worm."

"Shore 'nough," answered Jake. "Men will work for a man like 'e. But that other himage!" His voice was saturated with contempt.

They turned to their work again, but neither could forget the theme the captain had provided them. In spite of his kindness the words of the other man lingered in their thought: "If you dawn't like un, you knaw w'at you can do." The words filled Jim with uneasiness. "A poor man be a slave, no matter w'ere 'e be—drove by 'is masters," he muttered.

"W'at's that, comrade?" asked Jake.

Jim felt his face redden, but he repeated what he had said to himself.

Jake looked at him as if trying to determine the path his thought had taken before it forced him to speech. "There be too many like thicky night man," he said slowly. "It seems to me they be dirtyin' their awn nest."

"W'a's tha mean?"

"If they wadn' as blind as adders, they'd see they bayn't in Cornwall. They awverlook that America bayn't England."

"Spayk on," urged Jim.

"There be a diff'runt sperrit 'ere, Jim—outside the boardin' 'ouses, that is. I dawn't knaw as I c'n say w'at I mean, tell e w'at I see. Folks 'ave a diff'runt look, they talk diff'runt. They seem t' feel that they be on top instid of at the bottom. The whole country be theirs for the gettin'." Jake shook his head. "I can't say it, comrade. Maybe it's w'at liberty do for mun. Because they can vote for a President, they be as important as 'e be. W'atever 'tis, I'm shore I see it."

Jim was staring with rounded eyes. "Oosh," he said, but no more.

"An' they bosses dawn't see it. Back 'ome, if you dedn' like Cornwall, all that be left be the collieries of Wales or York. 'Ere, if you dawn't like Michigan, there be a dozen other states just as big w'ere you c'n mine."

"Aas."

"An', boay, they be big. One day from Plymouth t' Liverpool, an' that's England. 'Ere, four days from New York t' Michigan, an' that bayn't a half of America. A man's sperrit can grow an' spread in a country like this."

"Hi never thought of that afore."

"There be somethin' else they dawn't see. These mines

be owned by Americans. Likely anough the day will come w'en the big jobs will go to Americans. Diff'runt comp'nies own mun now, like Cornwall used t' be. W'en they combine there will be big jobs. Remember the Great Consols back 'ome? The cap'ns will be awnly messenger boays for the hoffice then. Remember, too, this copper wadn' found by no Cousin Jack. 'E was found by a school man—a hengineer, they call un. Men of that sort will run the shebang."

" 'Oo told e that?"

"No diff'runce 'oo tol' me, if 'e be true, my son."

Jake's short reply precipitated a silence that was broken only by the scrape of their shovels on the sollar and the low rumble of the dirt against the side of the car. Jim knew that Jake made friends with subtle ease. He had no fear of title or position, and people in return appeared to enjoy his keen observations and gentle aphorisms. His grasp of issues always amazed Jim, and apparently it attracted others. Men gave him their confidence. Following a moment of surprise at Jake's remark, Jim started thinking of the numerous jobs Jake had mentioned. Jim excluded them from his field of operation, thinking that only single men could take advantage of them. Also he framed objections to the removal of the captains from their places of power.

"There be other good men 'ere besides Cousin Jacks, t' my way of thinkin'," continued Jake, "an' we sorta turn up our nawses at mun."

" 'Oo be they?" asked Jim.

"They Swedes, Eyetalians, an' the rest," returned Jake.

"Most of they never seed a mine till they come 'ere," objected Jim. "They bayn't practical miners."

"You'm sayin' more'n us really knaw, comrade; but, if that be true, they can learn—an' do."

Jim laughed. "Did e hever see one of they beat a drill?"

"Hi knaw thy pride, comrade. I've seen thee beat a drill, an' foo there be 'oo can equal thee. But I seed a machine in the shaft drill a 'ole faster than thee cus do un. 'E beat an' twist both at once. All a man 'ave t' do be turn the 'andle an' keep the 'ole clean."

Jim was not slow-witted, and he saw Jake's point. The look of puzzlement that shaded his face had another cause. He was proud of his skill, as his fellow Cornishmen were too. He had never said a man wasn't a miner because he couldn't use a hammer, but he regretted the loss of the art that made Cornishmen feel superior. The machine would lower one group and elevate the other. He looked around the drift. Ample room for a machine, he thought. So in the shaft; so in the stopes. Every feature of the mine was bigger than in the Old Country. Different mines, different methods, but the workman will be a miner just the same. Jake called him out of his reverie.

"If Cousin John edn' careful, pride will be 'e's downfall. God A'mighty dedn' lay no 'ands on Cornish minin' cap'ns."

Jake himself was as good a miner "as ever stood in leather," but he showed no feeling one way or another as he talked. If machines supplanted hammers and Swedes or Italians became bosses, he showed no regrets.

A remark the captain had made stuck in Jim's mind in spite of the talk about methods and men.

"W'at did the cap'n mean by things bein' onaysy, do e s'pose?"

"W'at did a mean w'en 'e said times will pick up?" retorted Jake. He stopped his work and turned a smiling face toward Jim. "Comrade," he said, "when I 'ave a choice like they two—" He turned back to his work in playful impatience with, "Aw, gose 'ome with e."

Jim chuckled in spite of himself. Still, he had heard men talk about the bad times. Single men were leaving the town for other places. Men with homes and families were grave and depressed. They sought one another out for counsel, having a common problem. They discussed other copper towns where the mines had a record of continuous operation. These were not taking on new men. Down on the Iron Ranges new mines were being opened almost daily. Surely there was work to be found, but uprooting a family was not easy.

Jake sympathized with Jim, knowing what was in his mind continuously. Jim mentioned the iron mines to him and asked what he thought about trying them.

"I knaw, my son, I knaw," he said. "A lot of places be bein' born, but 'ow many be stillborn? Us never 'ear about they."

The most difficult feature of the situation was that nobody knew anything with certainty. Nobody dared ask the captain about it: it was a company secret. All of the men concerned had been ejected from their firesides once before, and their uneasiness was distressing.

Sitting on the side of his bed, dressed and ready for chapel, Jim said, "W'at do e think of un now, comrade?"

"Hi dawn't knaw more than you, Jim," answered Jake, "but I knaw I can look at un with a aysier mind. 'Ave e thought of this? This place be twenty year ol'. That do make un a good place t' live—'e's settled like. There be plenty of copper in the bal. The footure of the place depend on that. The business men of the place dawn't seem t' be worryin' that I knaw by. Let's put one rumor agin another. A foo weeks ago was talk about a new shaft an' a haddition to the stamps. My son, Hi'm for stayin'."

Jake looked steadily at Jim for a moment and then went on.

"I wish I could make thee remember one thing: Thee bayn't in Henglan'—thee's in America! That's the important thing. Hev'ry foot of ground 'ere be bustin' with opportoonity. There be jobs hev'ryw'ere. Remember the lumberman? 'E hoffered us all jobs with no askin'. If you dawn't b'lieve me, ask Hallen or the schoolmaster."

Again silence.

"That edn' answerin' thy questions, but it ought t' ayse thy mind w'ile the rumors be goin' about, about the mine."

Jake was in dead earnest. He knew the issue was a big one in Jim's mind and could not be treated lightly. He wanted to be wise in what he said. He was sure Jim would never go back to England again to live. America had already done too much for him. There were other things he had wanted to say to Jim for some time, and he thought that this was his chance to say them.

"If I made up my min' to stay 'ere, old as I be—stay in America, I mean—I dawn't think I'd stay underground. An' you'm younger than me. The towns around some of these pits will grow. New diggin's will be made close by. Growin' towns mean more jobs. The mines will 'ave more surface works, an' then, there's the lake. Shippin' will mean ports, an' that mean work. Remember w'at Ol' Parent said: 'Cousin John always look for a sheave wheel, but there be better ways of makin' a livin'.' "

A reference to Jake's father seldom failed to produce a smile. Jim smiled now and said, " 'E's nobody's fool," and Jake thought he was making progress.

But Jim found it difficult to content himself with Jake's ideas. He had never thought of doing anything other than mine work. It was his bird in hand. If he hoped to get Pol "out" he would have to stay with mining until she came. Time enough to think of another calling with her to advise him. He reviewed the tales that he had heard at Uren's house, tales of the West—mines and farms and growing towns. They be for men 'oo can turn their hand to mun, he thought. The old world be too strong in me. I bayn't no pioneer.

Then he replied to Jake, who had sat waiting for his response.

"W'at thee's sayin' be for the chuldern, seem t' me like. W'en their turn come, they can take up other trades. The fathers now must stick t' w'at they knaw." Then he said aloud what he had only thought before: "I guess I bayn't no pioneer."

For a moment Jake missed the connection. Then he surmised that Jim's thought had been going farther afield. He chuckled and said: "Thinkin' of the Wes', be e, comrade? Dawn't like the guns an' gamblin' an' Indians. I dawn't like they Indians myself, but the gamblin' an fightin' might be interestin' t' see."

Jim caught the twinkle in his eyes. "Art tha goin' t' scoose gamblin', comrade?" he asked, laughing. "That be goin' purty far for Wesaleen upbringin'."

When he laughed, Jake's thought was, The fust skirmish be winned. That's capital. Aloud he said, "Hi wonder 'ow bad gamblin' be!" He stopped for an answer, but Jim merely looked at him, wanting him to answer his own question. Jake went on: "The farmer do gamble with the weather. 'I'll bet on gettin' a crop,' 'e say an' he go t' work. 'I'll bet on doin' so-an'-so t'morra,' you say, an' t'morra be the trickiest day in the week for all of us. A bit back you throwed all you 'ad on the table: you risked a long journey, left 'ome be'ind, tackled a new climate. An' ev'ry day you go underground— a brave gambler, comrade." Jake closed one eye and lined the other on Jim's upturned face. "An' you'm more of a Wesaleen than I be," he said.

Jim did not answer. He was wondering how two men— himself and Jake—could be so different. They had lived under the same roof, their homes were as much alike as homes could be. They had attended the same chapel and been taught the same Sabbath learning. With him, the seed fell into the ground as it came from the hand of the sower. With Jake, the seed went through a sifting, was sorted, and some was thrown away. Jim felt that he was clay in the potter's hands; Jake was himself a potter.

The time had passed faster than either of them realized: without their knowing it, chapel time had come and gone. Jake pulled his lever from his pocket, laughed and said, "Thee's committed a hawful sin, my son."

"W'at's that?"

"Thee's missed church."

"I 'ave comp'ny," challenged Jim.

"My sins bayn't so big nor black as thine," said Jake.

" 'E edn' as bad as 'e look," said Jim. "My mind be too stirred up t' worship, I fear."

"Very good, my son," said Jake, "but I be shore—as shore as a man can be, that is—that your big worry be for thy gran'chuldern t' worry about, not for thee. My 'air won't git gray awver that."

His deepest wish was that he might help Jim see things less gloomily. He admired Jim's fidelity to his convictions but wished he could see more happiness in life. Jake knew what Jim's religion meant to him, but to his own way of thinking it put heavier burdens on the youngster's shoulders than any man should bear who had so many real loads to carry. Jake's philosophy had not asked a full explanation of all its tenets, but he refused the elements that clashed with everything that seemed so much a part of life. He said, "A man can't work in the mine and carry the sin of the world too." When he spoke again it was with this desire uppermost in his thought.

"Jim, boay, you need conversion," he said. "Thy 'eart be right, but thy 'ead need a change. You need a church w'ere some man do praych laughin', an' sunlight, an' hope. You be a sinner, Jim, a sinner agin thyself, takin' things too ser'ous, lookin' on the black side of ev'rything. You need a praycher like me, awnly better."

"A man can't 'elp—"

"Aas, 'e can. That be a hexcoose. Thee's been twenty year makin' w'at thee got from thy mother worse. Thee's made a bushel of gloom t' hide under. The twenty year of—"

"The Book—" began Jim.

"Thee dussn' knaw w'at's in the Book, comrade," said Jake, stopping him. "Hi dawn't nuther. Hi wish a lot of times t' read un t' see if 'e be the gloomy thing the Methodies 'ave made of un."

"W'y dawn't e?"

" 'E'd be a waste of time for two reasons. Hi'd find out I be right in the fust place. In the secon', the Methodies wouldn' hark to me."

After dinner Jim went out, not knowing what better to do. He did not know whether he wanted to think or to free himself from thinking. Jake saw him go, but said nothing. He watched Jim go down the street and wondered if he had been too blunt. "I 'ope I dedn' spayk too plain," he muttered.

The air was full of spring. A breeze that had the touch of velvet soothed Jim's face. He looked at the grass in the tender green of its new life. The buds he saw on shrubs in the vacant lots he passed were ready to burst. By this time, he said to himself, the flowers be out back 'ome. There be lambs in the fiel's. Spring be a time of birth. Pol came to his mind, and his eyes lost the impress of external things. Suddenly he heard women's voices from behind and recognized that of the captain's daughter, who was the chapel organist. He stepped aside to let them pass.

"Good afternoon, Mr. Holman," she said. "I missed you from the choir this morning."

"Yes, miss," Jim answered.

"I was afraid you had left town. So many have gone, I hear," she said, turning to her friends.

"No, miss. Not yet," replied Jim.

"I hope you won't go. We need you in the choir."

"You won't need a choir, miss," answered Jim respectfully, "if the mine shut down."

She ignored the remark and turned to her companions again. "I don't see why the men get frightened so easily.

With the first whisper they begin to run. You won't run, will you, Mr. Holman?"

"No, miss, not till I 'ave to."

"I don't see why the officials don't stop a rumor like that when they hear about it," she said. Then, blushing as though she had said too much, she hurried on.

Jim walked another block and turned a corner. He was at the door of his old boarding house. The door was open and Mrs. Uren was at the table "doing away" the dishes.

"It's Jim," she said to no one in sight. "Mercy, 'aow you scared me! Hi dedn' 'ear e comin'."

" 'Ow do, missus?" said Jim. "Is Bob in?"

"In 'ere, Jim," came Bob's voice from the washroom.

Jim walked through the kitchen, opened the door, and saw Allen stripped to the waist, his face and head steeped in soap and water, his body glistening to his middle. Allen changed the water and rinsed his hair, washed the soap from his face and neck, and then seesawed the towel around his body. His digging shirt was lying on the form; his pit trousers he still had on, but he stood barefooted on the bare floor. Beside his pit clothes on the form he had spread a paper, and on the paper were his street clothes in the order of his bath and redressing.

"Sit daown, my son," said Allen, "w'ile I finish washin' hup. 'Ad t' work t'day—a bit of shaft work."

Jim sat down and watched him finish his cleaning. His face came out of the towel ruddy and shining, his thin, blond hair a tangled snarl. Jim noted the slenderness of his body, the bulging and smoothing muscles in his arms and back as he moved. His skin was as pink as a child's. Allen donned his shirt, put the tub on the floor, spread a towel between it and the form, kicked off his breeches and sat down. Again a lather for feet and legs, and the man of the mines was clean.

Allen lowered his voice and dropped his Cornish. "Cleanliness is next to godliness," he said laughing. "Who said that, Jim?"

"Hi 'eard a praycher say Wesley did. I dawn't knaw."

"Well, it's not true, no matter who said it," said Allen, humor sparkling in his eyes. "You know I'm clean, but you wouldn't say I am godly. I like to break the Sabbath too well for that."

"Aas," said Jim, catching Bob's good humor.

"I have been working on the Lord's Day, and if I hadn't been underground I might have been doing worse. Awful man!"

"Aas."

"I might have been carrying a gun or dangling a line, coaxing a fish. Fish are foolish things, Jim. They never learn from experience."

"There be lots like mun 'oo bayn't fish," said Jim.

Allen pulled himself up straight and said: "Clean, but not godly, my son. You are an eyewitness." His mock seriousness made Jim smile.

"Not godly, if you like, Bob," said Jim, "but not far from the kingdom."

"Lucky for us, there's no telling where that kingdom begins. When I'm fishing or hunting sometimes, I think I am in the center of it."

Jim sensed his own change of mood under Bob's light raillery. Evidently Bob was not disturbed by the rumor that had dipped him in gloom. If Bob knew about it—and certainly he knew—he was not letting it bother him.

"And speaking of my kingdom, my son, makes me think. How would you like to go for a tramp next week?"

"W'en?" asked Jim.

"Next Sunday. There won't be preaching. The schoolmaster is going, and I asked Jake. He said 'Aas' as you do— 'if Jim will go.' "

Bob grinned mischievously as he imitated Jake's Devon-

shire brogue. "Four will be better than three, and besides"—
Allen stopped midstream, knowing well what Jim was thinking—"if the weather is like today's the sky will deserve a
psalmist's praise. There are no more beautiful skies than
these over Keweenaw and Lake Superior."

Jim was all attention but said nothing.

"And spring, boay, spring is stirring up miracles and mys-
teries in the woods. You will find the master a real prophet
out there."

Allen's face was a study to Jim. His eyes glowed, and his
face was suffused with something hard to describe. What
could there be out there to enthrall a man like that?

Jim felt something stir inside himself, something like a
new conviction. He recalled the schoolmaster at home and
his sermons on leaves and stones. He remembered Bill Downs,
the hedger, who hesitated to trim the overhanging hedge
growths after the master had preached. Why shouldn't he
know something of the miracles Allen spoke of and the
master preached about, and enjoy them too? He felt himself
being carried toward this new goal like a chip on a stream,
and for the first time in his life was sure that consent to it
would be a pleasure.

"Bob," he said, "I'll go."

Bob was hanging up his digging clothes. With his shirt in
his hand, still reaching for the nail to hang it on, he turned,
his face aglow with warmth and understanding and said:
"Jim, Hi be glad, my son, some glad. Thee will find that,
w'ether a man look up or daown, 'e'll find more than his
'eart c'n 'old if 'e awnly 'ave heyes t' see." That he had
dropped back into Cornish was proof enough of the emotion that stirred him.

The shirt was put in its place and Allen said, "Let's go up
to my room."

Jim sat on the bed while Allen adjusted a tie and combed
his hair. Talking into the glass, he said, "How is Pol?"

"Brave, thanks, Bob."

"That's a good word, Jim, and used in the right place to my mind. Some of those maidens deserve it."

"Aas," said Jim.

"I dawn't want t' be personal, but how long will it be—"

"Three or four weeks at the most," Jim answered.

"It's the custom here for a new father to set up the drinks or pass out cigars," said Bob. "Something to think about, Jim."

Jim looked studious for a minute, but in no way troubled. "I 'ave four frien's 'oo'll knaw about un. They all smawk pipes, an' none of mun drink. I'll lead mun to the store an' the poor box. 'Ow's that?"

"Looks like you hold the winning cards," said Allen laughing.

When Allen sobered again, Jim said, "W'at do e think of the mine, Bob?"

Bob's silence on the subject had given him comfort, but he could not resist the question. Bob might not know more than the rest of the men, but his judgment was sound.

Bob looked at the boy and read worry in his face. He was not unaware of the stories that were being told or of men leaving for other camps. He knew Jim's plans well enough to understand how he would be tortured by it all. He concluded that a simple direct answer would serve better than a discussion of the arguments passed to and fro at the store and in the house.

"Jim," he said, "I have faith in this country, in this mine. I am staying here."

"Thanks, Bob," Jim said simply, and arose to go.

"Don't forget next Sunday, boy," said Allen. "I'll see you again before that."

Jim found Jake sitting with Hunt and Harry, apparently talked out. Jake got up as he come in, and the pair went to their room.

"W'y dedn' you tell me about nex' Sunday?" asked Jim, trying to look calm and natural as he spoke.

"Afeared," said Jake teasingly. "Be e goin', comrade?"

"I be," said Jim.

" 'Ave e got a gun?" asked Jake, trying to be solemn.

Jim grinned sheepishly and only shook his head.

"Hi can see Simon Rattenham glaze at thee with 'is one good heye, traipsin' off into the woods on a Sunday."

Jake rocked on his chair and slapped his knees at his own joke. When he spoke again his voice was serious although his eyes still shone.

"But I be some glad, my son. Some glad. Workin' in the gloom can make a man nearsighted. Livin' in the gloom can make un nearsighted too. I be glad. Some glad."

Chapter Nineteen

Mr. Frost, Jim's teacher, was pleased with the progress his pupil was making and told him so. He knew the boy's primary reason for learning to write and praised him for his application. "Separation from a bride is a powerful incentive to learning, Jim," he said smilingly.

"If she 'ad comed with me, I might never 'a' wanted to," Jim answered. "That's true."

Frost toyed with the leaves of a book in accompaniment to his words.

"This is the first time I ever helped two lovers keep tryst by mail," he went on. "I might do better next time."

Jim reddened but enjoyed the teacher's friendliness and humor. "I shall always be thankful to e," he replied.

"You see, Jim, I never taught an adult beginner before. That has been a new experience for me. I can't tell you how eager I was for you to report your first letter. I had set that as my first goal." Frost's eyes glowed, and Jim's filled.

Jim turned away for a moment, then said, "For me too—an' for she." Jim blinked away the tears that threatened, and smiled. "Lucky for me," he added, "some important words be short an' aysy wraute."

Frost nodded his understanding. "Your job now, Jim, is words, words, and more words, and spelling."

"Aas, I know, but there bayn't no letters for some of my words, an' some book words 'ave too many letters—like buttons on the tail of a man's coat."

Jim offered his comment simply enough, but Frost saw the difficulty. Also he realized that time and practice would overcome it, and he could trust Jim to keep on. He thought of the pressure of his work and wondered if he might not dismiss Jim, leave him to his own incentives now that he could help himself. To be able to write his wife and read what she wrote was all that Jim had come for. He had opened the way for the boy; now the responsibility was Jim's.

Frost shook his head. As Allen said, he thought, "There is something about the boy I like." Frost believed that he could do more, and that Jim would appreciate it. Jim was capable, eager, honest. He had a mature mind and would progress rapidly. The others I have taught, I helped to make a living, he thought; I am helping this boy to live. He determined to go on. While Jim worked over his simple lessons in spelling, penmanship, and composition, Frost could open other fields for him.

He is a miner, Frost reasoned, if not a worker in rock by direct phrase, his life is one of intimacy with it. So he talked to Jim of seams, fissures, strata, dikes, water. All these were familiar to Jim's toil if not to his understanding. Frost talked of them simply, conversationally. Water was both destroyer and builder. It dissolved as it flowed, and it filled its own passages with the substances it carried. It was to the earth in part what the blood stream was to the body. Jim knew water as a problem. He had seen the most primitive ways of handling it. He had helped bale it from shallow pits and dragged knotted rags through tubes of wood or iron to dispose of it. His father's generation had hailed the Cornish pump with its bob and plunger. Jim exchanged his knowledge for that of the teacher's. In this way Frost went from geology to physics in his conversation.

Before Jim could read at all well, he got his foretaste of history in the same way. He was an Englishman, so Frost talked of England: its peoples, what they had brought to the little island, how its national life came to be. The language, the literature, the law of England—these he spoke of as her greatest gifts to the world. There was reason for the Englishman's pride, thought Jim, although the fellows who came near to blows about it in their arguments did not know it. "Once an Englishman, always an Englishman" was not as hollow as it sounded when they said it.

For Jim, history began with the first memory of his grandfather and the tales he had told of his childhood and youth in Cornwall. This small stream widened as his own experience broadened, but that was all. Back of his grandfather was oblivion. Within his own memory the Crimean War had occurred, but where was Russia? Chinese Gordon had been killed in Khartoum, but where was China? Where was Egypt? What had taken Gordon to either place, Jim did not know. He mentioned these things to Frost, and Frost said, "You'll come to that, Jim."

"Aas," Jim said. "Some day." And then: "I 'ope that day be long anough for all I'm puttin' hoff."

Then Frost asked Jim if he planned to bring his wife to America.

"Aas," said Jim, "I do"—his first avowal. Hearing himself say it brought a flush to his face. Why did he say Yes, to what seemed so nearly impossible—Yes, to what was at the time only a vague dream? He felt as though he had spoken an untruth. The teacher did not see his embarrassment, so he began to talk on a new theme: America took the place England had had. When he had done, the young Englishman felt less regret that he had been transplanted to American soil. To his fancy, America became the morning of a new day for the rest of the world.

Eagerly Jim said, "I wish you would tell me somethin' about Michigan."

"The history of Michigan—the part of it you are interested in—is short, Jim. The future of Michigan is beyond all I can say or think. But we will give it a session."

The night following the teacher's talk about Michigan, Jim sat in his room with a paper on the small square that had served him in his practice, in preparation for a letter to his wife. To date, he had been content to say simple things, the only things he could say he knew—also the things that he knew would be the answers to the first questions she would ask were she by him. Now he was bursting with a desire for broader expression. He wanted to tell her some of the things he had heard, to paint the dreams that arose in his mind in response to the master's talks. He felt a new, his first real, sense of security, and he wanted to share it with Pol. He felt an inner response to the appeal of America that he had never felt when England was mentioned. True enough, England stirred his emotions because of what she had been and still was to him; but America held out hands full of opportunity for the future. He would tell her about it! But the task was beyond his skill. Writing was so slow, and the words that came to his mind were so tumultuous. Would he never be able to do it? He wondered.

While he sat looking beyond the wall into his dreamland of hope and accomplishment he heard a knock, and Mrs. Jenkins' voice saying, "Come in, Mr. Hallen, playse." Then Allen's voice reached him asking, "Is Jim 'ome?"

"Jim!" she called. "Mr. Hallen t' see you."

Jim opened the door and invited Bob in.

Allen looked around the room, at the new furniture, noted the absence of clothes hanging around the wall, saw the new trunks, the clean, inviting bed with its thick heavy comforter. He lifted a chair from the wall and set it near the window so that he could look out into the settling dusk.

"You look t' be comfortable 'ere, my son," he said.

"Aas," said Jim, "we be."

Allen noted on the bed the paper and board that Jim had

laid aside on hearing his voice. "I see the paper dawn't 'ave a scratch on un. 'Avin' trouble with thy A B C's?"

"W'y dost tha say A B C's?" asked Jim, laughing. "Hi be past that stage."

"Thee will never get past that stage, partner—not if thee get t' be a Shakespeare."

"T' tell the truth," said Jim, "that be my trouble. An' nobody can 'elp me, I fear. 'E's my job from now on, shore 'nough." Jim stopped to consider his explanation. "Hi wanted t' tell the maid some things the maister 'ave been sayin'."

Allen did not respond. He thought it better to let Jim use his own judgment as to how much he told. While he waited he watched the wheels on the headframe of Number Two revolve in response to the bell. Slowly at first they turned, the spokes crossing as the wheels ran in opposite directions, making a series of X's until, at last, the spokes disappeared and the rims were empty circles apparently motionless and unsupported against the sky. Then they reappeared, becoming plainer and plainer until they lazily came to rest. As darkness crept across the sky, the spokes disappeared again, and the rims become mere pencil marks. A little longer, and the rims were invisible and the shafthouse stood an uncrowned pyramid, outlined but featureless.

Jim remained silent, trying to determine whether he should tell Allen. Allen might think the things he had wished to write were not suitable to a letter, or he might suspect him of wanting to show off his new learning. Cornishmen were suspicious. But Allen, he reflected, was different from any Cornishman he had ever known. He would understand that it was the happiness of his new discovery Jim wanted to share with his wife. The sort of prospecting he was doing was neither for boasting nor for secrecy, but for divulgence with those close to one that they might rejoice with him.

At last he told Allen what he had wanted to say. Allen listened closely, deeply gratified that the master's words were producing their desired result. "W'y," said Jim, " 'e showed me 'ow the air weighed fifteen pounds to the hinch, with a glass of water an' a piece of paper! Did e hever see that, Bob?" Bob nodded.

"Because of that pumps can sen' water up t' grass!"

"Oosh."

"The insides of the earth 'e make as wonderful as the outsides," said Jim.

"Or the stars that be awver un, my son."

Again they dropped their talk for minutes of silence. Allen drew his pipe from his pocket and lighted it. While the match still burned, he crossed the room and lighted a candle that stood on the dresser. He went back to his chair and to his silence.

"A day or two ago," said Jim slowly as though half afraid to trust what he thought to open speech, "I drilled an' blasted rock in the bal. Now I be undoin' the work that took a million years t' do! The maister said they rocks run once like boilin' water or was dissolved like salt or settled in places like sugar in the bottom of a cup."

As he spoke a new light shone in his eyes. He had been suddenly transferred from the dull, commonness of labor and the narrow limits of his mine and village life to the ever-widening world of the man who lives and learns. No wonder he wanted to tell Pol, thought Allen. Literacy means a new birth to him.

Aloud, Allen said: "Jim, boay, you 'ave tasted of several fields of knowledge now. Which one interested you most?"

"I never thought of that, you," said Jim. "I awnly wondered 'ow I'd find anough time t' learn much about all of mun." He looked at Allen with childlike shame and said, "I 'ave wraute down a foo things so as to remember mun."

Allen smiled understandingly and said, "Brave, my son."

Then he smoked on in silence. Jim allowed him his reverie, thinking it always paid to wait for anything Allen said. Once he had said Allen should have been a preacher; at this moment he thought Allen would have been in his element as a teacher.

But the thought going through Allen's mind was not for utterance. He was comparing his own approach to learning with Jim's. His own was the step-by-step, the graded method, suited, as was thought, to his physical and mental development. The doors to knowledge were inched open to his requirement and ability. Knowledge was let through faster and faster as he grew. He was in his late teens before his appreciation was fired and education was both privilege and benefit. When that happened he went to work. He became a student. Jim, however, brought a mature mind, full-grown hungers, wide-eyed amazement, keen enjoyment, a man's sense of value to the things that had bored Allen and to which he had often to be flogged. Allen smiled at the memory. He thought he should not say what he was thinking. Jim was a unique experiment.

Jim saw the smile and said, curiously, "W'at izza, Bob?"

"I was thinking of the grand experience you be 'avin', my son," he said with slight evasion.

"I shall never be able t' pay Frost back," said Jim.

"Yes, you will, my son," said Allen earnestly. "Yes, you will."

Without trying to fathom Bob's meaning Jim asked what had become of the Swede the master was teaching.

"'E lef' t' go t' school, t' be ready t' study in a minin' school when fall come. 'E come t' the master t' make 'e's English better. 'E was very well schooled afore 'e come 'ere."

"W'ere's the minin' school?" asked Jim.

"Pennsylvania, I b'lieve."

"None closer?"

"Not that I knaw by," said Bob. "W'en 'e come back 'e

won't mine no more like you an' me. 'E'll prob'bly boss the whole mine, w'erever 'e land."

It was Jim's turn to be quiet. The Swede filled him with amazement. Breaking loose from his job to go to school! Daring to set up a ladder that reached the top, and then daring to climb it! America, he thought, his lips moving to the word. America and the teacher! Something in the combination caught his fancy. America and the teacher! For that Swede, the teacher was the most of America! He thought of it a little longer and then said, "W'y do he do it? The taycher, I mean. 'E take Swedes, Eyetalians, Jews, Cousin Jacks if they'll come, give mun 'e's time an' strength an' learnin' for nothin'!"

" 'E's 'ard t' see, maybe, w'at a man like Frost get aout of 'e's job. But 'e's paid, no doubt. W'en 'e see your heyes get bright, see your hand shape words and 'ear improvement in the way you say them. W'en 'e think w'at a 'appier man you'll be an' more useful, a 'aow much better citizen—maybe 'e feel paid. No tellin'.

"Frost be American. 'E's grandfer was a Revolutionary soldier. 'E fought for American independence. Frost knaw America can't thrive if Eyetalians stay Eyetalians and Swedes stay Swedes, an' all the rest. 'E might get some pay there.

"They taychers 'ave a big place in communities like this. Some of mun dawn't knaw it, but he do." Allen nodded in the direction of the teacher's house.

He blew a mouthful of smoke toward the candle and watched it rise in the warm air over the flame.

"You knaw, Jim, the sooner we get awver boastin' that we be Henglish, and tothers that they be this an' that, the better; for, shore as life, our chuldern won't be w'at we be. They will be Americans. Us shall live t' see the day w'en they will intermarry."

"They'll mix, thee's mean, Eyetalian with Swede an' English with Finn?" asked Jim aghast.

"I b'lieve so, my son."

"Will that be good?" asked Jim.

Allen laughed at the horrified look on Jim's face. " 'E won't be fatal, boay," Allen said; "but 'aow bad 'e be, be for aour gran'chuldern t' worry abaout. The schools will 'ave a big job."

"An' the chapels," added Jim.

"Hi dawn't knaw abaout they," said Allen.

Again footsteps sounded on the little stoop, followed by a knock on the door. Then came Mrs. Jenkins' voice:

"Come in, Mr. Penglaze."

"Is Jim 'ome?"

"Iss," she said, "in 'is room."

Hearing, Jim went to the door and invited the visitor in. Penglaze did not speak to Allen, and showed displeasure when he saw him.

Allen arose to go. "Take my chair, William," he said. "I'll be goin'."

"Hi'll sit on the bed," said Penglaze.

Allen laughed. "Do e expect Jim t' sleep in un after you've set on un?"

Penglaze had no retort.

"Dawn't go, Bob," urged Jim. "Dedn' e come awver fur somethin' special?"

"Awnly t' tell 'e t' 'ave the missus make 'e a pasty for the trip an' maybe one for the master. 'E do like mun an' 'e's missus dawn't make mun. Good night, Jim. Good night, William."

As Allen went out, Jake came in. Jim felt a sense of relief. Why, he could scarcely tell. Dislike for Penglaze like a shadow passed over him. The man's uncompromising bluntness disturbed him. He wondered what William wanted.

Penglaze was uncomfortable, too. The relief he felt at Allen's going was cut short by Jake's arrival. Not that either would deter him from his mission. Nor was his discomfort enough to make him defer his purpose for a better time. It was merely the difference between the backless seat on the bed and the chair Allen had offered him. What he had come to do, he would do. If he fell short of that, he would default the cause he had adopted. To await another occasion was to show a weakness he would not countenance.

The two partners waited in silence for their guest to announce his wish. Both knew he had not come merely to make a call. Jake had been indifferent to Penglaze since their words at Uren's. Jim met him and spoke to him at the Class and Sunday school. There and elsewhere, his words with the Class leader were as few as he could keep them.

"Hi comed awver t' see e abaout the Class," the leader began. "Hi be givin' of un up. Hint'res' in un dawn't seem t' be strong. Maybe 'e need a new leader, a new voice. Hi thought a younger man might be better."

Neither of the younger men doubted Penglaze's sincerity: he had taken the Class as a matter of duty; in the same way he would surrender it. Nor could either detect any hurt or regret in his words. He was not seeking praise or encouragement: alike, these were foreign to him. Penglaze spoke seriously, his eyes searching Jim's face in the candlelight.

"W'at do e say, Jim?"

"You want me to take un?" asked Jim.

"Oosh," answered Penglaze.

"Hi can't," said Jim simply.

"W'y can't e? You be a Christian, bayn't e?"

"Hi be too young t' begin with; an', besides, I dawn't 'ave the gift."

"Try un for one Sunday—next Sunday—an' see 'aow 'e go," urged Penglaze.

"Hi be goin' away next Sunday," argued Jim, "with Allen, the taycher, an' Jake 'ere."

Penglaze's face darkened. He knew the teacher's inclination for days abroad in the woods. He knew Allen's Sunday custom. As Class leader it was his privilege to offer rebuke. "Goin' Sabbath-breakin', are e, boay?" he asked.

Jim did not answer, but he saw Jake's far-away gaze return to the room he occupied. He looked at Penglaze but remained silent, waiting.

Undaunted, if he had observed the change in Jake's attention, he continued under the urge of a Class leader's duty as he conceived it.

"Your comp'ny bayn't good for e, my son. Sunday bayn't no day for traipsin' the woods."

"Hi can't do un, maister," said Jim, ignoring the remark. "Shan't."

"You 'ad best watch an' pray lest you enter into temptation," admonished Penglaze.

Jim did not answer, but he wished heartily that his visitor would go. Then Jake spoke.

"William," he said, "you 'ave got yer answer. An' you've awvertalked yerself. You'd bes' be goin'."

"Hi dedn' come t' see you, an' haren't talkin' t' you," said Penglaze.

"No, but you'm talkin' about me an' yer betters. You'd better go."

Jake arose and went to the door. Jim got up too, following him. For an instant Penglaze hesitated, but he took his hat and went.

When the door closed, Jake turned to the kitchen, where Harry and his wife, Hunt, and Spargo were still sitting. In the doorway he stopped. Both husband and wife smiled and said, "Come on in, Jake."

"No, thankee," answered Jake. " 'E's bedtime. Hi wanted t' ask the missus if 'er will make three pasties for us Saturday so that us can 'ave mun for Sunday."

"Iss, you," said Mrs. Jenkins.

"Aren't e afraid you'll choke on un, comrade?" asked Spargo, "on a trip like that? Wuss things 'ave 'appened in the Scripters."

Jake laughed with the others, but all he said was, "Thankee, missus, an' good night."

Inside their room again Jake said, "Thicky one be as welcome to me as a missed 'ole." And with that the Penglaze incident ended.

Chapter Twenty

AFTER BREAKFAST, which the missus had prepared the night before, Jim and Jake were ready to go. Each put a pasty into his pocket, and Jake carried an extra, carefully wrapped in paper, in his hand.

They found Allen already at the teacher's house, his coat pocket bulging with the crib Mrs. Uren had made for him. Mr. Frost put Mrs. Jenkins' contribution into a small knapsack he always carried when he tramped, and they were off.

Allouez was not yet awake. The four men walked and talked quietly lest they disturb the last sleep of the cottages they passed. Not a curtain was raised; each house was sealed and still. Many windows were still insulated against the winter, now all but gone. Steam and smoke curled lazily from pipes and stacks of the mine. Everything proclaimed the day to be the Day of Rest.

They followed the road going north for a distance to which no one seemed to be paying attention, when the teacher left the road for the woods. A hundred yards, and they were among trees of the primitive forest. Jim and Jake followed with a sense of novelty, wondering at times how their companions could know or keep their way.

The trees stood still in the breezeless sunshine, their shadows marking off the forest floor in a tangled arabesque

of threads, cords, cables that tripped the eye and shortened
the step or lengthened it like a visible obstruction. A smile
or humorous ejaculation followed as each saw one of the
others a victim of the illusion. For a long time no one spoke.
They all joined themselves to the silence, half regretful that
their footfalls or stumbling disturbed the sanctity of the
forest. Jake spoke at last, his eyes twinkling with the assurance that he and his partners were feeling and thinking
alike.

"Hi reckon us be allowed t' spayk in 'ere. 'E be Sunday
'ere hev'ry day."

"Oosh," answered Jim.

But Jake did not add anything. The spirit of the place
or the hour or the day restrained him. All were content with
the constant change that met their eyes: trees with buds ready
to burst into leaf and trees with no knowledge that spring
was so close at hand; boulders here and there to be avoided;
ascents and descents, soft, yielding earth underfoot and knife-
like exposures of rock.

Finally a squirrel scurried across their path and circled a
tree bole to chatter at their intrusion. A chipmunk rattled
some dead leaves in his fright and disappeared as he had appeared, suddenly. An occasional rabbit startled the trampers
as he bounded from cover for a few yards to sit and watch
with solemnly suspicious eyes the invaders of his domain.
A breeze arose as suddenly as these, as if startled too; and the
travelers accepted the token as their permission to talk as
they pleased.

Now they climbed; now they slithered and skittered down
a sharp slope; from closely growing trees they stepped into
open spaces. In a protected confluence of two knolls, Allen
and Frost stopped. Before them was a small mound of snow,
and near it a patch of flowers, their petals of cream and pink.
Ever so slightly they nodded through the brown sodden
leaves.

"The first I have seen," said Frost. "Our American edelweiss."

"W'at izza called?" asked Jake.

"Arbutus," said Allen. "Trailin' arbutus. Some places 'e's called graound laurel or Mayflower."

"Back 'ome, Mayflowers grow on bushes," said Jake.

"They be lilacs 'ere, my son," explained Allen.

" 'E's as purty as a primrose, to my heyes," said Jake. "Edna, boay?"

" 'E's a purty flower," answered Jim. "Did e hever see flowers an' snaw so close t'gether?"

"They be light sleepers an' hearly risers, comrade. Wake up with the lightest touch of spring."

The schoolmaster turned and looked at Jake, and Allen smiled; but Jake noticed neither.

At times, for short distances, the four walked abreast; at times in pairs, and again in single file. The partners walked together or with Allen or the teacher in turn. They kept no order.

Jim remembered what Allen had said about the teacher and listened intently to all he said of the trees or shrubs or animals he saw. Outdoors was just another book in his library, it seemed, a book he read carefully and well. Jim asked himself, 'Ow do a man come by it all?

Once, when he happened to be beside the teacher he asked, "Do e knaw all they trees by name, Mr. Frost?"

"Most of them, I think," the teacher replied; "but that is not as difficult as you surmise. You would soon learn most of them, Jim. My father was a teacher of botany, you see. When I went to college I made it my first choice. I don't know whether I inherited my love for outdoor things from my father, or whether I learned to love them from him."

"W'at's the difference?" asked Jim seriously.

Frost laughed and said, "You asked a hard one then Jim —too hard to answer now."

The planless freedom of their journey limited their talk to mere patches of words. From such as he got from the master, a wonder began to emerge in Jim's mind. The man knew more of the things about him than any man Jim had ever met before. Indeed, he had never met one who took more than a poacher's interest in wild beasts or a mill man's interest in woods. The women tended the little flower "knats" around the cottages at home, and the blooms they nursed were few in number. Of those few the women knew only the names. The teacher went farther—farther than Jim could follow him. The question Jim raised was, What is the use of it? He wished he might ask Frost but was afraid a blunt question might offend. He thought, P'r'aps I'd better ask Allen.

Then the teacher spoke again. "Beginning to feel at home in Allouez, Jim?"

"Feel at 'ome in a boardin' 'ouse?" laughed Jim. "I feel aysier as I knaw more people an' they knaw me better."

Frost glanced at Jim and wondered if he should say what was in his mind. Talk was difficult circling trees, keeping branches from slapping one's face, stepping over roots, stones and fallen tree trunks. He abandoned the idea.

Then he stopped. "See!" he said. "There is a maple trying its best to grow as a maple should; but it can't. It is over-topped by its neighbors. Shortly a storm may give it a chance —those older ones will break and fall. Then the maple will get its chance at the sunlight."

To Jim and Jake the excursion was like being truant from school. They were absorbing a sense of freedom they had never known before. Perhaps the squirrels running from tree to tree and leaping from limb to limb in fright or ecstasy, or the birds darting from bud to bud or sending messages to mates that were out of sight, or the wind that kept the trees nodding in majestic courtesy to one another, imparted something to them.

Atop a steep slope Jake took Jim by the arm and stopped him. " 'Ow 'bout a race t' the bottom, comrade?" he asked. "Take off yer billycock an' let's go."

Allen and Frost were already at the foot of the grade when Jake shouted, "Look out below," and started.

Jim followed, surprised at Jake's exuberance and laughing at the spectacle he made. When Jim joined the others Jake said: "It was they w'iskers 'old e back, comrade. Dawn't the Scripters say if somethin' or other—w'iskers maybe—keep e back, cut min off?"

For some time the men climbed steadily. All were warm from the exertion, but they kept on until their route flattened and they picked their way through the trees on level ground. Here the trees were stunted and wind-blown. Their boles and limbs were atrophied and gnarled. They were gaunt, poorly fed. Their few branches grew out from one side, pointing in the same direction. Rock broke through the thin soil and snakelike roots humped and twisted over the stone. Jake and Jim were giving full attention to their footing and had not noticed that to their right they might look directly into the sky. Suddenly Allen shouted. The partners looked up and saw him standing on a huge rock in an open space, his arms raised, his head bare and his light hair struggling in the wind.

"Behold Balboa on Darien!" he called.

Neither knew anything of Balboa or of Darien, but they looked in the direction he pointed and saw that the rock on which Allen stood was on the verge of a precipice that dropped abruptly, hundreds of feet, and that in the sweep of his arm were miles of forest, and beyond that Lake Superior. They were on the crest of Keweenaw Ridge.

The natural response to the scene that spread before them was silence. The sheer drop at their feet was enough to hush them, but added to that were the miles of forest, the soft shore line of treetops bordering Torch Lake and beyond that,

Superior. Distance, silence, beauty! No wonder they were stilled.

Allen got down from his rock, picked up his hat, and with the others surrendered himself to the spirit of the height. At last he approached the crest of the cliff and, pointing, said: "See the road down there? Like a piece of yellow string."

Cautiously Jim and Jake neared the edge and looked. Something moved on the road and stood still.

"Bear," said Allen, and from his pocket took a small telescope. "Take a look," he added, and handed the glass to Jake.

"With the glass, 'e's a bear," said Jake. "Without un, 'e's a emmet."

"The glass bring un too close for comfort," said Jim, and returned the instrument to Allen.

Allen seemed to ignore the ledge as he looked into the abyss, but the partners felt the powerful pull of the depth and instinctively drew back, afraid of the magnetism it exerted on them.

They all buttoned their coats against the chill of the wind that blew from the lake, and sought a place to sit where they would be sheltered but also could enjoy the warmth of the sun and continue to look over forest and sea.

"I was just thinking you Cornishmen ought to feel at home here," said Frost. "This strip of peninsula is like your Cornwall with its rocky, hilly moors running from end to end, its wealth of copper, and water-beaten on three sides."

No one answered him.

"With the difference," he continued, "that Cornwall has had its day, and the day for this peninsula is just at sunrise. Copper and iron for centuries to come!" He stopped to marvel at the idea he had expressed. "And the iron, it is said, extends under the lake to Canada."

" 'Oo knaw that?" asked Jake curiously.

"An' how will a be worked if 'e's there?" added Jim.

" 'E might as well be hunder the 'Lantic Ocean, t' my mind," said Jake.

Frost was amused at the interruption but did not attempt to answer Jake's skepticism. He chose to go on with what he foresaw.

"And west of us and north of us are the wheat fields of the Dakotas and Canada. This lake is the highway over which it will pass to market. It is the Sabbath on the water today, but the end of the Sabbath is near. The time is close when these waters will know no Sabbath. Canals are being cut, railroads are coming, fleets are being built, and cities around the borders of the lakes are growing like magic."

"W'y be things so oncertain?" asked Jim.

"Things are not uncertain, Jim," answered Frost; "they are only new. The future of this country, of these lakes is as certain as tomorrow's sun."

"That be a money man's dream," said Jake.

"Money men be dreamin' of this country all right, comrade," said Allen; "but thee's knaw, Jake, 'e can't make money an' not give some t' we."

"Dawn't worry, Bob, about me," said Jake when what he meant for humor seemed mistaken for argument. "I be planning t' bide a bit an' do some dreamin' too."

By this time the warmth of their climb had worn off, and the chill air began to touch them with discomfort. They rose to go. With their backs to the cliff, the teacher said, "If the trees were not so close and dense we could see the lake this way too."

Again they entered the woods, Frost leading the way. Talk became a secondary interest; too much attention to their steps was necessary. Frequently they stopped to observe a newly arrived bird or a plant face rare among the leafing population of the peninsula.

"You see," Frost remarked to Jake, "growing things have

no choice of where they will grow. Wherever their seeds alight, whether dropped or blown, they try to grow."

"Then Jim an' me be growin' things," said Jake. "Us was blowed out of Henglan' an' lighted 'ere. No choice." He smiled wryly. "Choice or no choice, though, us be in luck."

They stopped to let a pair of porcupines amble across their path. The creatures paid no attention to their spectators.

"Hoogly, but wise," said Jake. "Mindin' their awn business."

"Always in full armor, they bayn't afeard of much," said Allen.

Of a sudden, like a mirror flashing before their eyes, they came upon a small lake. Along its shore were snow-white birches looking like wax candles set for a forest ceremony. Their reflection in the water was as clear as the reality, detailed to the last twig and bud. Not a ripple disturbed the border-line illusion. Again the party stopped to enrich eye and mind and memory.

For a half-hour they threaded their way as they had done for most of the morning when, just as the lake had appeared, a road lay in their path. It was a poor pattern of a highway, rutted deeply, with pools of water extending from rut to rut, here and there. A ridge ran between the ruts, showing that scarcely anything but teams passed over it. At times the four men walked abreast but more at length, walked single file, which reduced their talk to scattered bits. Still the road was a relief, and the four responded to it with easier steps.

" 'E need t' be stoned a foo times," said Jake, recalling the custom in Cornwall.

" 'E'll be a long time afore that 'appen," said Jim. "The roads 'ere be endless." He was slow in letting the distance he had traveled from New York become ordinary.

Allen was interested in their words. "This be a turnpike, my sons—a bonanza. Thirty year ago 'e wadn' 'ere." He stopped and faced the pair. Pointing to the ruts at his feet, he said, "Thicky scratch in the groot do mark the beginning of 'ist'ry."

Allen's comment was a signal for every man to dream.

"They fust days mus' 'a' been discouragin'," said Jake. "No way in; no way out."

"Hi never thought of that," answered Jim.

"There will be a plod t' tell about that some day," said Jake thoughtfully.

"Back 'ome the roads was like the 'ills—been there halways," said Jim.

"The present be too full t' think much of the past, my son," said Jake. "There mus' be some ol'-timers 'ere 'oo seed they things come."

"You'll be disappointed, boay, if you think they fust citizens will tell e much," said Allen. "I thought they could make good talk; but they was too busy with a dag, or a shovel, cuttin' down trees or shovelin' a pit, to get the answers to your questions. Besides that, in thirty year they 'ave forgot." Allen's look showed the discouragement he had felt. "You would 'ave t' fill in with your awn fancy, an' that edn' hist'ry."

Jim found himself looking at Allen as a child looks at a teacher when baffled by a sum. But Allen said no more.

Once more the vast silence, the unbroken solitude, of the place that had appealed to him earlier in the morning came to Jim's mind. This road was a sort of line drawn between the mysterious past and the present. On one side of it was the long waiting, the aimless wandering of beasts, and the scarcely more aimful wandering of primitive men, the unrecorded births and deaths of beings who left only footprints on the forest mold. As the leaves burst their buds, ripened and fell, so they came and went. It all belonged to the same void as the wind and stars. Almost as completely swallowed up in it were the doings of the first whites who came to save red men's souls for a white man's heaven. Their heroic and unrewarded labors were lost to memory after the flight of only two centuries.

On that same side were many of the battles of whites and reds, the futile resistances of the reds for self-preservation and the total expulsion of the pale invader. No one would ever know the copper-hued monarchs who, in pride and confidence, had commanded that white tide in vain.

On the other side was what? These men could not tell. Already their adopted country had advanced beyond their comprehension. Their thoughts were limited to what was nearest to them. How deep the mines had been sunk already in the short span of three decades! Quincy atop the cliff at Hancock was already deeper than Dolcoath. The two-thousand mark was already passed by a score of others, and prophecies were common that some would pass a mile before they were done. That seemed like an insane fiction. Allen had told Jim the first locomotive to puff west of the Appalachians had run between two Michigan towns not a generation before. (And he, Jim, had ridden by train from New York to Lake Superior!) He had also said something about Chicago being only forty-five years old, and Jim had been bewildered by the size of it. With such things for measures one might cite a future as fabulous as he wished. That rutted road marked off a vague, empty yesterday from a pulsing, vital tomorrow.

For some time the sound of running water had been reaching them, and they now spied it through the trees. Between the road and the stream the ground was soft and swampy. They continued along the road until the water was lost again to their view. Suddenly Frost turned into the bush, separating the low growths with his hands for passage. He led on until he reached an open spot as big as a town lot which stretched solidly to the water's edge.

It was evident to Jake and Jim that the master and Allen had been there before. They had noticed that at no time did

Allen seem to be following. Indeed he as often led the way as did Frost.

They crossed the clearing to the water, where a large flat stone lay unshaded in the sun. To their right they could hear the stream fret and complain at the obstructions in its path. From the thicket it emerged in rags and tatters of foam which now circled the pool that embraced half of the rock the men chose to use as table and chair and couch. Restfully and timidly the little islets of froth drifted here and there until, caught by an invisible tow, they slipped again into the forest and were gone.

The four stood gazing into the water as if expecting a mermaid to rise from its clear, dark depths. Here the waves and falls and spray of the upper course of the stream rested after their long struggle with roots and stones and fallen boles, gathering strength for their last run to the lake. The shrubs that bordered the retreat were still as though in reverence, the wind being restrained by the outer bulwark of the thicket. Peace was in the air of the place, and a quiet that reached the innermost depths of a man, that made him aware of the immensities that dwelt beyond the rim of his universe, yet touched his world and him.

Allen, without raising his eyes, in a voice low but clear, said, "He leadeth me beside the still waters."

Neither of the others looked at him for any connotation of his words. As he said them, they were accepted by the rest.

"That will serve as grace," said Frost. "This is the end of today's journey." He looked up at the sun and added, "It must be close to noon."

"W'y look hup?" asked Jake. He lifted his belt from his waist, showing a convincing slackness, and then pulled his lever from his pocket. "Aas, 'e's after twelve," he said.

"Time t' eat," added Jim.

The Cornishmen drew their pasties from their pockets, untied their crib bags, and extracted their meal, as Jake said, "all in a piece."

Jake held his up admiringly. " 'E's a purty thing to a 'ongry man," he said. He broke the pasty in the middle and laid a half on the bag spread on the rock. "Tetties, mayt, an' a smill of onion make un fit for a king," he added in tribute.

"A bit of turnip 'elp a lot," said Jim.

"Hi'll take parsley in mine, comrade, if I can get un," said Allen.

While Jim and Jake looked at their pasties with hungry appreciation, Allen scanned his with discouraged eyes. "The Cousin Jinnies be famous for awnly one bit of cookery, an' some be no good at that," he said wryly.

"Did e ever see a Cousin Jack w'at couldn' beat a drill, comrade?" asked Jake.

Allen laughed but immediately sobered. "Hi wonder if fish do like pasty!" he said.

His pasty, a hard, overdone, shapeless thing, splashed and sank. "There," he said. "Maybe after 'e's soaked a week they can eat un."

Bob joined in the merriment of his friends and accepted contributions from them. Frost made up for the shortage with sandwiches and topped off Mrs. Jenkins' generosity with cake for all.

"In spite of that thing," said Bob, nodding toward his submerged meal, "a pasty is a great invention. 'E's a whole meal suited to a man's pocket w'en 'e 'ad t' climb ladders in the mine."

"True anough, Bob," said Jake; "but you be onjust. Thicky one 'ave 'e's points. You could drop 'e down the shaft fust an' find un waitin' w'en you got down, smilin' a welcome an' un'urt."

Jake and Bob loaded their pipes and, to all appearances, set their minds to the leisurely twist and spread of their smoke. Jim lay back on the rock, pulled his billycock over

his face, put his hands under his head, and let his muscles
sag. He tried to analyze the sensations of the day. Foremost
came the feeling of freedom from responsibility. It was a
strange, indecipherable thing. He did not remember ever
feeling it before. Never before had the world of people been
shut off from him or had he been shut off from it as he was
just then. Allen and Jake and the master were gone, all
parted from him by the ancient silence "back of the road."
He was freed for the day from the mine, the call of the
whistle, the small urbanities of the street. Sure enough, there
was a lot to enjoy, to learn, to puzzle over in the woods, did
one want to do it; but the odd sense of release, to be lost
to everybody and everything but himself—that was the thing.
Did all the men who traipsed the woods take the enrichment
they offered, feel in the wind the breath of a measureless past
on their faces, expand to the clouds above and the horizons
around them as if released from their bodies? He doubted it.

The stillness of the place called him back. It spoke to him
in the very sounds it made. The water had not stopped its
murmur and the soft network of the new foliage still whispered. He listened to it as his muscles began to hurt from the
hardness of his couch. The stream and the shrubs had murmured and whispered so when there had been no ears to hear.
All the sounds of all the seasons had followed one another
through the years and the centuries. Was there such a thing as
silence? Silence here meant only the loss of man-made sounds.
The forest was full of sound—always. Jim wondered. Yes,
there was silence underground, he thought. And then he
denied it. He had been alone in the mine in places where no
drafts stirred in the drift or water dripped from the back,
where there was no timber to creak; and yet there were
sounds. Then he wondered if a man could stand absolute
silence. No, the road did not mark off silence from sound,
only one kind of sound from another—the laughter, the
cries, the voices of men from the notes of joy or fright of lesser

things, of breeze or storm, when only the stars looked on and heard.

For the first time that day he thought of Pol. The cliff, the woodland, the vast impulse of spring, the road and its implications, the effect of tramping an earth almost untouched since God had made it had shut out his old world, including his religion and her. How could that happen? He would tell her about it—but could he? He had no words or skill for a task like that. He must wait till she came. That meant he would never tell her—tell it as he wanted to tell it now. It would stale while he waited, or grow beyond its present bounds. Then it would be hopeless. He had never dreamed he could forget her or forget what day it was, but he had done both. What did it mean? To the question he asked, nothing inside him rose in rebuke; and he was glad. He wondered if he might take her on this trip some day. He fancied her on the cliff, her hair surrendering to the wind, her skirts ablow and her holding his arm while she looked and marveled as he had done. What did Allen call it? It was more like Pisgah to Jim. And the road! Those monstrous ideas that reached back to the birth of the world. He would see her eyes widen as he knew his own had done. And the wind, or whatever it was, that swept his care away and left himself—free. He could not tell her these things; he must wait. The rock was wearing into him, and he sat up.

Jake took his pipe from his lips, and Jim waited on the portent he knew so well.

"I feel like— 'Oo was a, comrade? 'E said, 'Let us make three tabernacles.' I could bide 'ere a long time."

"Then thee't 'appy, Mr. Sabbath Breaker," said Jim.

"I 'ad forgot 'e was the Sabbath, shore 'nough," said Jake.

"Me too until a minute back," confessed Jim.

A splash in the water broke the quiet. A spotted, sparkling arc flashed before their eyes and disappeared. At one end of the arc was just a tremble of the dark amber surface; at the other ripples broke sharply from the spot where the fish had plunged from sight.

"You won't need no ravens t' bring your crib, comrade," said Allen, "with this creek runnin' afore your tabernacle door."

Allen got up and moved to the edge of the bank and looked into the water. He turned and beckoned to the others. "Walk light like," he said, "an' look 'ere." They looked and saw. "I fancy I shall come back soon," he added. "A mite of bread an' a bit of fire on that rock with they in a skillet be worth a Sabbath day's journey, I'd say."

So that was what Allen carried in the pack he always wore on his Sunday trips. I wonder w'at sort of cook 'e be! Jim smiled at his own idea. P'r'aps a long anough trip be all a man need t' eat 'e's awn cookin'. For a moment Jim encouraged the plan to accompany Allen some day. What about trying a short journey alone!

The four men strolled around the small enclosure in silence, each refreshing himself at the springs of solitude. Back to their starting point again, they sat down once more. There was two hours yet before they would meet the stage, and they could walk the distance in much less time than that.

Frost broke the silence. "I wonder if David was a fisherman, Bob. I always think of him when I come here. You did too, before we ate. Right?"

"Yes," said Bob, "I did; but nothing I have read suggested he ever saw a fishhook."

"And he never saw forests like these stretching across empire after empire."

"No. His cedars were just drift timber. We have cedars here that were trees when he was a boy."

Allen was looking into some oblivion, not turning his head to Frost's remarks or to emphasize his own.

"He never felt a new earth under his feet, either," said Frost.

"No. The ground he tramped was stale with the footprints of centuries."

"Too bad his harp can't sound again today—and here."

"You ask too much, Silas, or too little—I don't know which," said Allen. "The Davids and Shakespeares are wisely scattered, as I see it. That gives encouragement to any man to try his hand. I'd rather see a little more of the po—I mean the fisherman in every man."

Quietly, as if for himself alone, Frost recited:

> "To him who in the love of Nature holds
> Communion with her visible forms, she speaks
> A various language."

He stopped for the effect of his words upon his own spirit, and Allen carried on.

> "For his gayer hours
> She has a voice of gladness, and a smile
> And eloquence of beauty, and she glides
> Into his darker musings, with a mild
> And healing sympathy, that steals away
> Their sharpness, ere he is aware."

"Go ahead, my son," said Bob.

Frost did, uttering the words he chose as if to himself alone:

> "Go forth, under the open sky, and list
> To Nature's teachings, while from all around—
> Earth and her waters, and the depths of air—
> Comes a still voice."

"The man who wrote that was popular while I was in school," said Allen; "his poetry was on everybody's lips. But that much was all I wanted. The rest of it is like a Dartmoor bog. He threw a little nosegay of rhetoric to what we have seen today and then had us walking through the biggest graveyard in the universe."

Jake had listened to all this without a word. He removed his pipe to say he wanted to speak. " 'Ow far do a run from 'ere, Bob—the creek?" he asked.

"Abaout two miles, I judge," answered Bob.

"Let's go an' see un," said Jake. "Us 'ave the time. Too much rest bayn't good for mortals like we."

Allen glanced at Jake suspecting something off key by the remark, but Jake's face showed only an innocent interest in the lake's welcome to the little stream.

Watches were examined, and they agreed.

A half-hour, and the lake came in sight. A turn in the road, and the little river was at their feet. It made a disappointing end. Just before it left the tangle of woods, it fell over a ledge, making an enchanting little fall. It crossed the road in a shallow spread, spreading more and more as it approached the lake. All its attempts to make a channel for itself were defeated by recurrent storms.

For some time they stood in silence looking over the empty waters. The waves that broke at their feet were scarcely audible. Without a word Allen turned away, and the homeward journey had begun.

When the lake was out of sight, Allen told the story of Houghton's explorations and death. "Not far from w'ere us was standin'," he said. " 'E was in sight of the shore w'en 'e died." Bob told the story simply. No one asked where he had learned it; no one doubted a word he spoke. Houghton was a personable being to him, close and warm like some one he had really known. Allen seemed to reach back and touch hands with the man who had died a martyr to a passion for useful knowledge.

"W'y did a do it? Was a hordered?" asked Jake.

"No, Jake, not ordered; 'e was drawve. As missionaries be drawve, only"—Allen was speaking slowly, choosingly—"for somethin' closer t' crayture comfort, somethin' that ain't shook aout of a man by a change of hopinion; somethin', boay, that would make men feel safe t' spen' fortunes, build taowns, 'omes, an' schools."

" 'E wadn' lookin' for a fortune for 'isself?"

"Hi dawn't knaw w'at was in 'e's mind, my son, but I daoubt it. 'E belonged to a new breed of men 'oo be startin' up, 'oo will spend their lives learnin' 'aow t' make 'omes pleasanter, work aysier, 'ealth shorer, an' sickness less fateful. Some may get rich, but foo will. The best of they will give little mind t' money. 'Oughton belonged t' they."

When Allen was done, they walked in silence, watching their shadows lengthen in the open spaces. No one heeded the distance they were traveling until the master said, "Just beyond that charred tree is the stage road." He pointed to the all but limbless bole standing distinct against the sky. It split in halves a cleft in the slope they were steadily climbing. In some years-old forest fire it had lost bark and branches save for a few scraggy stumps. On its tip sat a lone crow, as black as his watchtower, keeping a self-appointed sentry.

" 'E be w'ere 'e can see an' be seen, I fancy," said Jim.

"No knawin' aow many heyes below look t' 'e for safety," said Allen.

Not far beyond the tree, the road dropped rapidly between the steep sides of the cleft the tree had marked. It led across a small creek and through a patch of bog in which the current appeared to lose itself. A hundred yards, and they were on the stage road. They found places to sit while they waited for the stage.

"If we 'ave missed the coach, thee must think up another plod, Allen, boay, t' make the road short like the last," announced Jake.

"Us might walk on a bit," said Allen. "There's a coat's diff'rence atween this shade an' the hopen spots. The coach will catch us."

When the stage overtook them, they found that they had it to themselves and were glad. They sank to the seats gratefully. "My legs 'ave growed old in a day," said Jake, and with that speech languished.

The trees that overarched the road hastened the nightfall. Whenever their way dipped into a hollow, everything about them disappeared in a fog. A slight ascent, and the air was clear again. The horses had no difficulty in keeping the road, and the driver appeared to take no responsibility for their direction. Allen's voice called the nodding heads and swaying bodies to attention by saying, " 'Ere is w'ere you seen the bear."

Jake and Jim looked out to get a view of the cliff but could see only a wall of blackness that seemed to blend with the sky.

Finally Jim was in familiar surroundings. He recognized the spot where Tom was found the night of Walters' death. This far he had often walked when loneliness had bound his spirit or some problem had pressed for solution. He had made friends of the night silences, of the needled, snow-laden wind, of the creaking sounds of the forest in winter. He knew now that the other seasons would extend their friendship too.

When the lights of Allouez came into view, it dawned on Jim that nothing had been said about supper. The missus did not have any idea when they would get home. Nor had he had when they left in the morning. He was hungry.

Frost's voice calling to the driver wakened Jim from his reverie. He asked the driver to stop as they were at that moment nearest his home. He clambered from the coach, saying the while: "Come, my sons, com'es on 'ome with me. My missus will 'ave a bit of craouse for all of e. How's that, Bob, for a make-believe Cornishman?" he asked, laughing.

"Brave, you," answered Bob. "An' they words be sweet saounds t' three 'ongry tramps."

Chapter Twenty-one

ONE ADVANTAGE OF BEING night-shift—and miners agreed it was the only one—was that a man could lie abed as long as he wanted to on Monday morning. Jim and Jake had left word that they were not to be called for breakfast, so that they might get all the sleep they needed.

Jake awoke first. He knew it was late by the shadows on the wall opposite the window. He looked at them with an indifference that was a luxury. Finally, to gratify his curiosity, and, as he said, to laugh at his watch, he drew the timepiece from under his pillow. Sure enough, it was ten o'clock. His movement awakened Jim.

"W'at did Solomon call folks 'oo sleep too much, comrade? You hought t' be 'shamed."

"W'at time izza?" asked Jim.

"Ten a'clock," said Jake accusingly.

"I can't 'elp un, you, if 'e be noon. Thicky trip made me tireder than a doubler."

" 'E filled my legs with rheumatics," returned Jake. "They 'urt like growin' pains."

"Us 'ad better walk some more t' take mun out," suggested Jim.

Jake agreed, but neither made a move to get up. Instead, they stretched and yawned until wide enough awake to review their excursion.

"Hi be too lazy for that sort of thing," Jake began. "Hi like sidewalks, good roads, an' folks about me. 'Untin' an' fishin' never was to my taste—'edge'ogs an' bears."

"Did e ever 'unt?"

"No."

"N'r fish?"

"No. But I 'ad hopportoonity an' dedn' want to. A man mus' be born to un or come by un young."

"I was wonderin'," said Jim. "Mr. Frost an' Bob seem t' come by un natural like."

"Aas," returned Jake. "But you knaw they 'ave other int'rests in un, more'n you an me an' most folks."

"True, but you knaw chaps 'oo couldn' tell *B* from bull's foot 'oo love t' fish an' 'unt."

"Oosh," said Jake, " 'e's a gift," and lapsed into silence. Minutes passed before he spoke again. "The 'igh spot, t' my mind," he said musingly, "wadn' the top of the cliff. 'E was the plod Bob told of thicky man w'at drownded. Bob talked like 'e knawed un. W'en 'e spawk of they rocks on the shore an' the cliffs, you'd think 'e seed mun made."

"Aas, an' the lake too. To me, the cliff an' lake must always 'ave been there. They glacyers must 'a' been hawful things!"

"Hi wonder if there be any now!" said Jake.

"Seem like there must be w'ere there be snaw all the year round."

"That's so," said Jake. "Hi'd fancy seein' one."

For a time, the partners lay looking at the ceiling and the shadows, each content with his own musings. Jake was enigmatic as always. The look in his eyes told nothing of what journeyed to and fro in his brain. He was lying in a hidden place, looking out upon a world that was unconscious of his presence. Ideas engaged Jim's brain obviously. Problems wrote themselves plainly on his face. Still, Jake was first to form his thought to words.

"I told e w'at sterried me the most, comrade. W'at did you get out of the trip?" He grunted at something that amused him. "Allen on the rock lookin' into Canaan, I s'pose."

"You'm close, comrade," answered Jim, "but you missed by hever so little."

Jake turned over so as to stare questioningly into his eyes.

"Your Canaan notion be right, but the place w'ere 'e come be wrong."

"Spayk on," ordered Jake.

" 'Twas w'en us crossed thicky road," said Jim, and stopped. He knew he could not tell all it had meant. Ideas had come like clouds; they came from and went to—who knew whence and whither? They were monstrous, mysterious, intangible, and reached from unknown to unknown—beyond the horizons of the world he knew. The things he might have mentioned, something inside him forbade utterance. He wanted an explanation for them himself before he submitted them to conversation, even with Jake.

"I see," Jake muttered. "I see, I think. On one side of the road, nothin'; on tother side all America's goin' t' be. But w'at did a do for e?"

"Gived me peace of mind, comrade. I bayn't afeard no more."

"Then the trip be wuth all 'e cost," said Jake. He took time for his approval to have full weight with Jim before he went on. "Another convert to the bush," he said teasingly. "But you'm welcome to un, comrade. Hi'll drift along with the crowd." He smiled at Jim to prepare him for what was to follow. "Remember w'at Allen told the taycher w'en they was 'obnobbin' awver their book learnin'? 'E said, 'Shakespeare dedn' 'ave to go to Denmark or Venice to write about mun.' "

" 'E might 'a' wraute better about mun if 'e 'ad," said Jim.

Something amused Jake tremendously, and he laughed heartily. " 'Oo be you an' me t' mention Shakespeare?" he asked.

" 'E be dead, I fancy, an' can't answer back," retorted Jim.

Still laughing at his own joke, Jake swung his feet over the bedside and began to dress.

For several weeks Jim had been conscious of a deepening anxiety. He knew Pol's time was near at hand. He also knew the possibilities of the ordeal. He had had a sister once. He recalled his last look at her. She held her babe in her arms in the box the village carpenter had made for her. He relived it over and over again: the long slow walk from the village to the parish church; the long procession and the men stepping out of the line to take their turn to carry the coffin. He chilled to the marrow at the thought of it. What would he do if anything like that happened? or if the child were left to his care? If the worst happened, his Pol would be put away with him in a foreign land! He had heard that the first child was always dangerous. He almost dreaded the coming of the letter that would tell the tale. At times he saw it with a wide black rim. "Oh, God," he said, "I could never hopen un!" And then a remark of Jake's came to his mind: "More folks live than die; there be more good than bad; more light than dark."

He tried hard to adopt Jake's philosophy. Even now the child might be born. He hoped it was a boy. Mary Ann would choose a girl, of course. He tried to be generous, but in spite of himself he always thought in terms of a boy. In fancy he played with him, walked with him, explained things to him. He had never seen such things done, but he dreamed rather in terms of the things he himself had wished for—of the companionship a son ought to find in his father. Among the people he knew, the family was left to the care of the women. Fathers and sons became partners when the boys were big enough to work underground. His boy should know his father, and he would strive to know his boy. His boy should read and write, learn of peoples, times, events. He would know like Allen and Mr. Frost. What a man he would be! No mining for him, thought Jim.

Here his mind turned to Allen again. Allen was a miner, and he made mining a lighter trade by what he knew. But— Whenever Jim considered this side of Allen he came to the same full stop. He couldn't understand Bob. Honest and open, he was, 'twas true, but why was he in the mine? Why had he stayed underground these years? Bob told a lot of things; but he kept one secret, Jim was sure.

So Jim thought and waited.

Since he had landed in Allouez, Jim had received a letter a week after Pol had learned his address. It came almost unfailingly on Wednesday with an occasional arrival on Thursday. Pol had never failed him.

The week came at last when no letter arrived on either Wednesday or Thursday. Friday passed, and a Saturday.

Monday came, and Jim was day-shift. When he came home that night he found a letter lying on his dresser. Mary Ellen, knowing his anxiety, had fetched it from the office. The writing was strange to him, but the twopenny-halfpenny stamp told that it had come from England. The postmark said Callington.

Jim's fingers trembled as he picked it up. Who, in Callington, would write to him? " 'E look like a man's writin'," Jim said aloud, " 'eavy like." He tested its thickness. It was a small letter, just a note. He held it up to the light as though a word might show through and brace his courage. Then he tore it open and looked at the bottom of the page to see the name of the sender: J. M. Davey, M.D.!

Slowly Jim read, puzzling out the strange script. Why didn't people write alike, clearer, plainer? The letter was brief and to the point:

Dear Jim:
You have a son. Born last Wednesday. Sound in every part. His mother doing well. You must have her come to you as soon as you can. Times are still bad. Good luck to you.
Very truly,

Jim finished the letter and sat down. His brain seethed with questions the doctor might have answered. Likewise the tumult of ideas that had assaulted and besieged him for weeks past became active again, inspired by the message in his hand. He swept them aside to think of his boy. He was to have a chance to bring his own dream to pass. He had a boy to bring up! Jim thrilled to the thought. And then he remembered what an old Downgater had said at Fools' Corner: "Raisin' a cheel be like takin' a scram; 'e be all luck." Jim wondered.

Jim excused the doctor because he knew him so well. The old man had brought Jim into the world, and Pol, and all of their generation in the parish. Another baby was nothing to him—even though it was Jim's baby. What was there for a doctor to talk about? All he saw was births, sickness, and deaths. He had no time for much else. No wonder the doctor became untalkative. Stoke churchyard came to mind. How must a man feel when his medicines fail? Jim did not want his boy to be a doctor.

Jim's mind seemed to be swirling on a sea of happiness. Pol was well! He had a boy! The closing of the mine, small pays, lodgings, nowhere to go, no games to play—all were unimportant. The brief letter contained the tonic tones of the score that filled his heart with gladness.

"Well, my son, w'at do a say?"

Jim looked up to see Jake standing in the door.

"You look like a man caught staylin' a sheep," said Jake, smiling.

"Pol 'ave a boay," Jim answered simply.

"Be that all 'e say?"

"The maid be well an' will soon be hup."

"Brave! That's brave, comrade. Now, Jim, the big job's a'ead. Pol mus' come out."

Jake uttered his conclusion as though there was no longer any argument about the matter. He repeated words he had heard just a brief time before: " 'E gived me peace of mind. I bayn't afeard no more." His friendly smile accompanied his words, and he watched their effect. Jim raised his face to Jake and said, "That's w'at the doctor say, too." Jim smiled as he quoted the letter, but only for an instant. Serious again, he said, "But I'll 'ave t' learn patience, comrade."

"By the time 'er's well 'nough t' be bothered with sich things," said Jake slowly, "p'r'aps a way will turn up. Us'll see."

At the dinner table, Jim was quiet. He had no words suited to his experience even had he wished to talk about it. But it never occurred to him to make an announcement of it. Jenkins and his wife were gossiping of the events of the day. The children spoke as they needed something; then only. So they had been taught. The meal was almost over when Jake spoke. With the first word Jim looked up, knowing that Jake's motive was mischief.

"Back 'ome they do call my father Parent," he said, using his West Cornwall accent in deference to the boarding boss and missus. "Forty year ago, my holdes' brother was borned. The ol' man was so praoud 'e went up t' Fools' Corner an' said, 'Hi be the parent of a man child.' From that day on 'e was knawed as Parent. Strange 'aow folks differ. Now 'e seem t' me like, if I was a father, Hi should be like Parent. But look e at that one! Hi b'lieve 'e be 'shamed."

Harry and Mary Ellen laughed and spoke in unison while Jim's face crimsoned.

" 'Ave the word come, Jim?"

"Aas."

"Izza a boay or girl?" asked Mrs. Jenkins.

"Boay," said Jim.

"An 'aow did the missus do?"

" 'Er be doin' well."

"If your wife be like me, 'er wanted 'er first a maid," continued the woman.

"The women be all alike," said Harry. "A man must 'ave some luck some time."

"A woman hought t' 'ave some reward for 'er labor," retorted Mary Ellen sharply.

Harry veered for safety. "If 'e grow t' be a good boay, the mother will 'ave 'er reward. With a mother like you, my dear, yoor boay will be a good one."

"That's brave, 'Arry," said Jake, and pushed back his chair.

Jim was glad the discussion was over. Boay or maid, he thought, 'e be in 'e's mother's arms for a long time.

With no further comment Jake went for his hat, lighted his pipe, and went out.

Jim's first impulse was to see Allen; but before going out he would read his letter again. Slowly he made sure of each word. When he reached the doctor's name he said aloud, "Hi be some glad. Some glad."

"Talkin' to yourself, my son?" asked some one at the door.

"Aas," said Jim. "Hi dedn' 'ear you come. I was goin' awver t' see e w'en I read un. 'Ere, see w'at e say." And he handed Bob the letter.

"I 'eard the news, Jim. Hi met Jake."

"Aas, 'e was trumpeter for me at the table," said Jim, smiling.

"But I'll bet 'e 'ave throwed 'e's trumpet away afore naow," said Allen.

"Aas, you," agreed Jim. "Nobody helse will knaw from 'e."

Allen entered the room and sat down. For some time he remained silent, like a man perplexed and trying to find a path through a wilderness of circumstance. He seldom appeared so. Rather, Jim had thought Allen to be the most self-sufficient man he had ever met. He tried to analyze Bob's silence. Whatever it was, it was something unusual. Bob was worried. Finally Jim said, "W'at izza, Bob?"

"Jim, I 'ave a surprise for e. I leave fur England t'morra. In two weeks I sh'll be in Plymouth."

Jim knew he stared in surprise, but all he could say was, "Aas?"

Thinking of the little Bob had told him of his father's affairs and wondering if they had come to a settlement, he asked, "Do e think you'll stay there?"

Instantly Bob said: "No. Hi dawn't b'lieve anything would keep me there now, Jim. Hi worked that all out afore I come a citizen 'ere."

Jim's puzzlement did not lessen, however. Jake had intimated once that Bob had had a maid, and Jim grieved that his friend had to stir again his painful memories by returning to the old scenes and associations. The question, however, of the girl still being free and increasing Bob's perplexity did not enter Jim's mind.

"Jim," said Bob at last, "I 'ave somethin' t' say. P'r'aps you won't agree with me. You might think I be a meddler."

"Hi always think kindness of you, Bob," said Jim stanchly.

"That's fine, my son. Hark t' me then. Hit will take another year of savin' for e t' 'ave anuff t' get a 'aouse furnished. An' t' get the maid aout, longer still."

"Hi knaw it."

"That be a long time."

"Aas."

"Longer for thee than for most folks."

Jim said nothing.

Allen took an envelope from his pocket and fingered it dubiously. He knew he was walking on dangerous ground, but the fewest words were the best.

" 'Ere be a 'underd dollars fur the furniture," Allen said, and he laid the envelope on Jim's knee. "Hi dawn't need un. Hi 'ave nobody dependin' on me, an' there be nothin' 'ere for a sober man t' spend un on."

Jim's lips quivered, and his eyes filled; but he said nothing. Crowding his mind with this unexpected offer was the thought that England, Cornwall, home were being relin-

quished forever by the act of taking it. The little village of
his boyhood, his parents, his friends, the lanes, the hedges,
and the other treasures of the old parish would stay mere
memories as long as he lived. And more, all the problems that
he had pondered during the past months, and supposed the
coming months would clear and make easier to bear, thrust
themselves into his mind with a tangible thrust. He had never
quite realized what they had meant to him. In that moment
he understood the men who went from day to day without
having to make a decision. As long as the hope lingered that
they might go back—could go back—they put off making up
their minds. He would not censure them again.

And was Pol ready to come? Would she be happy here?
She might long for the primroses and snowdrops and honey-
suckles as Mrs. Jenkins did. Still more might she grieve over
having left her mother and the maidens she had grown up
with. He had not tried to question her seriously about coming
to America because the possibility seemed so far off. He had
no doubt that she would come. No matter how great was her
devotion to her village and friends, her devotion to him was
greater; but the suddenness of this was overpowering. To
know that her heart ached for anything would be bitter grief
to him. Would it not be better to let time prepare her for
the separation?

"Two weeks, my son, an' Hi shall be in Plymouth," Allen
repeated. "That be awnly fifteen miles or so from Callin'ton.
Hi can run aout an' see the maid. I 'ave a henvelope for she."

Jim's throat tightened until it hurt, and tears ran down
his cheeks in spite of him.

"Dawn't say nothin', boay," said Allen. "I understand. You
can save faster if you 'ave awnly one 'aouse t' keep. You can
pay me as you be hable."

Jim hid his face in his hands, and the pent feelings of
months vented themselves in unaccustomed sobs. This kindness, his anxiety to see his wife, the longing he had felt to be

with her in her trial, the sudden opportunity to have her with him! A home! The child! One after another, these thoughts came and came again. Gratitude, joy, perplexity in turn tied his tongue but unleashed his emotions.

Allen waited for the boy to compose himself. He watched him become calm and at last raise his face and smile.

"Jim, Hi 'ave 'ad my dreams of a 'ome; but they 'ave been scat t' bits, an' I'm afeard can't be mended. Hi shall learn the truth awver there. Hi be 'opin', Jim, that all I've 'eard bayn't true, 'opin' I shall find—" He stopped as if no words suited the deep longing of his heart. "Hi 'ave two reasons for goin', an' reward be waitin' fur me in one. Hi shan't go hunderground no more."

Jim listened, wishing with the solicitude of prayer for his friend.

"W'en I left, the maid's parents forbid 'er t' write t' me. Like my father, they regarded me as a hapostate, unworthy, bad. Hi wrote 'er but 'eard nothin'. They watched her that close, I thought. After two year Hi stopped writin' an' awnly rumor come t' me. Then I 'eard she 'ad married—married a praycher. A month ago it come to me that the tale wadn' true. Jim, I be goin' t' see fur myself."

Allen's last words fairly quivered with the intensity of his purpose. His passion made a different man of him. His reserve, his separateness from the common frailties of the men about him were gone. His self-control, that Jim had thought never deserted him, left him now a victim to his longing.

"W'en I come 'ere, Hi refoosed the advantages my schoolin' might 'ave give'. W'ile I waited, anything would do. I 'ad mined, on and off, in my boyhood. Father let me—t' learn the worth of money, he said—and I could mine again. An' then, w'ere Cornishmen was, I was shore t' 'ear from 'ome come times. You remember 'aow the praycher knawed me. W'en I 'eard she 'ad married, I gave hup."

Allen stopped, fearing that his reference to mining might offend his listener.

"W'en I said that, Jim—abaout minin', I mean—I meant no reflection. Minin' be as honorable as praychin' or lawin'. Not that. A man's dooty be w'ere 'e can do 'is best, an' Hi be schooled fur somethin' helse."

"Hi wadn' thinkin' of that, you; I—" Jim checked his words, fearing that he could not say what was in his mind at the moment. He had accepted Allen's assurance that he would return while matters of his father's estate were his only concern; but Allen's love story shook Jim's faith, or, more to the point, added to his fear. In spite of Bob's strong denial that he would stay in England, Jim feared that the farewell would be a lasting one. He had hoped that for years to come Bob would be within hailing distance to share life with him and help him translate it.

Jim's question threatened again, but he suppressed it. The unforeseen things that Jim feared might happen, Bob knew as well as he. So why mention them? Hadn't Allen said he had thought it all through? And yet, the girl might have a powerful influence. His love for her was sufficient to take him back: might it not be sufficient to keep him there if she asked it? Circumstances could change a man's mind so thoroughly. Allen had doffed his English citizenship and adopted a new one. Jim himself had almost settled that question from outside pressures. And the heart had a way of making a man falter in spite of his clearest judgments.

Allen's mind was not far from the path Jim's was following. He had crossed the water, too. The old scenes were in his eyes. Old memories were absorbing him. He was thinking of his love, which had begun, it seemed to him, when he and the girl were children. It had grown in depth, sweetness, beauty as carefully tended flowers or fruits grow and sweeten from year to year, but— A chill that almost made him shudder dispelled his dream. His face showed the bitterness of his thought. Little places have long memories. The village would not have forgotten. Small communities have too few diversions. To make the situation worse, he himself would be a constant reminder. His habits would always be patent and would grate on the code of his neighbors. He would be discussed annually and prayed over. Stewards would visit him and leave him less stewardlike than when they came. Being one's self—his sort of self—would increase his affliction from day to day.

And more. His stay in America would make living in Cornwall difficult. America's vast ranges would make the confines of the old place crampingly real. His mind roamed the vast field of American enterprise, its opportunities, its future, and in comparison set a picture of Cornwall before his eyes. Allen did not seek words for his thought, he only drifted in fancy from one limitation to another.

"No, Jim," he said, as if Jim had taken part in his mental journeys. "I couldn' stay. Dost tha see, I'd be a furriner in my awn parish. My ideas be too fixed, an' my habits too strong." The gloom lifted from Allen's face, and a smile took its place. "Hi've seen the boays leave this, thumbin' their nawses w'en they said good-bye. In six months they was back, hopin' nobody would remember their last words w'en they left. They was changed an' dedn' knaw un; Hi knaw I be."

In that moment Jim remembered Allen's comment when Mrs. Jenkins' homesickness was told. " 'Arry must let 'er go back after a year or two. That's a sure cure—almost," he said.

Allen got up to go. Not another word was said about the money, the home furnishing, or Pol. He held out his hand. "Good-bye, my son. You will 'ear from me."

"Good-bye, Bob. A good passage to e."

"Say it for both ways, Jim. I shall be back."

Jim watched him to the corner, then went back to his room. If awnly the light I seed in 'e's heyes on the cliff shined in mun now, 'e'd 'ave a 'appier journey.

He sat down with his letter and the money in his hand, his mind seething beyond his control. Either one was sufficient to take all of his attention, and they had come to him within an hour of each other. There was nothing he could do about the first. Pol and the baby were far away; they had been reported well and progressing. All thought about them was pure guesswork that might be right, that might be wrong. He might make himself deeply miserable or uncertainly happy. He had better curb his thought on that matter.

Allen's envelope, his words, his purpose were different. The money meant that there was much to be planned, much to be done. He was glad there was time enough for the attention it deserved. He thought of the bit-by-bit method by which he and Pol had equipped their family life back there, and the opportunity he had now of doing a complete job of it at once. There had been happiness in that; he and Pol would realize just as much in this—perhaps more. "Us be in great favor," he muttered. And then he added, "Thankee, Bob— for she too."

"Now for the hanswer," he said, and set himself to write. "Fust there be the cheel, an' then 'er comfort. That's the way 'e should be." His face brightened as he determined the order of his letter. "An' then Hallen—'e's gift, 'e's crossin', 'e's call." Jim realized that his thoughts were outstripping by far the best he could do, but still, he was singingly grateful for that, meager as it was. He wondered if the letter could reach Pol before Bob got there. Bob might delay a day or two in Plymouth. Even though Bob got there first, he could trust him to broach the subject in the best way.

When Jim had finished his letter he found that a few lines had to suffice for all the words that had flooded his mind. The gush of his thoughts confused him in his effort to pencil them. Some of the things he wished to say just because it was a man's part to say them—the disposal of their goods for instance—he had to let pass, had to leave to her without comment from him. He should discuss her booking, give her advice based on his own experience, but he could not. Perhaps more important than all the rest, he should help her with the decision Allen's call would make imperative. Like Jim himself, Pol must have thought that the time when she might leave for America, if she ever did, was a long time away. Here too his pencil failed. He looked at his completed page— a page of small words and mere bits of what he wished to say—and shook his head. He had been too happy, too grateful, however, to feel that he was defeated. Just as Pol had strengthened him for their parting, just as Allen had aided him here, so their combined efforts would do for him now what he could not do for himself. In spite of the letter that disappointed him, Jim was happy.

Jim heard Jake come up the steps and waited for him to come in. Jake spoke first. He saw the letter, which he knew Jim had wanted to be alone to write, and said, " 'Ard at it, comrade?"

"Done," replied Jim. "A poor job, done poor."

"A sort of a miracle to my mind," said Jake.

" 'Tis so, comrade, by rights, but 'e edn' the miracle t'night I wanted un t' be."

Jake noticed with deep relief that his face was bright in spite of his words. He had hardly dared guess the state he would find Jim in after the news he had received and after he had tried to reply by letter.

"Two bigger miracles 'ave 'appened," continued Jim, "—one in Englan' an' one 'ere." He handed Bob's envelope to Jake.

Jake did not open it. He only smoothed it between finger and thumb, its soft resilience telling him what was in it.

"Bob left it," Jim explained.

"Aas, I knaw. 'E asked me about un."

Jim looked his question.

" 'Ow you'd take un. If you'd be touchy an' refoose."

Jim did not answer.

"Did a tell e the res'?"

"About Pol? 'E did."

"W'at nex'?" asked Jim.

Jake looked at Jim a moment and then, with visible feeling, said, " 'Ouse and 'ome."

Chapter Twenty-two

JIM AND JAKE WERE UNDERGROUND at coach time in the morning. Since coming down, neither had felt chatty. With few words they had scanned their job for the day and set to work. "A short 'andle an' a pile a dirt dawn't call for plannin'," Jim said. Jake agreed, tapped out his pipe, and they were off. Suddenly Jake straightened up, drew his watch from his pocket, and said, "'E's gone, comrade."

"Aas," Jim said, and they bent over their shovels again.

Allen's going occupied their minds to the full. It was a big event for both of them—too big to be quickly or lightly dismissed.

Jim was afraid Allen's farewell might be final. He might stay in England. With a woman in the case, 'ow's a man t' knaw? If Allen came back he might not settle on the Ranges. He would have no further need of newsmongers among Cornish miners. So, married or unmarried, Bob might choose to live anywhere he could put his abilities to their best service. Jim shook his head in misgiving.

Then a memory brought a morsel of hope to Jim. Allen was speaking to Frost, speaking of the young foreigners of Allouez: "When they need help the most, nothing is done for them," he said, his eyes as accusing as his words. Recalling what Frost was doing, Bob's expression suddenly changed.

347

"I'm sorry, Silas! You know what I mean. It's not a one-man job." This came back to Jim. "That might hold un to the Range," Jim murmured. And yet, in spite of his argument, in spite of Bob's stout assurance, Jim was far from confident that he would see him again.

Jake stood up, braced himself with his shovel and waited for Jim to come to attention. "The boay—Allen, that is— started the fust chapter of our book, 'ave kept 'is name on ev'ry page since—almos', an' now 'e 'ave ended un."

"Aas," replied Jim. "A chapter be ended, shore 'nough, an' 'e done un."

Again their shovels kept time as they slid on the sollared floor and kept pitch as the rock flicked from their shining points into the car.

Jim lived that first day through again—the elastic-sided shoes, soaked stockings, the snow, Allen! "Fix mun hup, 'ead an' feet—diggin' clo'es an' all," he said. And then assuringly to them, " 'E won't sell e w'at you dawn't want." And then in a still lower voice, "If you run short afore payday . . ." Jake's comment to Tom as they left the store was clear, too: "Dawn't think, my son, 'is kind be numerous. Us be lucky t' meet un." That was the beginning of the chapter.

The end— Jim's thoughts were almost audible. The end was w'en 'e put they bills in my 'and! He grunted in approval of his thought: "They bills was my citizenship papers, shore 'nough."

The citizenship matter had a fascination for him, but it had something else too! "I dedn' want t' leave Englan'," Jim conceded. "Now I must live in America! 'Oo said a man's a free hagent?"

That was a path his mind had followed often during the past weeks. Try as he might, he could not banish a yearning, an affection for England—for Cornwall—for the roads and lanes and fields of one parish. Then he restated what the master had said about America. "My feelin's be moved by one, my head accept t'other," he concluded. "That keep a man divided, in a way, but 'e won't for long. I sh'll sing 'America' with a full 'eart."

The evening of the day Allen left, Jim was still casting and recasting the issues that had grown so large, become so insistent. "If Pol won't grieve too much," he said. "If 'er will see an' feel as I be learnin' to!" He had said that before, as he had all the other things he had said today, and as he was saying even now. But he had not laughed before, laughed at himself as he was doing now. "I be glad the folks an' Jake be out. They'd think I'm maze," he said, aloud, "—laughin' to myself! Well, I be. I been judgin' Pol by Mary Ellen, Mrs. Uren, an' me! The things I see an' knaw, 'er will see quicker'n I seed mun, an' most of mun won't need t' be pointed out to 'er."

Jim sat down by the window to indulge the change of mind and spirit his thought of Pol had brought to him. He looked out the window with a new vision. Shaft houses, enginerooms, shops took on a new significance. He tried to imagine their cost. The people who had built them had faith in their future, their service, their productivity. They were intended to serve more than a generation. And there were the buildings of brick on Main Street that to his eyes looked new. They had by no means served their day. What would happen to them if the mine closed down? Thousands of dollars had been put into those buildings! Thousands put into their stocks! Hardware, furniture, clothing! What if they had to move! And if the miners left, the store people would have to leave. Jim wondered if this was the line of reasoning Allen used when he dismissed the idea of the mine closing. He felt his spirit lighten and a happiness take possession of him that he had not felt before.

As he turned from one phase to another of the big event, he sat with Pol in his arms in his new home. That made Allouez the center of the universe to him. Beside them, in a little homemade cradle, such as he had seen many times back home, was the boy. Pol's hand sensibly stroked his hair, and her subdued laughter sounded like silver bells in his ears. "W'at do us 'ave t' worry about, 'ere, my son?" she asked. "Back there somebody helse 'ad whip an' reins in 'is 'ands. 'Ere, us do a bit of drivin' ourselves! Laugh, Jim. Hi want t' 'ear e laugh! Us be t'gether—an' the boay. Us 'ave 'ouse an' 'ome again—an' somethin' t' live for."

Jake broke in on Jim's reverie—thoughtful, considerate Jake. He understood the turmoil of Jim's mind, and that Jim needed to be alone. But not for too long a time. He stood in the door, almost invisible to Jim. Jim had let the night fall around him while he dreamed. "W'at do the book say about lovin' darkness more'n light, comrade? Maybe a ol' bach could strike a light for e."

"You'm a big 'elp halways, Jake, thee's knaw that," answered Jim. "I bayn't thinkin' nothin' new. Us 'ave talked un awver again an' again. Then they was awnly dreams; now they be hawful close an' real."

Jake waited for him to go on; he wanted to know more. When Jim remained silent, he said, "W'at more, boay?"

Jake had entered the room and seated himself on the bed. Jim was still outlined against the window and the starlight. He answered slowly: "W'en you come in, I was wishin' the boays was 'ere. Us would sing thicky tune us singed on the boat: 'Nearer Home.' "

Jake got up, scratched a match, and found a candle. He lingered over the small task, coaxing the wick to burn with the shortening match, his mind absorbed with the import of Jim's wish to sing. When the blaze was to his liking, he said, "If all I 'ear be true, the song would fit they, too."

"W'a's tha mean?"

"Bill an' Joe be sparkin' a bit, I'm told. Never could keep their heyes off the maidens for long, they two," said Jake, with more humor than censure in his voice.

"Yankee maidens, likely."

"Likely. But—"

Jake stopped and looked at Jim wonderingly. A moment ago he had wanted to sing "Nearer Home"—now doubt was disturbing him again. Jake understood Jim's uncertainty. In spite of his faith in Pol, the thousands of miles from home, the climate, the changed way of living, made him anxious, uneasy. Jim's heights of hope and lowlands of fear were only moments apart. Jake spoke again.

"I knaw w'at you'm thinkin', boay. Did e ever mind they Swedes an' Heyetalians, they Finns an' the rest?"

Jim shook his head.

"Think of they for a bit. It will do e good. You spayk English—of a sort, 'tis true—they dawn't. They 'ave a new language t' learn, new customs, new hev'rything. If they dawn't change—an' some dawn't, some can't—they be hexiles. Their chuldern grow up furriners in their awn 'ome. Boay, your lot be aysy by compare. 'E take real courage for they t' come 'ere! No wonder they live in locations! But that dawn't save mun worry."

Still Jim listened.

"Hi bayn't nobody t' praych, but, comrade, I envy e no little. 'Ev'rything new,' you said once, remember? It was our fust night in the bal. New timber, new tracks, new cars, new drifts! You an' Pol be new, an' the cheel—new as a dewdrop. A fresh beginnin' in a new worl'. If 'twas me, I'd be makin' resolutions."

Jake's eyes were eloquent with sincerity. Jim wondered, as he so often did, how Jake thought of so many things. Some mus' be told things t' knaw mun, he thought; Jake see mun without bein' told. He had a way of speaking at critical moments, and what he said usually dropped like a plummet, cut like a knife, blocked an argument like a dam. He quoted Scripture to stop the mouths of carping Wesleyans; store gossip, he frequently killed with a phrase. When the boarding-house crowd denounced "furriners" Jake said: "They'm no furriner than we! They'm just furder away from 'ome an' 'ave a 'arder job t' do."

There was admiration in Jim's voice when he said, "You'm Ol' Parent awver again at 'is bes'—an' more."

"You mustn' flatter," replied Jake. "Parent was a good man."

Jim felt his anxiety increase as the days passed. He and Jake had spells of talk. The one subject occupied them; they seemed to think of nothing else. Jim was nervously eager. Sometimes Jake soothed him; sometimes, rebuked him. "The days will all 'ave twenty-four hours to min. Frettin' won't make mun shorter," he said, "an' you just as well take mun a minute at a time."

They were drilling one day—Jake twisting the drill. Jim's hammer hit the drill a glancing blow that missed his partner's hands by a hair. Jake let loose, leaving the drill in the hole.

"Let's trade places, my son," he said. "The best man in the worl' can't beat a boryer with 'is mind four thousand miles away."

Jim flushed: he was as proud of his skill with a hammer as a painter might be of his brush. Jake did not let him strike again that shift. "Us dawn't go so fast, but 'e's safer," he said, and winked.

Allen had been gone more than four weeks when Jim found a letter on his dresser. As soon as he recognized Pol's writing he thought Bob had had time to make his call. He tore the letter open and tried to devour its lines. Again and again he backed up to be sure of their message. "More haste, less speed," he muttered. "W'y dedn' the maid put the most important thing in the fust line?" Perhaps she did. She spoke of the boy first—a paragraph about him—all marvel and mystery. Then Allen's call and many lines about that—her surprise at his appearance, his marvelous offer, and her fear to accept it. At last the words he sought! "I will come. A wife should be with her husband—a boy with his father." Not a word of grief about leaving, no word about friends, about flowers or fields. "I want to be with you," she said. "I'll write again when arrangements have been made." No worry about the journey, its difficulties, its length. Not a question!

Jim read it a second time and went to the kitchen, where Jake was blacking his boots for the Sabbath.

"Pol's comin'," he said, his voice broken with excitement. He held up the letter to witness what he said.

"Of course 'er's comin'. W'at did e spect? Do e remember that 'richer, poorer, better, worse, sickness, 'ealth' thing you both said afore the passon? Hi do. Hi was there. An' so was you." Jake stared at Jim in mock rebuke, while his tones rumbled in bass merriment. "W'at a man you be for a dummon t' come to! No more faith than a haythen. Seem like I knaw Pol better'n you."

He stood before Jim with a shoe enveloping one hand and a brush in the other. He resumed his job again. A few whisks, and he put the shoe down and picked up the other. Jim reached for the one Jake had finished and looked it over. The heel had been slighted, was dull. Holding it out he said: " 'Alf done, never done, comrade. Folks see e from be'ind as well as from afore."

Jake ignored the banter save for the merriment that shone in his eyes. He daubed the shoe he held in all seriousness for a few minutes as if to comply with Jim's remark. He laid aside one brush for another but, before using it, looked unsmilingly at Jim and asked, "Do thicky letter mean another boardin' 'ouse in Allouez?"

Jim tried hard to counter with as humorless a look as Jake's and said, "If 'e do 'e'll be hultraselec', as the shopkeepers say."

"That leave me out," said Jake. He gave the shoe his whole attention for a few strokes before he spoke again. " 'Owever that may be, comrade," he said, "there be a lot t' do gettin' thicky 'ouse ready."

"Aas," replied Jim. "I knaw."

They had talked that matter over already and had come to some conclusions; but everything had had to wait on the letter from Pol with her consent to come. Jim had obtained an option on a house; now he would sign the lease for it. Mary Ellen had promised to give him a list of the things necessary to begin housekeeping. Harry had volunteered a man's judgment wherever it might help, and Spargo said he wanted "t' 'stablish a new 'ome in the republic—the awnly way I'll hever do un." Jim was grateful, but he confided to Jake that he wanted to do all he could himself.

Jim warmed to his job, thinking of Mary Ann's surprise and her words when she saw how well he had done. He fancied leading her from room to room and watching her eyes glow as she saw his thoughtfulness of her comfort and happiness. Beds, sheets, blankets, he would buy; but the comforters and counterpanes she must select. Stoves, tinware, kettles, he could get; but the dishes, she must choose. So with the furniture. He would not buy a picture or a knickknack of any sort. A woman do live with 'er hornaments an' niceties, he reasoned, and so he told his helpers when their suggestions did not suit.

Jim mentioned his plans freely to Jake, who always listened with deep interest but not always without humor. "I be glad you 'ave regard for a bach'lor's jedgment in sich things, my son," he said. Jim was eager to see his rooms filling, and occasionally Jake said, "Not too fast, my son—not too fast!" and then, "After word 'ave come that she've started, you still 'ave two weeks an' more."

Three days after Mary Ann's letter arrived, one came from Allen. Jim had been waiting impatiently for that, too. He fancied that there might be some things his wife would not tell, to spare him anxiety that Allen would—her health or the child's. Allen might notice and want to warn Jim. The envelope was postmarked Camborne.

Dear Jim:

I have been to Downgate and have talked with your wife. Thanks to your letters, I was not a stranger to her, nor was she to me. In praise of her I say, "Lucky man!" to you. I saw the boy too, and repeat, "Lucky man!"

Your wife asked a lot of questions, naturally enough, which I tried to answer. I advised her about the journey, which she discussed bravely and, I could see, with self-control. She knows what it means well enough but has made up her mind on the matter. Her greatest concern seemed to be the riddance of the household goods. However, she knew more about that than I did. She thought it might take two weeks to arrange the sale.

I left for Launceston the same day and reached home the next.

My affairs, which seemed so tangled when I left you, were easier to adjust than I expected. Jim, I shall go back to America a happy man.

Business and some pleasure will take me to Plymouth again in ten days, when I will get your wife's booking for America and Calumet. I'll make things as easy for her as I can.

Downgate is a dreamy little place—a spot one might easily yearn for. Every house and garden looked like home, hedged in and shaded for security and comfort. But I was not misled, Jim. I remembered how many fathers and sons you said were away from those houses as you are. A man can't live on scenery and tradition. Where you are is bread and to spare—and scenery, straight from Genesis. You are helping make a new tradition on a bigger scale.

My trip was pleasant enough. I tired of the long train ride—not accustomed to sitting so long, you know—but the voyage freshened me again. The run from Liverpool to Plymouth was just a short postscript at the end of a letter.

I don't know when I'll be back, but it won't be long. I want to go to London for a few days. I was never there.

Things are going to your liking, I hope—the house filling with furniture, and your eyes with the vision of home. I don't know where I shall settle; but you will hear from me, I promise. It will be somewhere on the Peninsula.

Be of good cheer, my son, and good luck.

Regards to Jake.

Bob

P.S. In Downgate I heard your lingo for the first time in full chorus. The children piped and shrilled it, women trebled it and

the men tuned up in it from tenor to bass. I was the only dis-
cordant note. I was a foreigner, fifty miles from home—an alien
in Stoke Parish.

B.

This was the longest letter Jim had ever received, and he
spent the whole evening on it before he was sure he had its
meaning. Finally he thought he could read it to Jake.

At the end of the letter Jake said, "Brave, comrade—'e's a
real frien'." But when Jim read the postscript Jake's face wore
an injured look. "Pot callin' the kiddle black," he said. "A
pig's squeal be moosic to a butcher."

"There bayn't no poetry wrought in our tongue that I
knaw by," said Jim.

"There might be volumes, an' us wouldn' knaw," said Jake;
"but I'd chance the same guess on 'e's western stuff."

They laughed together at Jake's retorts to the distant Allen.

"Things seem to be workin' right in your 'and, comrade,"
said Jake; "but I be wonderin'."

" 'Bout w'at?" asked Jim.

"Somebody meetin' the maid in Castle Garden!"

Jim's face paled. He had not thought of that yet. He had
been occupied with the beginning and the end of the journey
—Allen and Pol over there, the house and the things that
help spell home, here. His happiness bestrode the distance
with only a passing glance at the trying ocean days and the
wearing ride on the train. Certainly he wished he could spare
her both; but that was impossible. Pol would brave it, adjust
herself to it, meet the necessities of it, and not flinch. That
had to be as the coming of her babe had to be. She would
smile and take each day, and all it brought, with courage.
The best he could do was to meet her where the railroad
ended, at L'Anse, cross the bay with her and, with a pride
that swelled his heart even in prospect, conduct her home.
But Castle Garden! It was a black shadow that for a moment
blotted his dream.

Castle Garden was a wound in his memory. Not from his having had trouble getting through, but from the sights he had seen! People of all tongues herded in pens like beasts— one family, two families to a pen; families unable to speak to each other. Men, wild-eyed and frightened, beat on the gates with their hands to get attention from a man in uniform, from any one free in the runs, called with strange words to get information, to explain something, to get release. Women sat on their bundles sodden with helplessness and fear, small children holding to them and wailing in fright. Some one had failed to come, a message had been delayed, an error had been found in a ticket—something beyond their understanding. Thus they were terrorized. An old woman counted her beads in a corner to ward off whatever the madness of the place portended. As Jim and his companions had threaded their way after their guide, a man approached waving a paper and calling a name: "Mrs. Johns! Mrs. John W. Johns!" A voice beside them screamed: " 'Ere I be! 'Ere! I be Mrs. Johns!" The woman pressed her face between the slats of her cage in her eagerness. The boys stopped at the sound of the Cornish accent. The man with the paper began to explain, but the woman was in a heap on the floor. Castle Garden!

"W'at should us do?" asked Jim.

"The bookin's be s'posed t' take care of ev'rything, but thee's knaw they bayn't perfec'."

"Aas."

"You can't go t' New York t' meet the maid; so the best us can do be to write a 'otel man an' ask un be shore t' meet 'er an' the babe."

Jim did not answer.

"Write thicky man w'at took care of we. No matter what 'otel 'er ticket call for, give 'e the right. 'Ave the maid met."

"As soon as us knaw the boat," Jim said. But his words were heavy with the dread of Castle Garden.

Jim's job of furnishing was nearing its end when Pol's letter came. He puzzled his way through it and found that, this very day, Pol had said good-bye to Downgate. The scene was easy to construct: the trap at the door, Pol's mother, Jim's father and mother, a dozen neighbors—kisses and tears. Then the road to Plymouth. He recalled his own sensations as houses, spires, farms, mines, came to view and slipped away—forever—as days slip into eternity. This was no easy day for her. He tried to adapt a phrase, "Greater love hath . . ." but he could not shape it to his purpose. And yet, somehow, those words expressed his appreciation of her devotion. Suddenly he realized that Pol was hours ahead of him. At that very moment she was in Liverpool. Her boat was at the dock. She would board it in the morning! He got up, reached for his hat, and went to the schoolmaster's.

"If I dawn't himpose," began Jim, "will you write a letter for me?"

"With pleasure, Jim. But why—"

"Hi can't a'ford no mistakes in this one."

Jim told what he wanted, and Mr. Frost wrote. When he had finished, he read his lines to Jim.

"Now an envelope for a reply. You will want to know that he got your letter and will do what you ask."

"Thanks," said Jim, and left.

The letter posted, he went to his own house to read Pol's letter again. It was not long. Like the last, it was tuned to hope. Courage rose from every line. Jim went to the window that overlooked the town. Night was less than an hour away. Shadows were deepening in the hollows through which ran Hill and Gratiot creeks. The forest was losing its outline, the trees merging solidly into a black bulwark that now made him feel secure. As the crescent of his view drew nearer, lights began to appear in windows. The houses drew closer together, and he fancied the little place became more friendly, its Finns and Swedes and Italians and Cornishmen more comradely. The village was putting its arm around him, claiming him, owning him. He was no longer a frailly attached temporary boarder in the place. He had become a part of it, he was here to stay!

A man approached through the shadow and rapped on the door. The knob turned, and Jake walked in. "Hi thought you'd be 'ere, comrade," said Jake, "so I made bold to come in."

"Thee't welcome, thee's knaw," Jim answered. "Pol sail t'morra. 'Er left Downgate t'day."

"That's good, my son. I be glad."

"The letter be gone t' New York, too."

"That'll 'elp, I 'ope."

They stood at a window looking out into the night and enjoying each other in silence. At last Jake spoke.

"Hi 'ad a word with the cap'n t'day."

"Aas."

"An' with Spargo, too."

"Oosh."

"Jack's partner be leavin' in a week or so. An' I shall be movin' on, too. Jack wondered if you'd like t' work with 'e."

Jim was silent. He wondered why life liked to make gifts with flaws in them. He had feared Jake would leave when Pol came, but he could not blame him. When he had needed Jake most, Jake had stayed with him. Now Jim's home was established, Jake would go to his brothers. Jim grieved in spite of his understanding. He did not argue. He knew Jake always read both sides of the slate.

"Jack suit me, comrade," said Jim, and the matter was ended.

He lighted a candle, and the two walked from room to room. In the kitchen they stopped and scanned the pots and pans, table and chairs, cupboard and stove, in silence. Back in the front room again, Jake said, "Hi be thinkin' of a miracle, my son."

"Spayk on, comrade, spayk on."

Jake's hand moved in a half-circle to include the whole house in its sweep. "As 'e be," he said slowly, "as 'e be, 'e be awnly a 'ouse full of things. A fortnit, an' 'e'll be more'n that. 'E'll be 'ome."

Jim felt the surge again that had filled him as he had watched the night fill the low places and then called the stars to watch. He swallowed hard, set the strength of his will against the strength of his emotion, and repeated, " 'Ouse an' 'ome."

TITLES IN THE GREAT LAKES BOOKS SERIES

Deep Woods Frontier: A History of Logging in Northern Michigan, by
Theodore J. Karamanski, 1989

Orvie, The Dictator of Dearborn, by David L. Good, 1989

Seasons of Grace: A History of the Catholic Archdiocese of Detroit, by Leslie
Woodcock Tentler, 1990

The Pottery of John Foster: Form and Meaning, by Gordon and Elizabeth
Orear, 1990

The Diary of Bishop Frederic Baraga: First Bishop of Marquette, Michigan,
edited by Regis M. Walling and Rev. N. Daniel Rupp, 1990

Walnut Pickles and Watermelon Cake: A Century of Michigan Cooking, by
Larry B. Massie and Priscilla Massie, 1990

The Making of Michigan, 1820–1860: A Pioneer Anthology, edited by Justin
L. Kestenbaum, 1990

*America's Favorite Homes: A Guide to Popular Early Twentieth-Century
Homes,* by Robert Schweitzer and Michael W. R. Davis, 1990

Beyond the Model T: The Other Ventures of Henry Ford, by Ford R. Bryan,
1990

Life after the Line, by Josie Kearns, 1990

*Michigan Lumbertowns: Lumbermen and Laborers in Saginaw, Bay City, and
Muskegon, 1870–1905,* by Jeremy W. Kilar, 1990

Detroit Kids Catalog: The Hometown Tourist, by Ellyce Field, 1990

Waiting for the News, by Leo Litwak, 1990 (reprint)

Detroit Perspectives, edited by Wilma Wood Henrickson, 1991

Life on the Great Lakes: A Wheelsman's Story, by Fred W. Dutton, edited by
William Donohue Ellis, 1991

*Copper Country Journal: The Diary of Schoolmaster Henry Hobart,
1863–1864,* by Henry Hobart, edited by Philip P. Mason, 1991

John Jacob Astor: Business and Finance in the Early Republic, by John Denis
Haeger, 1991

Survival and Regeneration: Detroit's American Indian Community, by
Edmund J. Danziger, Jr., 1991

Steamboats and Sailors of the Great Lakes, by Mark L. Thompson, 1991

Cobb Would Have Caught It: The Golden Years of Baseball in Detroit, by
Richard Bak, 1991

Michigan in Literature, by Clarence Andrews, 1992

Under the Influence of Water: Poems, Essays, and Stories, by Michael Delp,
1992

The Country Kitchen, by Della T. Lutes, 1992 (reprint)

The Making of a Mining District: Keweenaw Native Copper 1500–1870, by David J. Krause, 1992

Kids Catalog of Michigan Adventures, by Ellyce Field, 1993

Henry's Lieutenants, by Ford R. Bryan, 1993

Historic Highway Bridges of Michigan, by Charles K. Hyde, 1993

Lake Erie and Lake St. Clair Handbook, by Stanley J. Bolsenga and Charles E. Herndendorf, 1993

Queen of the Lakes, by Mark Thompson, 1994

Iron Fleet: The Great Lakes in World War II, by George J. Joachim, 1994

Turkey Stearnes and the Detroit Stars: The Negro Leagues in Detroit, 1919–1933, by Richard Bak, 1994

Pontiac and the Indian Uprising, by Howard H. Peckham, 1994 (reprint)

Charting the Inland Seas: A History of the U.S. Lake Survey, by Arthur M. Woodford, 1994 (reprint)

Ojibwa Narratives of Charles and Charlotte Kawbawgam and Jacques LePique, 1893–1895. Recorded with Notes by Homer H. Kidder, edited by Arthur P. Bourgeois, 1994, co–published with the Marquette County Historical Society

Strangers and Sojourners: A History of Michigan's Keweenaw Peninsula, by Arthur W. Thurner, 1994

Win Some, Lose Some: G. Mennen Williams and the New Democrats, by Helen Washburn Berthelot, 1995

Sarkis, by Gordon and Elizabeth Orear, 1995

The Northern Lights: Lighthouses of the Upper Great Lakes, by Charles K. Hyde, 1995 (reprint)

Kids Catalog of Michigan Adventures, second edition, by Ellyce Field, 1995

Rumrunning and the Roaring Twenties: Prohibition on the Michigan–Ontario Waterway, by Philip P. Mason, 1995

In the Wilderness with the Red Indians, by E. R. Baierlein, translated by Anita Z. Boldt, edited by Harold W. Moll, 1996

Elmwood Endures: History of a Detroit Cemetery, by Michael Franck, 1996

Master of Precision: Henry M. Leland, by Mrs. Wilfred C. Leland with Minnie Dubbs Millbrook, 1996 (reprint)

Haul–Out: New and Selected Poems, by Stephen Tudor, 1996

Kids Catalog of Michigan Adventures, third edition, by Ellyce Field, 1997

Beyond the Model T: The Other Ventures of Henry Ford, revised edition, by Ford R. Bryan, 1997

Young Henry Ford: A Picture History of the First Forty Years, by Sidney Olson, 1997 (reprint)

These Men Have Seen Hard Service: The First Michigan Sharpshooters in the Civil War, by Raymond J. Herek, 1997

The Coast of Nowhere: Meditations on Rivers, Lakes and Streams, by Michael Delp, 1997

From Saginaw Valley to Tin Pan Alley: Saginaw's Contribution to American Popular Music, 1890–1955, by R. Grant Smith, 1997

Toast of the Town: The Life and Times of Sunnie Wilson, by Sunnie Wilson with John Cohassey, 1997

The Long Winter Ends, by Newton G. Thomas, 1997 (reprint)

Bridging the River of Hatred: The Pioneering Efforts of Detroit Police Commissioner George Edwards, by Mary M. Stolberg, 1998

A Place for Summer: One Hundred Years at Michigan and Trumbull, by Richard Bak, 1998

Michigan in the Novel, 1816–1996: An Annotated Bibliography, by Robert Beasecker, 1998

All–American Anarchist: Joseph A. Labadie and the Labor Movement, by Carlotta R. Anderson, 1998

"Time by Moments Steals Away": The 1848 Journal of Ruth Douglass, by Robert L. Root, Jr., 1998